FROM LION'S JAWS

FROM LION'S JAWS

CHÖGYAM TRUNGPA'S EPIC ESCAPE
TO THE WEST

GRANT MACLEAN

山
Mountain

First Edition
Printed in the United States of America

ISBN 978-0-9950293-0-9

Contents

Maps, Illustrations

Hand-drawn maps and illustrations by Chögyam Trungpa Rinpoche, courtesy of Diana Mukpo

1. Map of escape route (following page; see also *Resources*)

2. Dudtsi-til monastery, Surmang (facing page 24)

3. Dorje Khyung Dzong retreat center, Surmang (facing page 44)

4. Kham/East Tibet (page 61; see also *Resources*)

5. View of monastery with travelers (facing page 86)

6. Bridge over the Alado Gorge (facing page 116)

7. The perilous route to Rigong Kha (facing page 150)

Frontispiece: Chögyam Trungpa, Bhutan, 1968
(courtesy, Dan Russell)

For enlarged maps
see *Resources* p.315

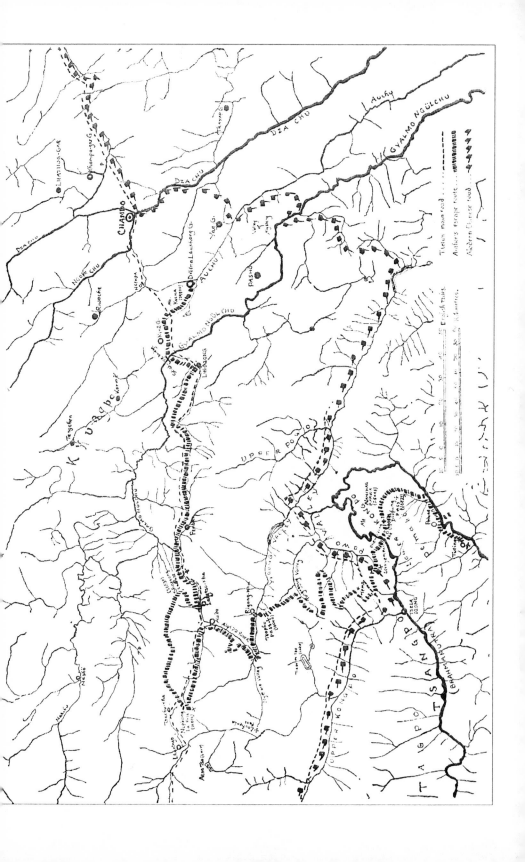

Prologue

On the morning of December 15, 1959, a young Tibetan sat high on a mountain slope, gazing despondently down to the great Brahmaputra River in the valley below. He was emotionally spent, physically drained and painfully thin from lack of food. Fleeing his homeland, he had been on the road for over eighteen months, the last three of them on a harrowing trek across a vast mountain wilderness.

He had not slept the previous night, deeply worried for the safety of the people who had followed him this far. As he'd journeyed on, hundreds of men, women and children had joined him, trusting that he – nineteen-year-old Chögyam Trungpa Rinpoche, the leader of a renowned spiritual lineage – could lead them to freedom. Over the months, they had together faced arduous challenges, terrifying obstacles and ferocious weather, had wandered lost among towering mountain ranges where humans had never been, and had recently been forced to take a dangerous route through rugged, unknown terrain while traveling in the dark of night.

Now, starving and utterly exhausted, they were riven by anxiety. That night, in flimsy craft they had made themselves, they would try to cross the legendary river, and do so under the noses of heavily-armed Chinese Communist troops. Then, if could they reach the far bank, they faced the appalling prospect of a midwinter climb over the great, soaring wall of the Himalayas …

❋

Earlier that year, having lain for millennia hidden and mysterious atop its snowy heights, Tibet had burst into the West's consciousness in a torrent of news headlines. The twentieth century's tumult had breached the walls of the legendary spiritual kingdom: the Chinese colossus, which had itself long lain remote and quiescent, had heaved itself into the modern age and was on the move, into Tibet.

In late March, its spiritual and political leader, the Dalai Lama, was on the run from Chinese Communists. It had been quickly labeled one of the "stories of the century."[1] Tibet, far off and exotic, had long fascinated the world, vaguely felt by Westerners to be the mystical Shangri-La. Now its "god-king" was in peril from the same forces threatening much of the world. The Cold War was at its frostiest, with Europe, North America and much of Asia jittery about what seemed to be Communism's unstoppable advance. As Tibet's young leader fled to freedom from a ruthless and mighty foe, he in many ways personified the West's own anxieties.

Yet, almost as soon as it had begun, the cliffhanger was over, the Dalai Lama safely in India. Journalists cancelled their travel plans, wrapped up the little they knew of the momentous event, and headlines faded as the world turned to more urgent matters. However, the story that emerged was an engaging one, and in later years has been told and re-told in articles, books and movies. It was a tale of nail-biting drama as the young Tibetan leader, his family and a small group of ministers made their dash for the border, Communist troops straining to cut them off. On a grueling ten-day ride, the group crossed Himalayan passes in weather that froze their hands and feet, grabbing sleep where they could in tiny huts and cow sheds.[2]

Beyond this arresting spectacle, and largely unnoticed by the world's press, the Tibetan exodus was already under way. It began with the country's Buddhist leaders. The mere existence of the religion was a provocation to the Chinese Communists: during a 1954 visit to Beijing, the Dalai Lama had been informed by Mao Zedong himself that all religion was poison – a sinister darkening of

Marx's view of religion as a comforting drug, an opiate. The Communists were set on undermining or destroying Buddhism in Tibet, hell-bent on converting or eliminating the country's leaders.

The Karmapa, head of the Kagyu school of Tibetan Buddhism, whose predecessor had been the personal spiritual teacher to the Emperor of China, had earlier crossed into Bhutan with a large entourage after a three-week ride. Other eminent Buddhist lamas had already left or were making plans to go. Then, as the news spread, thousands of ordinary Tibetans also took to the roads, simply fleeing the fighting, or heading south in search of sanctuary, somewhere they might continue to practice their religion.

For most Tibetans, Buddhism made them who they were. It was the wellspring of their existence, coursing through their lives and shaping the contours of their culture. When faced by the Communist onslaught, leaders and ordinary people alike felt that they had little choice but to flee. In regular displays of stunning fortitude and courage the exodus has continued to this day; tens of thousands of Tibetans have fled their homeland across the Himalayas, usually in the dead of winter when the ferocious weather reduces the chances of being spotted.

While some of these journeys have been recorded, a far larger number have gone undocumented and are now lost to history. Thanks, though, to the foresight of an Englishwoman, Esmé Cramer Roberts, one especially remarkable story was told, written down and published.

A woman in her sixties with an interest in comparative religion, Mrs. Roberts was introduced in 1963 to a young lama recently arrived at Oxford University from India, Chögyam Trungpa Rinpoche. Captivated by his wit, charm and grasp of English idiom, Mrs. Roberts suggested that they meet for dinner – then, over the meal, proposed that they publish a book on Rinpoche's life in Tibet. He agreed, and the following week they began work, shaping a narrative from his diary and memories. Although his English was still fairly rudimentary, and the chasm between their world views sometimes seemed unbridgeable, after two years they came up with a manuscript.

In 1966 the book was published under the title *Born in Tibet*.[3] It has since become a classic, with many hundreds of thousands of copies sold. In clear and simple language, it told of Trungpa Rinpoche's life in Kham in Eastern Tibet and his training as a high lama in its monasteries' rich spiritual and artistic heritage. With deep warmth he described the people and culture of the region he knew. In vivid anecdotes he portrayed the growing presence of the Chinese Communists and, towards the end of the book, gave an account of his escape to India. *Born in Tibet* afforded many readers their first glimpse into the heart of a land that had for so long been an enigma. It was also their introduction to Tibetan Buddhism, and to a lama who was to play a vital role in bringing those ancient teachings to a modern Western audience.

Although the book became widely known, Trungpa Rinpoche's account of his escape went largely unnoticed. Many readers came away with just a faint sense of what he and those who had joined him had gone through. It had been a cold and hard journey, the mountains high and snowy, and they had run out of food, but wasn't this how those things went on those kind of travels in that part of the world? Readers were in search of something else – clues to the renowned mystery of Tibet, its fabled spiritual power.

Perhaps, too, the narrative's spare and radically understated style was too much of a stretch – too even, too matter-of-fact – for Western readers reared on a steady diet of carefully crafted drama. Maybe we lacked the empathy to grasp what the refugees went through, surmounting privations that a Westerner finds hard to imagine: the long months of trekking through impossible terrain, the frightful weather, the gnawing fear. How could we grasp their cognitive fogginess about the route, the fact that they had no maps or compasses and little more than a sturdy belief that India existed at all, somewhere to the south?

And how could we relate to the extreme altitudes at which the story was played out? Surmang, Trungpa Rinpoche's monastery, was situated at about the same altitude as the summits of Mount Rainier and the Matterhorn. His birthplace was on a remote plateau which was only a thousand feet or so lower than the altitude of Mt. Everest's base camps, from which oxygen-equipped climbers set out for the summit. One of the story's dramatic crises came at an altitude several thousand feet higher. At these heights they were above most of the earth's atmosphere, nearer to the void of space.

The mountains were the wake up call for me. Seeing them in their full, three-dimensional grandeur triggered a flash of memory, then awe. First came the famed Himalayas with their stupendous peaks, then the expanse of towering ranges and deep, yawning valleys spreading across Eastern Tibet. Trungpa Rinpoche and his group of refugees had climbed these peaks, and made their way across this almost incomprehensibly harsh and chaotic landscape.

These mountains weren't the real ones. In the winter of 2005 I was exploring scenery around Mt. Everest in a popular flight simulator program when scattered memories of the escape story arose. Being able to immerse oneself in the three-dimensional scenery, in the sweep of massive mountains and valleys, if only in their computer version, brought home the vast challenges the escapees must have faced when crossing them.

Almost idly, the question arose: could one find landmarks of the 1959 escape in the simulator? The program's Tibetan landscape was fairly rudimentary, but the elevations and positions of peaks, ridges and valleys were accurate, and it seemed do-able. After several false starts I found the first landmark: Mount Namchag Barwa, the high, sacred peak overlooking the point where the escapees had crossed the Brahmaputra, with the river's unmistakable loop around it.

Drawn in by the discovery and by the resplendent vista, curiosity took over. If landmarks could be found, what about the waypoints, the route they took? Studying Rinpoche's hand-drawn maps and his detailed and precise account in *Born in Tibet*, along with a series of paper and online maps, gradually brought to light sections of the route. Then a program offering photorealistic satellite imagery of the entire earth's surface was released. Its vivid detail made everything clearer, and after some months' further research the entire route was in place. Seeing it from start to finish, its impact was inescapable: this journey had been a quite extraordinary one.

By 2009, the fiftieth anniversary of the escape, screenshots had been shared, the route confirmed.[4] Friends were now involved in the project, and we wondered how best to pass on the story in the anniversary year, how to convey its full potency. Clearly, the most direct and compelling way was through a video, a medium that could immerse the viewer, three-dimensionally, in the terrain the refugees had been through. It was an unnerving realization. I wasn't a movie-maker, and all I had were still photographs and the flight simulator and satellite maps programs. It turned out to be enough. Although skills and tools were basic, the story's intrinsic power fused with the scenery to bring the journey movingly alive.

By now it had become a personal journey. Re-reading the book to pinpoint landmarks had also meant trying to make out the story's shape. This was not always straightforward: the narrative's dramatic high and low points, its contours, were often hard to see. Rinpoche's utterly matter-of-fact style had been faithfully reproduced by the book's editors: strings of events were run together without highlight or emphasis – where a Western writer, seeking clarity, drama and tension, would have broken them up into a series of carefully-crafted paragraphs.

From this perspective, the original narrative was both understated and, notably in the book's escape sequences, under-edited. A striking example comes at one of the journey's crises, the crossing of the Brahmaputra. In the book, events spanning around twelve hours, most of them action-packed and anxiety-ridden, were packed into one very long, overstuffed paragraph – leaving the reader with the task of separating out one episode from another, then discerning which was more important, which less so.[5]

Retracing the escapees' steps brought both the story's shape and its back stories into clearer focus. Among them were the daily trials, the periodic disputes, the worries about food supplies, the unending search for knowledge of Communist troop movements and of possible routes to evade them, and the multitude of decisions – many of them a matter of life and death – that the leaders, Trungpa Rinpoche in particular, had to make. The video overflight of the journey, seeing the great, harrowing trek they had made, had been gripping enough; the earthbound human story turned out to be far richer and more charged.

Now drawn into the journey, I felt the refugees' struggles more acutely. My own journey started to merge with theirs, become bound up in it. Empathy arose and became almost painfully personal. How could ordinary folk have made such a journey, shown such breathtaking courage, such resilience and cheerfulness … how would I have done? At once inspiring and humbling, it cast a strong, probing light into my own life with its drumbeat of passing discomforts and complaints. At this point the story could not have been more personal.

What a journey it was, in many ways unique. It had been sparked by the young lama's decision to escape capture and probable execution. Knowing that his best hope lay in moving fast and unobtrusively, Rinpoche aimed to keep his group small, but even before he set out others asked to join him. As they traveled onwards more and more people begged to go along, until the group swelled into a mass of refugees three hundred strong – lamas and monks, villagers, peasants, nomads, men, women and children, mothers with babies in arms and elderly folk – along with many hundreds of horses, mules and yaks.

Most of the journey was on foot, the refugees trekking through some of the world's fiercest weather and most harshly spectacular landscape. Frequently at breath-grabbing altitudes, often in heavy rain, mist or snow, towards the end in the near-Arctic conditions of winter, they slogged through deep snow, swamps and nearly impassable boulder-strewn valleys, crossing countless mountain ranges. Much of their route lay across an unknown wilderness where the only tracks were those made by wild animals. Then, as the crisis approached, when food ran out and they began to starve, they were forced to travel at night to avoid discovery.

Trungpa Rinpoche is the story's natural protagonist. From the start it had been his escape, and would not have happened without him. Organically, he became the leader of those who asked to join him: choosing the route and finding the way, making the critical decisions, overseeing people's well-being and shouldering the responsibility for getting them through. Finally he became the chief chronicler of the journey, *Born in Tibet* its primary reference.

Apart from its raw power, the story has a number of intriguing elements. While it is a profoundly human journey of high drama and adventure, it is occasionally lit by shafts of magic. And we might find that we have periodically to remind ourselves that the escape was led by someone who had only just turned nineteen years old.

Trungpa Rinpoche's relative youthfulness, and the leadership qualities he displayed, are more comprehensible when we have some sense of the training that young lamas were put through (outlined in Ch. 1). They would, in traditional Tibetan society, be responsible for both the spiritual and political welfare of the people; high things would be expected of them and their training was correspondingly rigorous – to a modern sensibility, sometimes abusive and even brutal. Nevertheless, a boy of even average capabilities could, through the intensive training, become a skilled and compassionate leader; with a child of superior intelligence, who also felt affinity for the Buddhist teachings, the outcome could be impressive. While the young lamas' training does not tell the whole story – Tibetan Buddhists believe that reincarnation plays a significant role – it goes some way to doing so.

Even though most of the journey's key figures were Buddhist lamas, it was not all love and light between them. As danger grew and prospects darkened, hopes and fears churned up, and discordant views and disruptive initiatives boiled to the surface; blind obstinacy, cunning stratagems, disobedience, and outright sabotage – even from within Rinpoche's own circle – all made their appearance.

Still, as in history's myriad other accounts of perilous journeys, the brightest of human qualities shone out luminously, in Rinpoche's leadership and in the extraordinary courage and resilience of the refugees in the face of towering challenges, qualities that were somehow combined with kindness, compassion and good humor. It is, above all, a human story, one that burrows deep into the psyche and glows there long after we have put the book aside.

❅

It has taken over half a century, but the magnitude of the journey has finally come into focus. For that alone the story calls for a revisiting, but there are other compelling reasons to do so.

We now know that Trungpa Rinpoche omitted much from his account in *Born in Tibet*. He changed the names of people still in Tibet who might have been persecuted had their identities become known to the authorities. He veiled in secrecy his escape plans – and the occasional deception needed to carry them through – in case survivors in his home monastery were accused of conspiring in his disappearance. He left out parts of the story, many of them deeply moving, to protect those who fell by the wayside, people who might have wanted to make another escape attempt when the time was ripe. And he omitted key elements concerning his own leadership, gaps that can only be seen as stemming from a profound humility.

We have learned too that his interpreter edited out material that Rinpoche wanted to include, but which she deemed somehow unseemly or unbelievable.[6] Trungpa Rinpoche always spoke of Mrs. Roberts with respect and affection, and once described with warm irony her tactic for dealing with elements in the story that she found

unpalatable: when one came up in the narrative, she would suggest, in the finest English tradition that it was time for a cup of tea and, upon returning with the tray and pouring the tea, would take up the story at another point or from an angle which she found more agreeable.[7] We can't know specifically what was edited out in this way, but from later reports it seems clear that the banished material told of events that Westerners can find difficult to swallow – events seen as somehow non-rational, inconceivable or "supernatural."

In the spring of 2012, Gesar Mukpo, son of Trungpa Rinpoche, Walter Fordham, the director of the *Chronicles of Chögyam Trungpa Rinpoche,* and the author interviewed survivors of the escape in Nepal. In 2013 and 2014 the author interviewed further survivors in Scotland and the United States. Everyone we talked to gave generously of their time and recollections. By the end we had collected a trove of personal memories which has filled in many pivotal details and much enriched our sense of the story. Much of this came from Yonten Gyamtso, now living in Boudha, Nepal, with whom we spent over forty hours. Both before and during the escape Yonten was an attendant to Rinpoche, taking care of his practical needs, being entrusted with his most precious possessions and, at decisive moments, acting as his spokesman and protector. About eighty-five-years old at the time of our interviews, his recollections of details and events of his life in Tibet, India and Nepal – most of them new to us – were rich and colorful. (See *Resources* in the Appendix for a link to interviewee images.)

Akong Rinpoche, who was later to become abbot of Samye Ling Monastery in Scotland, was Trungpa Rinpoche's close friend and a huge source of support and encouragement on the journey. In recent years he offered his help in tracing the route while also giving us his recollections of the escape. Tragically, following years of signal achievements in the West and around the world, he was killed in Chengdu in southwest China in October 2013. The previous year his younger brother, Lama Yeshe Rinpoche, who was fifteen years old at the time of the escape, had also offered his unique perspective along with some riveting new details. In 1959 he went by his family name, Jampal Drakpa, the name by which he appears in the narrative.

Thanks to Walter Fordham's tireless sleuthing, we found Palya Washutsong in Kathmandu. Living in Boudha, not far from Yonten's monastery, she is a strikingly elegant woman in her seventies. She was, like Lama Yeshe Rinpoche, fifteen years old during the escape, and gave us sparkling anecdotes along with some heart-rending accounts of her family's experiences. She also put us in touch with her younger brother, Drupju Washutsong, now living on the American West Coast; twelve years old at the time of the escape, he clearly recalled many engrossing events, including one when his own life hung in the balance.

The journey was still vivid to these survivors, their stories arresting. They gave their accounts spontaneously, with an eagerness verging on joy at the chance to share them. We learned of personal and political frictions, of secret plans and disruptive counter-plans, of individual triumphs and anguish, of intriguing coincidences and supernormal divinations. Their stories sharpened our sense of the suffering, the emotions and the pushes and pulls of the desperate journey.

Their accounts fused seamlessly with *Born in Tibet*'s narrative while filling in many gaps that Trungpa Rinpoche had not felt free to talk about fifty years ago. In particular, the accounts illuminated the young lama's leadership under the pressures bearing down on him, stresses that grew remorselessly as the journey unfolded. Apart from the sheer physical strain of the journey, he, more than any of the others, faced the threat of imprisonment and death. There was the ever-growing burden of leading hundreds of frightened people, refugees whose discipline sometimes cracked under the strain, and the tensions from within Rinpoche's inner circle, among those who disputed his decisions and criticized his leadership, sometimes bitterly.

In telling their stories, both Yonten and Palya spoke openly and in the most ordinary way of the "magical" or "supernatural" events occurring on the journey. Their accounts have been included here as they were told, without analysis or judgement. In the same way, I have described other such events occurring before and after the escape, as reported by participants, witnesses or, later, Western newspapers. At times we posed skeptical questions. When we asked Yonten about an unusually hard-to-believe detail, he said – obviously amused, and with a touch of scorn – that he didn't care whether or not we wrote it down. A relaxed view of the mystical or miraculous seems to be widespread among Tibetan Buddhists: for them, the miraculous comes not from divine intervention, from powers gifted from on high, but is latent in the human mind, arising organically from years of intensive meditation.

Almost paradoxically, Yonten's and Palya's telling of magical incidents went with an earthy, skeptical mindset of their own. It appears to be something of a national trait. Palya's father made a note of at least one of Rinpoche's divinations, intending to check on its validity later.[8] When we asked Yonten about the escapees' spiritual practice and how it might have helped them face the journey's challenges, he said brusquely that they had no time for such things. It appears that, for many, all their focus, all their energy, was on gritty, practical details – the route, the next range to climb, the depth of snow drifts, the hazards of water and ice, their failing food supplies, the next trudging step forward.

As compelling as is the human drama, it gains much from our having a vivid sense – a clear visualization – of a principal actor, the Tibetan terrain. Yet the terrible grandeur of the mountain ranges they crossed, their seeming endlessness, may be beyond even the finest writer to convey.

Recognizing the reader's need for some visual grasp of the country, the scenery and the escape route, Trungpa Rinpoche drew pen-and-ink maps and elegant images for *Born in Tibet*, including two evoking the hair-raising challenges the refugees faced. Readers have found Rinpoche's maps invaluable when tracing his route; some have been tickled by his symbol for the then recently constructed Chinese road – which looks much like an unbroken line of tanks, their guns pointing towards the Tibetan capital, Lhasa, each small symbol painstakingly drawn one after the other.

Today, thanks to easy-to-access online satellite imagery, we can immerse ourselves in the scenery, and see clearly what the refugees went through in a way not possible before. This has given us fuller insight into the story, including the uncovering of challenges and incidents that Rinpoche did not think worth mentioning in his account. One example of this is the descent from Hungry Ghost Pass just south of Shabye Bridge, a dizzying descent down a steep, two-thousand-foot rock cliff.

This book's website offers photographs, downloadable large-size maps, along with paths and place marks for the satellite imagery, allowing the reader to follow the route; at more popular and accessible locations, there are links to photographs. Also available on the website is a link to a video of the journey – which comes with a strong spoiler alert (See *Resources* in the Appendix).

History teems with stories of adventure and survival, notably those of famous explorers, climbers and adventurers. Glancing at one of them can highlight some key facets of our story: of the refugees' accomplishments and of Trungpa Rinpoche's leadership.

One of the most celebrated journeys is that of the Polar explorer Sir Ernest Shackleton, whose Imperial Trans-Antarctic Expedition of 1914-17 was recently described as "The World's Greatest Journey of Survival."[9] After their ship was destroyed by Antarctic ice, the men were marooned, their only hope of rescue lying in getting a message to the outside world. Shackleton set out in a lifeboat with a small crew, sailing for two weeks across hundreds of miles of treacherous seas to South Georgia Island. Then he and a few companions trekked for thirty-six hours over a three-thousand-foot snow range to reach a whaling station, later returning by ship to rescue his marooned team.[10]

Every story of human courage, survival and adventure is unique. From this perspective it is pointless to compare one to another, to ask which journey was the more challenging, which the more arduous, which the greater. There are, though, parallels between the two accounts – and some very telling differences – that can cast light on the Tibetan journey, bringing it into sharper relief.

Both stories can be seen as playing out in three gripping acts: the first as their home grounds were crushed by overwhelming force, Shackleton's ship *Endurance* by Antarctic ice, Rinpoche's society by the Communist onslaught; the second as exceptionally dangerous journeys were undertaken in appalling conditions which also presented near-insuperable navigational challenges; and the final, climactic act as the travellers faced life-or-death crossings of snow-bound mountain ranges. Both men revealed extraordinary qualities of leadership, in their grasp of strategy and tactics, logistics and morale; both put their own lives at risk to save the people who had followed them; both died young, Ernest Shackleton at forty-eight, Trungpa Rinpoche at forty-seven.

Yet even leaving aside differences of time, place and culture, there is a striking contrast between the two leaders' backgrounds and experience. Ernest Shackleton, aged forty during his famous expedition, was an experienced Polar explorer and, like so many of the leaders of expeditions during the twentieth century's heroic age of exploration, he had a military background as an officer in the Royal Navy reserves. Trungpa Rinpoche was nineteen during the escape and, having spent most of his life cloistered in monasteries, had little experience of hard travel and none of leading an expedition.

The contrasts heighten when we look at those they led and the challenges the followers presented. When Shackleton announced his expedition, five thousand applied to join it. He selected fifty-six highly-seasoned men, hardened, skilled and disciplined. Many had military backgrounds, and in the Antarctic a near-naval level of discipline prevailed. Only once was there a problem, when a carpenter suffering intense pain refused to pull a sled. Accounts differ on how Shackleton handled this: one mentioned him issuing a blistering reprimand, another that he threatened to shoot the man on the spot.[11]

Trungpa Rinpoche had planned to escape with just four companions. With this small group, even leaving as late as they did in April 1959, he could have made a relatively swift and straightforward escape. But even before they started, the party had doubled in size, and then kept on growing as ever more people asked to join. He never turned anyone down, yet each new person and animal added to the difficulties and complications: slowing them down, forcing them into detours and onto routes they would not have chosen, sapping away their chances of survival and freedom.

The swelling numbers were just part of the picture. Even before the escape began, the young lama had to face down fellow monastics' challenges to his decisions, opposition that continued through much of the journey. And Rinpoche led a flock of refugees, many of whom had no sense of personal allegiance to their leader, and little grasp of the pressing need for discipline. As the escape neared its crisis, the refugees' heedlessness confronted their young leader with ever harder challenges until, at the crux, it brought down disaster. Every flare of dissent or indiscipline needed Rinpoche's personal attention, took time, patience and effort to pacify, and added to the already colossal pressures bearing down on him.

And of course, in sharp contrast to Shackleton's team and those of other famous explorers and climbers, the Tibetans' journey was not voluntary: they did not choose to leave their homes to put themselves in harm's way. For none of the threats posed by weather or terrain compared to the menace of the Communist People's Liberation Army. Fear of the PLA dictated all: its onslaught first forced the refugees to flee their homeland, and then shaped the routes they took, compelling them to avoid villages, roads and paths and to travel through an unexplored wilderness they would otherwise have never dreamed of crossing.

✳

It speaks volumes that when news of Rinpoche's escape reached Tibetan expatriates in India, almost all of whom had made their own grueling and often death-defying Himalayan journeys, they were in awe. Indeed, many thought the feat to be miraculous. For nine months – in truth a year longer than that, if the full story were known – Rinpoche had evaded the Communists, and led a large and growing group of refugees through the most rugged of their country's famously daunting mountain country, on routes no-one could remember having ever been traveled before. They had done so in the worst season of the year, sometimes at night, in the later stages eating their leather bags to survive.

If it was a miracle, it was a quintessentially human one. This, it seems, was how their fellow Tibetans saw it, the journey's achievements due less to some spiritual or magical power than to what their countrymen and women had accomplished through courage and resolve. While they had all been tempered to a natural toughness by their land and climate, they were wholly unprepared for what they faced. Yet monastics used to a cloistered, sedentary life, and a multitude of nomads and villagers, ordinary men, women and children, achieved marvels: men were roused to near-superhuman exertions: heroic mothers carried and cared for babies and young children, elderly people who trekked till they dropped.

Driven by a determination to escape oppression and to follow their teachers and religion wherever they went, they left behind what they knew and loved and, under the untried leadership of a young lama, took an astonishing leap into the unknown.

There was no outside help or divine intervention to call on as their situation grew ever more harrowing. They were on their own, people who went beyond themselves on an escape that was to be among the greatest, most heart-stirring journeys of them all.

PART I

1

Surmang

At the dawn of the twentieth century, an era which was to
change Tibet more radically than at any time in its long
past, an observer wrote: "No country in the world has
exercised a more potent influence on the imagination of men."[12]
Few would dispute this. Today, in spite of all that's happened, the
place still holds us in thrall, still somehow pulses with a magic and
spirituality gone from the modern world. It's a spell strengthened by
the land's potency, its remoteness and its stark, extraordinary beauty.

Over the years, many have sought some striking catchphrase to
describe Tibet. It has been called "the heart of Asia," "the roof of
the world," "the realm of magic and mystery" and "the cradle of
life" – several major rivers have their source there, including the
Indus, Yangtze, Mekong and Brahmaputra. Perhaps the most
resonant image is to be found in an ancient Tibetan text, where the
land is seen as "like a house of rock that appeared from nowhere."[13]

Around forty-five million years ago, the massive island that was
to be India slid northwards on its tectonic plate and collided with the
great Eurasian landmass, then ground underneath it. It was one of
the most colossal upheavals in the planet's history: as the edge of the
landmass was forced upwards, it formed a range of mountains over
fifteen-hundred miles long and, to its north, a lofty plateau. As one
writer put it, it was as if "a sea, the gigantic waves of which, driven
by northern and southern winds, have changed to stone at the
moment of their greatest fury."[14] The mountains, the Himalayas,
today include the planet's highest peaks; the Tibetan plateau and the

surrounding terrain is the world's most elevated and mountainous country. The "waves" have never quite settled: every year since their birth, the peaks and plateau heave themselves a few more inches heavenward, their rise often accompanied by the roar and tumult of earthquakes.

On its majestic heights, within its immense mountain ranges, Tibet is also the world's highest and most forbidding natural fortress. To the east, in the Kham and Amdo regions (parts of them now Sichuan and Qinghai), is a tumble of peaks strewn like dragon teeth across the path of visitors or invaders. To the north, guarding the land from Central Asia, is an alien world of marshes, quicksands and glaciers, the Kunlun mountains, the Gobi desert, and the deserts of Qinghai and Xinjiang. To the west and south lie the Himalayas, a daunting obstacle to traders, explorers or invaders wanting to get in or, in recent times, a dismaying challenge to anyone trying to get out. It's here – especially in winter when border guards retreat to their barracks, and when refugees prefer to travel – that you find the deep snow and dizzying peaks of the legendary Tibet, and its ferocious, Arctic-like weather. A winter crossing of these frozen heights is among the worst journeys in the world. The Himalayas are also a barrier to moisture-laden monsoon air from the south, and much of Tibet is extremely dry, supporting only a thinly spread population.

Overarching all is Tibet's harsh splendor. Its mountains dominate the land with what one bewitched writer called a "fierce majesty and barren grandeur."[15] Above them, its deep, striking sky shades from azure to ultramarine to a near-midnight blue. Its high thin air, cloud-free and pure, neither blocks nor retains heat, with scorching days usually followed by frigid nights; the sun's unfiltered radiation is so penetrating that frostbite and sunburn can occur simultaneously. The land has about it something intangible, intense and intoxicating.

Before the modern era, the land was quiet. Except around towns and villages, little could be heard except the wind, the occasional bellow of a yak, the bark of a distant dog, the far-off calls and songs of herders, or the drums, bells, horns and chanting from monasteries. Within this pervasive peace many people lived their lives within a spiritualized atmosphere, attuned to the slow rhythms of the seasons, the cycling of crops and of birth and death, and the religious ceremonies and observances which consecrated everything.

Seductive to so many, Tibet cast an overwhelming spell on spiritual seekers. They were drawn by its challenges, and by its remoteness and beauty, qualities that inspired what a nineteenth-century Western observer described as an "uncompromised faith, simplicity, isolation, calm and spiritual mystery."[16] Yet Tibet's general remoteness was not enough for a small elite, who traveled deep into the mountains in search of their highest and furthest fastnesses.

One of the most remote, and most spiritually renowned, of these regions was in the province of Kham, which lay far to the northeast of Lhasa, in the northernmost reaches of the Himalayas where they break up into the towering, dragon-teeth mountains along the Chinese border. Among its commanding peaks and deep, isolated valleys were superb settings for hundreds of monasteries and myriad meditators' caves. Many brilliant teachers and highly realized meditators were reputed to have come from this area.

Here there was only the occasional bird and wild animal, only the sounds of mountain wind, rain or snow, the murmuring of one's own voice, and the rhythms of breath and heartbeat. Here spiritual hermits sat in small huts or caves for years on end, meditating, supplicating and practicing an array of yogic techniques. These not only sustained them through the frigid depths of winter but also led, they believed, to ever more profound heights of spiritual realization. In this high, great space, everything seemed possible.

In early 1941, a small party of monks made their way through Kham's cold mountains, following directions contained in letters they carried.[17] They were seeking a small nomad encampment in a remote region far to the north. After coming across a group of nomads camped high on a sixteen-thousand-foot plateau, they spotted the letters' next indicators: a tent whose entrance faced south with a red dog standing guard outside.

While the monks were still some way off, a baby boy sitting on the ground outside the tent waved his small hand to them, then, as they dismounted and entered the yak hair tent, he broke into a big smile. When they spoke to the family, everything matched the letter's directions, including family and place names, but it was the warm reception they had received from the boy that clinched it for the monks. They had found the one they were seeking, for this was the eleventh incarnation of the Trungpa lineage of teachers.

Overjoyed, the monks presented the child with gifts, a sacred protection cord and the traditional white silk scarf – which he accepted and draped around the offering monk's neck in the traditional way, as if he instinctively knew the right thing to do. The monks later heard from other nomads that, on the night of the boy's conception, the mother had dreamed of a being entering her body in a flash of light. She had given easy birth in a cattle byre on the full moon day of the New Year festival. That day, a rainbow was seen over the encampment and a water bucket was unaccountably found to be full of milk. That night, several of the mother's relatives dreamed of a lama visiting them in their tents.

With everything confirmed to the monks' satisfaction, they hurried back to their monastery and sent off a report. It went to the author of the letters they had carried, the Gyalwa Karmapa, the head of the Karma Kagyu school of Tibetan Buddhism; he'd had the two visions indicating where the Trungpa reincarnation would be found, detailed in the letters. When the monks' report arrived, the Karmapa glanced at it and said, "This is the right person. You've found him."[18]

From then on, things moved quickly. The monks sent a letter to the Karmapa, requesting that he come to their Surmang monastery to enthrone the young Trungpa. They then dispatched a second mission to the nomad encampment. It was a critical expedition, and was led by the monastery's general secretary, Karjen, who was accompanied by a large party of lamas and monks. They were anxious for a quick resolution, but these things took time; in giving up the child the community was relinquishing a valuable commodity, and normally a large gift, either of money or land, would be demanded in return. But negotiations were swift and smooth: "everyone was very cooperative and modest and no-one asked for any gain for himself."[19] With matters settled, the mission set out triumphantly on the return journey, bringing with them their newly found teacher along with his parents.

As the traveling party approached Surmang monastery, the valley was cloaked in mist, a rainbow arching overhead. The group was met by a long procession of monks, and by outriders carrying banners high aloft who escorted them to the waiting monastery. Around them thronged many hundreds of excited villagers, townspeople, farmers and nomads, many of whom had traveled from far afield for the occasion. The monastery itself was in full festive mode, ablaze in color on flags and banners, and in the gold, saffron and maroon robes of thousands of rejoicing monks.

Among the joyous crowd was a thirteen-year-old boy, Yonten Gyamtso, thrilled by it all and brimming with pride to see his uncle Karjen, the general secretary, leading the procession. On the outskirts of events now, Yonten was later to play a vital role in the young Trungpa's life, indeed in his very survival.

Trungpa himself was now just thirteen months old. When he arrived at the monastery, he immediately recognized the monks who had been closest to his predecessor, the tenth Trungpa. Then, once the festivities were over, concluding with a great feast for all, the baby was put through a set of rigorous tests. Tibetans are a skeptical people, the monks perhaps more so – they are fond of quoting a saying that one should test the Buddha's words as one would test the quality of gold – and they needed to be quite sure that they had found the right child. Several pairs of closely matching objects, among them two rosaries and two walking sticks, were placed before the baby. In each case he selected the one belonging to his previous reincarnation. Various names were written on small, folded pieces of paper and he correctly selected the one with the tenth Trungpa's name on it. When he later tried to talk, his first words were reported to have been "*Om Mani Padme Hum.*"[20]

With everyone now convinced, they could proceed with the new Trungpa's enthronement. When the ceremony was held a few weeks later, Surmang's monks were delighted: one of the largest and most glorious events in living memory, it was witnessed by a glittering array of high reincarnated lamas, over thirteen thousand monks and a huge, ebullient crowd of people from surrounding areas. With all the pomp and ceremony of hallowed, ancient tradition, and accompanied by the sound of deep chanting and resonant horns, drums and cymbals, the child was carried into the assembly hall – a space aglow in bright murals and multi-colored brocade banners, the air laden with the smoke of incense and butter lamps. He was then lifted up to the lap of a high lama sitting on the traditional lion throne. The proceedings ended with the traditional Buddhist Refuge ceremony, when the boy's hair was cut to represent the transition from a worldly life to a spiritual one. At the very moment the Karmapa put scissors to hair a clap of thunder shook the hall, followed by a sudden rainfall and then a rainbow, all taken by those present to be highly auspicious signs.

With the ceremony over, the Karmapa left for his monastery and Surmang returned to its centuries-old routine, its teacher's reincarnation back home, fully examined and installed. The boy was now known as Chökyi Gyatso,[21] meaning "Ocean of Dharma," "Dharma" referring to the Buddhist teachings. As the eleventh Trungpa he was also referred to as the Trungpa Tulku (*tulku* meaning "incarnate lama") or in more personal terms as Trungpa Rinpoche (*Rinpoche* meaning "precious one").[22]

In Tibetan Buddhism, a *tulku* is an enlightened being who, for lifetime after lifetime, chooses to be reborn in order to continue teaching others. Although the *tulku* tradition was a profound and genuine one, it was open to decay and corruption. In Tibet, having a famous – or even a lesser – lama's reincarnation in residence gave monasteries a unique opportunity to amass wealth, influence and power. While great care would be taken in the search for, and testing

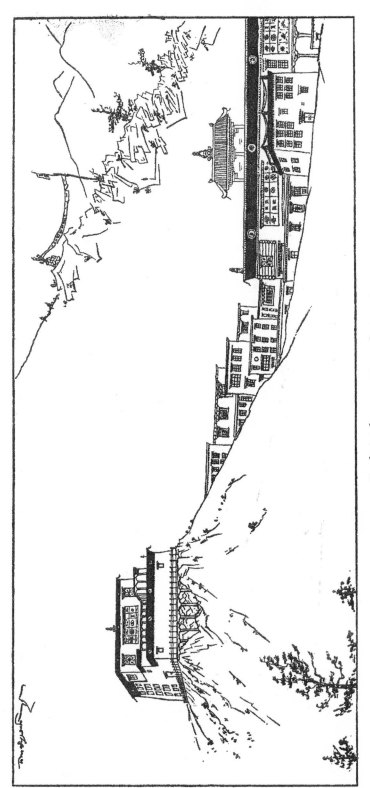

Dudtsi-til monastery, Surmang

of, leading teachers, with lesser figures from struggling monasteries the process could sometimes be quick and perfunctory.

Yet even with a master's vivid visions, and a scrupulous search and examination, things did not always work out as hoped. The ninth Trungpa *tulku*, the least charismatic of all the Trungpas, chose to spend much of his life sunning himself in the courtyard, or hanging out with his chums, drinking tea and taking snuff. As the eleventh Trungpa Rinpoche later put it, he was a bit of a "basic good old Surmang redneck."[23] One of the few clues that he was anything out of the ordinary came at his death. Having announced that he was going to die the following day, when the morning came he changed out of his everyday clothes into his yellow teaching robe, drew himself up into meditation posture and passed away.

Perhaps the most sensational case of the *tulku* tradition going adrift was that of the sixth Dalai Lama. Although he was both the spiritual and secular leader of Tibet, he preferred the life of a playboy, spending his days practicing archery, writing poetry or carousing with Lhasa's aristocratic beauties. Much of the poetry was blatantly erotic, but many saw in it veiled, highly advanced teachings showing the unity of secular and spiritual pleasures. His activities tipped the spiritual-political establishment into turmoil, and also enraged a puritanical Mongol warlord on whose support the establishment depended: unbothered by niceties, in November, 1706 he had the Dalai Lama assassinated.[24] Yet the Tibetan people loved him, and the sixth Dalai Lama continues to hold a secure and venerated place in their memory, as beloved for his tender poetry and simple humanity as for his power as a tantric yogi.

Although the infant Trungpa Rinpoche was now the supreme abbot of a major monastery, for the time being his life would be that of any new young *tulku* – cherished, protected and gently brought into the life and routines of the monastery, and gradually introduced to his spiritual and political inheritance through the sorts of stories that would appeal to a young boy.

Surmang monastery, and the Trungpa lineage itself, had arisen in the fourteenth century after Trung-mase, the son of an Eastern

Tibet king, sought spiritual guidance from the fifth Karmapa, the personal teacher to the Chinese Emperor. Following years of rigorous training, the Karmapa sent Trung-mase out to teach. He finally found a remote, sheltered valley in a beautiful region of the far northern Himalayas, in Kham, high in the border lands between Tibet's cultivated plains and the highlands where nomads roamed. Many mountains in the area rise to over eighteen thousand feet, while among its numerous rivers are the beginnings of the great Yangtse and Mekong waterways.

Here Trung-mase built himself a grass reed hut and settled down to meditate. Soon, people were flocking to request his teachings, and in time there was the call for a monastery. Trung-mase named the monastery "surmang," meaning "many-cornered," after his reed hut's irregular shape. Within his lifetime, Surmang expanded to cover a huge area, its two chief monasteries lying forty-five miles apart.

Trung-mase's closest students were ironically called the "three idiots," likely because they did without hesitation everything that their teacher told them to do. One of these "idiots" became the first Trungpa. Over the generations, with each Trungpa incarnation, Surmang's spiritual and political power expanded, while a brilliant artistic heritage flowered. In the seventeenth century the Emperor of China honored the fifth Trungpa with the title *Hutukhtu,* or Great Teacher.

The close links between the Trungpa line and the Emperor of China continued down to the first half of the twentieth century and the tenth Trungpa. As if to make up for the ultra-relaxed "red neck" life of his predecessor, he was a fervent practitioner: before meditating he would tie his hair to the ceiling and surrounded himself with stinging nettles, so that if he drowsed off he would be yanked or stung back to full wakefulness. A man of simple tastes and austere lifestyle, he despised court life. So, when the latest invitation to the imperial court arrived, the tenth Trungpa brusquely declined it, saying that he would rather give his blessing to a dog's skull than to the Chinese Emperor.[25]

The latest incarnation in the line, the eleventh Trungpa Rinpoche happily settled down in his new home. Every morning his mother took him to the monastery and in the evening returned with him to their home nearby. He had no lessons to attend to, and plenty of playmates – carefully selected from among the sons of respected officials – with whom he enjoyed snowball fights in the monastery courtyard. Rinpoche was a curious and occasionally mischievous boy, once getting into trouble for setting off firecrackers on the kitchen roof. In all, it was a golden, carefree time for him.

Rinpoche's days passed amid a swirl of shaven heads and the saffron and maroon robes of monks. Early on, though, his eye may have been caught by the dashing figure of a local boy in his early teens, usually to be seen on horseback around the monastery. Yonten was now a junior assistant to his uncle Karjen, the general secretary, and was being groomed by him to take over the position in due course – family connections were all-important where the plum jobs were concerned. He had come to the monastery when he was about ten years old, two years before the young Trungpa's arrival, and was very happy there. The family home was nearby, he loved his uncle and reveled in his job: he had learned to ride when he was four, and was thriving in his responsible, independent work as a mounted courier, carrying messages from and to the monastery.

When Rinpoche was five, the golden times abruptly ended. He was shaken to hear that a tutor would be coming from some far-off place to give him lessons. The monastic committee in charge of his training had decreed that it was time for him to begin his studies. They well knew that finding a reincarnated lama, a *tulku*, was only the beginning. Just as important was the long process of shaping him into a worthy heir of the lineage. This would require the most intensive training under the finest tutors, scholars and meditation masters that could be found. Only at its successful conclusion would the young *tulku* be qualified to carry on the high teachings and traditions he had inherited; only then would the future of the monastery and its material, artistic and spiritual wealth be fully secure.

Rinpoche had heard that his tutor had a scar on his forehead and, fearing the worst, nervously watched for anyone fitting the description. The man duly arrived and lessons started. It was the first day of winter; Rinpoche could hear the sound of snowball fights among his friends in the courtyard below, and was miserable to learn that he could no longer join them.

Then the beatings began. A Tibetan saying declares that *tulkus* are like gold, needing to be beaten until their full luster is revealed. The beatings were formal events: Rinpoche always knew that one was coming when the tutor lit incense on the shine, then did a prostration before him. As his world slowly darkened, his mother's visits grew less frequent until one day she told him that she was returning to her village. Alone in his room, he cried with grief, writing later: "I missed her as only a small boy can."[26]

In spite of Rinpoche's distress, he kept at his studies and began to show much promise. This did not satisfy the monastic committee, which decided that the monastery was too distracting for the young *tulku*. He and his tutor were dispatched to a remote hermitage, Dorje Khyung Dzong ("Indestructible Garuda Fortress").

Like the nest of the mythical, eagle-like garuda, his new home perched precariously on a ledge of rock high on a mountainside, held there by pillars; it was reached by a long set of stairs that zig-zagged up the steep face. Through the windows of his room Rinpoche could see a great spread of mountains and, in the far distance, was sometimes able to spot the smoke from his monastery. Although isolated, the hermitage's food was typically Tibetan, simple but nourishing. Yak milk and meat – their protein and fat much needed in the cold climate – were combined with rice, oats and Tibetans' beloved *tsampa*, roasted barley flour. Hot salted, buttered tea was served throughout the day.

Young Rinpoche's day now began at five in the morning and continued well into the evening. Astonishing his tutor and other teachers at the hermitage, he learned the Tibetan alphabet in a single session – although he said later that he was most interested in the grain and texture of the paper, and the shapes resembling tigers and dragons he saw there.[27]

In spite of Rinpoche's early fears, the tutor turned out to be a kind and gentle man, and they quickly formed a close bond. Going outside the committee's curriculum, the tutor encouraged Rinpoche's painting lessons, and on special occasions the two of them would go out for walks on the mountain. Out on the heights the tutor would tell him stories about the Buddha and about Rinpoche's predecessor, the tenth Trungpa.

In his seventh year, the monastic committee judged that Rinpoche was ready for a sizeable step. He was taken back to the monastery where a teacher was to give a reading transmission on all 108 volumes of the Buddha's sayings. For three solid months under tight discipline, two or three volumes were read aloud every day, usually at top speed. No-one could be expected to hear and absorb teachings read at that pace; it was understood to be a transmission, a passing-on. It could have been overwhelming for the boy, but he found it a "great experience."[28]

This was Rinpoche's first full-blown introduction to the wealth of teachings that awaited him, and to their quintessentially personal quality. Rather than looking outward to some deity for salvation, Buddhists look to themselves, to their teachers, and to teachings which have been handed down from one teacher to another, in an unbroken line all the way back to the Buddha himself. The teachings are transmitted less through belief or doctrine than through personal exertion and an intimate, heart-to-heart communication – a kind of tough love affair – between teacher and student.

Rinpoche would not know such a full-fledged relationship until he met his own guru. In the meantime, tutors were filling the role – and the monastic committee had another shock in store. They had decided to dismiss his kindly tutor on the grounds that he was too indulgent, was telling his young charge far too many stories rather than keeping him to strict study. The tutor had been like a father to Rinpoche, and the parting was almost harder for him to bear than when his mother left.[29]

The replacement tutor was a man of an entirely different stripe. He was very experienced, having been in charge of the monastery's young monks, but had somehow managed to combine this with a highly erratic temperament. Rinpoche was constantly criticized, but could never quite figure out what was expected of him. Some things would make sense, as when he swallowed his food noisily and was criticized for eating "crocodile style," or when he leaned back in his seat and was told to sit up. But often he was criticized even more heavily when he thought he was behaving perfectly correctly.

Perhaps more unsettling for Rinpoche, he felt that he was being taught to act in a false and artificial way. His teachers instructed him on how great masters of the past behaved, insisting that he imitate them: even if he did not feel that he was a completely religious person, they told him, he should always smile at people, keeping his eyes half-closed as if he was continually meditating. And when he met visiting dignitaries he must follow a set formula, first saying this, then that – instructions that regularly got him into uncomfortable situations when he tried to apply them. He was, he wrote later, "being made to be a charlatan ... asked to make a fool of myself."[30]

When they returned to Dorje Khyung Dzong the tutor changed Rinpoche's schedule, and upped the lessons' level of difficulty. In perhaps the hardest blow, he stopped Rinpoche's cherished painting lessons. Now study went on by lamplight well into the evening, and was tied to memorizing, with Rinpoche's accuracy tested the next morning. His sense of claustrophobia grew pervasive. Constantly criticized, rebuked and harangued by the tutor, Rinpoche could not escape his presence. And he himself was awash in doubt: how could someone with so many faults, so inescapably flawed, be the eleventh Trungpa? How could he possibly follow in the footsteps of – let alone live up to – his illustrious forebears?

The tutor even slept in the corridor outside Rinpoche's door, ensuring that he could not leave without being noticed. Rinpoche's only break from his suffocating prison came when he relieved himself. The hermitage's facilities were crude structures built out from the walls, with a hole in the floor high over a sheer cliff. Here

Rinpoche found simple, peaceful enjoyment in the rush of fresh air, and in the pleasure of knowing that at least here he was free of his tutor, and could defecate in peace.

Even outdoors, on the walks that he and his first tutor had so much enjoyed together, there was no lightening of the mood. The new man was a most serious and solemn character, all business, and his friends who visited him at the hermitage were much the same. They were all quite uninterested in the flowers, plants, animals and birds that Rinpoche loved, and he could not share with them small jokes as he had done with his first tutor's friends.

Without companions or playthings, the boy cooked up his own amusements. During the New Year festival, Rinpoche persuaded a young monk to get him some gunpowder, which he was then able to fashion into a fairly successful rocket. Thrilled by this success, he began working on an improved version – only to be caught in the act by the tutor who, although he did not punish him at the time, from then on took every opportunity to remind him of what a terrible boy he had been.

Around this time Rinpoche had a series of strange dreams. In one dream he found himself riding in a small truck, in another he saw aircraft neatly parked in a field, while in a third he was walking around a shop full of boots, shoes and saddles with unfamiliar shapes and styles, and which were covered in what seemed to him like dried blood – both styles and polished finish he later knew to be Western. He had never heard of such things or seen them in pictures. With no-one else to confide in, he described the dreams to his tutor, who swatted them away as nonsense.

When Rinpoche turned eight, the committee again accelerated his studies. He began formal study of Buddhist practice and history, subjects he loved from the start. He read the life of the Buddha, and was especially affected by the account of the death of the Buddha's mother. He read an illuminated manuscript of the life of Milarepa, Tibet's great yogi-poet, so often that he knew it by heart. The songs and stories moved him to the core, and he often wept or laughed as he read them. His tutor sneeringly asked him whether it was because he missed his mother, or whether he was trying to get out of the training's harsh discipline, but Rinpoche told him, "No, I'm crying because of what I am reading."[31]

He especially loved the story of Padmasambhava. Seen by Tibetans as "the second Buddha," he was an Indian saint who in the eighth century defeated the indigenous Bonpo priests and planted Buddhism in Tibet; shortly afterwards, the king of Tibet and the emperor of China signed a peace pact that ended centuries of warfare. Padmasambhava also introduced the *terma* tradition to Tibet. *Terma* are hidden treasures of sacred teachings, concealed in caves and rocks for future generations to discover when needed. These texts could only be found and deciphered by a *terton*, or treasure-finder, someone with sufficient spiritual insight to do so.

Rinpoche's obvious passion for the material and his questioning, probing style impressed both his tutor and the committee. They decided that he was ripe for another big step, ordination as a monk. The ceremony was followed by a short sermon, in the course of which Rinpoche was formally included in the *sangha*, or Buddhist community. He was then sternly reminded that his predecessor, the tenth Trungpa, had always rigorously held to the strict rules of a monk. Afterwards, the officiating lama confided to Rinpoche that he was the youngest novice that he had ever ordained.

Rinpoche then began a three-month meditation retreat. Sitting meditation was the key, calming the mind so that confusion could be seen and worked with. It is said that intensive practice allows the rich, previously unseen, qualities of the natural world to unfold, along with a deepening kindness and compassion. With further practice, the haunting sense of the impermanence of all phenomena sharpens into a vivid, living insight into their essential emptiness.

Rinpoche emerged from his retreat feeling heartened, more confident, more awake. His studies were going well, he had been ordained, he was deeply inspired by the great Buddhist figures, and now he had accomplished a quite demanding retreat.

But something more far-reaching had happened. He had realized that he did not have to feel shamed and beaten down by his tutor's criticisms – did not have to struggle with the endless demands and unpredictability of his world, or fight against the stifling claustrophobia they brought. He had accepted that his world just was that way, his life like that. He could relax with it, take it as it was. Now, rather than seeing harsh criticism and chaos as burdens, he took them as sparks of inspiration for further practice. From then on, as Rinpoche put it: "I just went on and on."

He later talked of the power of monastic discipline, and how it worked for him. When discipline is all-encompassing, everything simplifies. The mind, totally involved with things as they are, is unmoved by surges of desire, aggression or other emotions; in every moment, there is a sense of a living totality, free of pushing and pulling, hope and fear. Then one lives life sanely – or as Rinpoche put it, "sanely and saintly."[32]

The shift triggered a startling change in his teachers. As Rinpoche leaned more confidently into his world, and his questions multiplied and became sharper and more penetrating, his tutor said less and less. He seems to have become intimidated by his young charge. Then, as Rinpoche pursued his other teachers at the hermitage for answers, they began reducing the amount of material they gave him; they could no longer supply answers to his questions, and were openly afraid that they could no longer keep up with him.[33] Instead of being pushed by his teachers, he was now pushing them. But Rinpoche had not gone on the offensive: he was craving more challenge, genuinely wanted answers, and was disappointed that they were not offered. He was not at all happy with the teachers' new open, subdued and relaxed approach.

Looking back at Rinpoche's super-intensive training, it's hard to avoid the conclusion that the monastic committee, tutors and teachers had known precisely what they were doing. Like that of other young *tulkus*, Rinpoche's training was far tougher than that of a normal monk. Yet its methods had been tested over many centuries by a religion known for its gentleness and kindness. Perhaps it was tough love at its most potent: unflinchingly skilled toughness contained within a profoundly felt love. However the training worked – whether it had been like beating gold to bring out its luster, or super-compressing rock into brilliant diamond – it seemed to have worked for Rinpoche. He had learned truths about himself and his world that would serve him well, far beyond the monastery walls.[34]

Back at the monastery, Yonten had also spread his wings. Now in his early twenties, he had been given increasingly important errands that took him ever farther from Surmang. The journeys tested his mettle to the extreme. In an area where roads were few and maps rare, he had to know a variety of routes through a maze of peaks and valleys. Out in all seasons, he learned how to survive appalling weather. And he had become a skilled horseman; one of the few people at the monastery to have his own horse, he had chosen the fastest and most reliable one available.

He needed it. Far more nerve-wracking than weather and terrain were the brigands infesting the area. These were tall, swaggering Khampas, fierce yet jovial men with red cloth braided into their hair. Crack shots and able swordsmen, they lived for loot and, when booty was to be had, cared as little for the life of a young man as they did for that of a high lama. Yonten learned to ferret out the latest information on bandit sightings, then time his travels accordingly, carefully choosing routes around likely points of ambush. For self-defense, he carried a long Khampa knife; much like the ancient Roman short sword, it was a beautiful object, usually with an engraved scabbard. It's been said that Khampas love their knives more than their cattle herds; Yonten certainly treasured his.

In Rinpoche's ninth year, a famed teacher, Jamgon Kongtrul of Sechen, visited Surmang. Rinpoche was captivated by him. Unlike all the previous teachers he had met, Jamgon Kongtrul was a large, natural, jolly man who made no distinction between the highest lama and the lowliest novice, speaking openly and freely to all, giving generously of his time to anyone he met. Physically large, he had a vibrant sense of humor which sat easily with a deep sympathy and understanding, and brimmed with funny and engaging tales about gurus and lamas. And he did not gaze through half-closed eyes – he did not even sit upright all the time, as Rinpoche had been so sternly enjoined to do, sometimes lying down when he gave teachings or met guests. The boy was overjoyed. All the doubts he had entertained about himself and the Buddhist path were dissolved on the spot. He had met his guru.

The Kongtrul and Trungpa line of teachers had a unique bond. Jamgon Kongtrul's previous incarnation had been the guru of the tenth Trungpa, Rinpoche's immediate predecessor, while, in turn, the tenth Trungpa was the guru of the present Jamgon Kongtrul. He told Rinpoche that he was to be his teacher, just as the tenth Trungpa had been his own, and warmly recalled the previous Trungpa's kindness to him, saying how happy he was to give back to Rinpoche what he had received – as the Tibetans say, "returning the owner's possessions."[35] One morning, as Rinpoche entered Jamgon Kongtrul's room, the sun's rays fell on him, which the master said was a very significant sign. After this he gave Rinpoche teachings that moved him to the depths: "I felt that he was giving me back the spirituality he himself had received from the tenth Trungpa."[36]

As joyful as were their times together, at one point Jamgon Kongtrul made a troubling remark. He said that the world was changing, that it was in darkness and that people were surrounded by suffering. He himself had been fortunate to live in a country that was so happy, and he hoped that suffering would not come to Rinpoche and his generation; people like Rinpoche were the hope for the future, like flowers in bud that must be carefully tended so they could bloom. When Jamgon Kongtrul left Surmang, he said that Rinpoche should at some point join him at his own monastery to "receive the full cup of spiritual milk."[37]

After the master left, Rinpoche and his tutor returned to the mountain hermitage. To fill the void left by the departure of a man he had quickly come to love, Rinpoche threw himself into his studies with even greater vigor. Meanwhile, his relationship with his tutor had matured. They now found some ease and pleasure in each other's company, going on walks which both enjoyed. While the tutor still did not think it right to compliment Rinpoche on his obvious progress, he suggested that the boy start giving short sermons to the young monks and laymen at the hermitage.

And so by his ninth year Rinpoche had undergone a sweeping transformation. He had taken to the teachings like an eagle to air. He had begun to feel that he could, after all, be the Trungpa *tulku,* someone with a strong and vibrant sense of the teachings, well able to pass them on to others. He had been revealed as a *terton,* or finder of hidden spiritual teachings. And he had met his guru, someone with whom he had formed a uniquely close bond – one that really did seem to echo back over lifetimes. Around this time a quiet, diffuse joy must have settled over Surmang. The Trungpa lineage was intact, the monastery's future assured, the luster of its gold visible to all.

In early 1950, a few months after Rinpoche began to teach, news reached the hermitage that three Chinese Communist officials had arrived at the nearby town of Jyekundo, the province's chief trading center. They announced that they had been put in charge of the entire area, including Surmang itself.

It was a high-handed proclamation, but few in Surmang were much concerned by it. The monastery's influence had until recently extended to the heart of Chinese power, to the Emperor himself, while Kham's proximity to the border had left ancient memories of the violent – yet fleeting – passage of Mongol cavalrymen, Tibetan government troops and Chinese warlords. They had heard of the Communists' rise the previous year, but they had seen a long cavalcade of dynasties come and go, and there was little reason to think that this one would be different. And anyway, the area had for some time been under the control of a Chinese overlord, a man happy to let them get on with their lives as long as the heavy taxes he imposed kept flowing into his coffers.

What's more, the Communists had come unarmed. There seemed little cause for alarm. Relations between Tibetans and the newcomers remained cordial, and the life of the monasteries, the province and its people went on much as they had done for a millennium or more.

2

Closing Storm

Throughout much of the last century, Westerners viewed Tibet as a sort of Shangri-la, a peaceful, snowy, mystical realm where dazzling heights of wisdom were attained by beings of almost super-human insight and fortitude. In some ways the view was accurate, the country's remote mountain regions the site of thousands of monasteries and myriad caves where meditators shut themselves in for years on end. Yet for the land at large, and for East Tibet and Kham in particular, the reality was often a quite different one.

In the eighth century, under King Trisong Detsen, Tibet ruled over a vast military empire, stretching from Persia in the West down through Northern India – encompassing all the states in between – and extending deep into China in the East. So far-flung were its conquests that contemporary chroniclers spoke of the Bay of Bengal as the "Tibetan Sea."[38]

In 779, to crown his prodigious empire, the king declared Buddhism to be the state religion,[39] and invited the great Padmasambhava from India to teach it – and also to subdue the stubborn Bonpo priests opposing the religion's establishment. But, after Padmasambhava returned to India, the Bonpos bided their time until the great king's death, and then strangled his successor. The new Bonpo king relentlessly hunted down Buddhists, coming close to altogether erasing the religion from Tibet. The holocaust went on unabated until, during public festivities, a Buddhist monk drew a bow and arrow from under his robes and shot the king between the eyes.[40] In the maddened Bonpo rampage that ensued, the unified state shattered, its great empire collapsing with it.

Amid the wreckage, Buddhism gradually regained its strength in Central Tibet, and in 1155 the first Karmapa built his monastery near Lhasa. Then, a century or so later, the all-conquering Mongols swept in. As fearsome as they were, it was a fairly bloodless invasion: Tibet's broken, fragmented state made it easy game, while Genghis Khan himself had enjoyed amicable meetings with Tibetan Buddhist missionaries, placating his feelings towards the land. The Mongols annexed Kham, and then adroitly appointed a succession of Buddhist viceroys from each of the different schools to rule Tibet. As years passed and the invaders settled down, they converted *en masse* to Buddhism, making it dominant in Tibet and, in time, the Mongol empire's official religion. Ringing through the centuries, history's greatest land empire, and its most formidable warriors, had been conquered by one of its most gentle religions.

In the relatively stable era that followed, a new school of Buddhism arose: the Gelugpas, led by the Dalai Lama. Peace reigned until, in the seventeenth century, the fifth Dalai Lama's regent joined with a Mongol chieftain to suppress the other schools and to impose Gelugpa rule over all Tibet. In 1637, after three years' civil war – during which a thriving and powerful Surmang was singled out for attack and the fifth Trungpa jailed[41] – the Dalai Lama was installed as supreme temporal and spiritual leader of a re-unified Tibetan state.

Yet after the Dalai Lama's successor, the wayward sixth, was assassinated, Nepalese Gurkhas took advantage of the chaos to launch their own invasion. The weakened Tibetan government had no choice but to call on the Chinese emperor for imperial troops to expel them.

It was a fateful call. Political links between Lhasa and Beijing had been forged, and they soon began to tighten. From the start the connection was fraught with confusion and misperception: the Chinese assumed a natural superiority and authority, while the Tibetans were unshakably confident in the power of their own history, religion and culture; the Chinese saw their representatives in Lhasa as viceroys with imperial authority, the Tibetans took them as ordinary ambassadors and politely ignored their edicts.

The sense of sturdy independence was even stronger in eastern Tibet, where Khampas had always vigorously defended themselves against all comers. In spite of this, an early outcome of the central government's new Chinese links was a 1724 agreement between Lhasa and Beijing that ceded parts of Kham to China – a mischievous bend of the Yangtse River, the agreed border, placed Dudtsi-til, Surmang's founding monastery, a few miles inside China. Khampas blithely ignored the new imperial authority and, as much as they venerated the Dalai Lama, paid equally little attention to decrees arriving from far-off Lhasa. On the whole, though, except for the occasional squabble between the central government and its sometimes obstreperous province, peace was maintained.

The dawn of the twentieth century gave Tibetans their first glimpse of what lay in store for them. In 1904 the British, worried about Russian designs on India, decided to pre-empt a possible incursion from the north by sending a small military expedition to Lhasa, on the way mowing down ill-equipped government troops using recently-invented Maxim guns.

The incursion was fleeting, but it brought tragedy to Kham. The Chinese, shaken by the foreign threat to its power, for the first time declared sovereignty over Tibet. To assert this authority they sent an official to Kham, who was promptly assassinated. The imperial response was ferocious. General Zhao Erfeng – known forever after to Tibetans as "Butcher Zhao" – led a punitive expedition into Kham, destroying monasteries and massacring people, often by decapitation or mass live burials. Surmang did not escape the destruction. Some terror-stricken people fled almost as far as India, finding refuge in remote valleys of the Himalayas, never to return. It was all a somber foreshadowing of what was to come.

In 1911 China's last imperial dynasty fell – as did Butcher Zhao's head after his troops mutinied. In the ensuing power vacuum, the Dalai Lama declared full independence, proclaiming that Tibet had

never been subordinate to China. The Lhasa government followed
words with deeds: to regain its authority in East Tibet, it launched an
attack on Qinghai in 1932. The government troops, ill-armed and
under-trained, were easily repelled by a Chinese republican force
under General Ma Bufang.[42] A few years later, Lhasa tried again, this
time being forced back by Khampas hoping to establish a
democratic republic within China. In this ungovernable, semi-lawless
mountain country, thieves and brigands began marauding freely.

This was the world into which Trungpa Rinpoche was born.
Although the King of Nangchen was Surmang's traditional ruler, the
republican General Ma Bufang was now Kham's effective overlord.
He showed scant interest in trying to govern the wild and intractable
Khampas, focusing instead on extracting heavy taxes when and
where he could. Due to its talented statesmen and merchants, the
region had, from the fifth Trungpa's time on, become wealthy and
powerful, and its people thrived. Here lay rich pickings for the
general and, borne aloft on Khampas' backs, he earned the
nickname "The King of Qinghai" for his grand style.[43] Years later,
Rinpoche spoke of people's suffering under his rule.

Ma also periodically persecuted Buddhists, combining his distaste
for the religion with his lust for money to lucrative effect. After the
discovery of the current Dalai Lama's reincarnation in northeast
Tibet, not far from Surmang, Ma tracked the child down and then
held him ransom – only letting him leave for Lhasa after the
payment of one hundred thousand silver Chinese dollars.[44] A
Muslim, General Ma was a loyal soldier for the Chinese republican
cause, leading his Muslim cavalrymen to victory, first against
Tibetans, then against Japanese invaders. In the 1940s he met his
final opponents, the Communists who, in a string of battles,
annihilated Ma's forces and sent him fleeing to Mecca.[45]

From the first, the Communist Chairman, Mao Zedong, had clear
designs on Tibet. Even before his armies' final victory over his

republican foes in 1949, he was actively discussing the "liberation of Tibet."[46] Like the emperors before him, he brushed aside Tibetans' own views: Mao simply assumed that Tibet – all of it – was part of the greater Chinese empire. Wasting little time, by the first months of the following year Communist officials had established themselves in Kham's provincial capital, Jyekundo. This news soon reached Surmang.

❋

At the Dorje Khyung Dzong retreat center, ten-year-old Trungpa Rinpoche was just beginning his studies of the advanced teachings of Tibetan Buddhism, the Vajrayana or Diamond Path. This path deepens insights gained on the earlier paths, deploying a variety of meditative and yogic techniques to accelerate meditators' engagement with the phenomenal world – their full embracing of its luminosity and its emptiness. Along the way, Vajrayanists say, as a natural by-product of years of intensive meditation, miraculous powers arise. But teachers are careful to warn students that these powers are not to be sought for themselves or exploited; then they become obstacles, and a real danger to the meditator and others.

One morning Rinpoche was deep in meditation when an urgent message arrived: Communist troops had been seen approaching the monastery. Nothing came of it, but they later received news of other troop movements; apparently no villages or monasteries had been harmed, and the soldiers had paid in silver for any goods acquired. Wherever the Communists had gone, they handed out large posters announcing that the Red Army had come to help the people, and assured everyone that feudal and monastic structures would be respected. A few days later, from his window Rinpoche could make out the distant glint of Red Army weapons.

All this was deeply worrying, and Rinpoche interrupted his meditation to consult with Karjen, the general secretary. As a precaution, they decided to safeguard Surmang's treasures by moving them to a more secure location. They would also position horses nearby in case of need. For the first time, the possibility of Rinpoche's escape had been raised.

Following his eleventh birthday, Rinpoche received an invitation from the King of Lhatok to go on a three-month teaching tour in his nearby kingdom. The traveling party consisted of thirty monks, organized and attired for pomp and display. Everywhere they went, young Rinpoche was greeted with traditional pageantry and festivals, which both he and the people hugely enjoyed. He had seen nothing like it since his enthronement: the vibrant display of rainbow banners, tall crimson hats, and gold, saffron and maroon robes; the haunting sounds of horns, cymbals and drums; and, suffusing it all, the smoke and incense that raised it all to the heavens.

The king hosted Rinpoche in his palace above the town. From the guest room windows, Rinpoche could see down into a newly built school nearby. Children were now being taught Chinese along with Tibetan, and were also instructed in drilling and marching, for which a monastery drum was used. A red Communist flag hung at the school gate; when it was lowered in the evening, the children were lined up in formation to sing the Communist anthem.

Rinpoche was intensely curious about it all, but he was troubled that a drum meant for sacred rituals had been turned to secular, militant purposes. And posters had been plastered everywhere, even on monastery walls, with slogans like "The Liberation Army is Always at the People's Service." Few were persuaded. Rinpoche heard that the people of Lhatok's initial openness to the newcomers had evaporated with the sudden surge of troop movements; and there was growing dismay at the rough, imperious way in which the changes were being pushed through.

After their invasion, the Mongols had calmed down and converted to Buddhism. General Ma had generally left people alone as long as they poured taxes into his coffers. But Khampas were coming to realize that their new overlords were of an altogether different breed – hard, relentless, driven by ideology, bent on shaping not just people's lives but their minds.

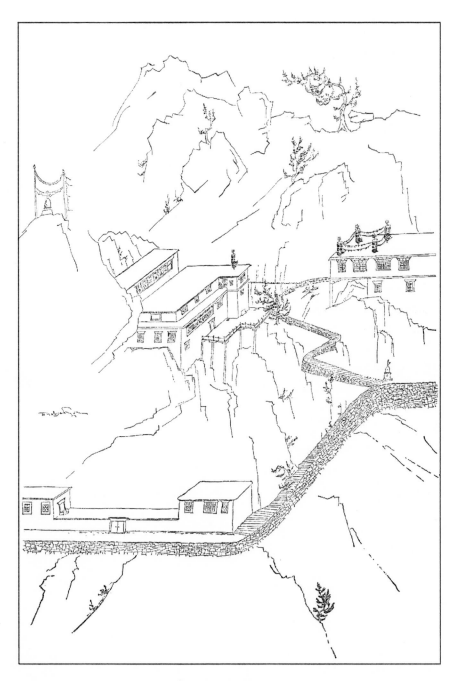

Dorje Khyung Dzong retreat center

It was a chilling shift. For well over a millennium, Tibetans had lived with the teachings of universal gentleness and compassion, teachings that had become rooted in themselves and their world. Now they were being force-fed a dogma about the clash of classes and an unending war over material possessions – a vision so alien that it might have come from another planet. Before, their world had been adorned with a myriad of multi-colored banners reminding them of the Buddha mind flowing through their minds, bodies and all the elements. Now a blood-red flag flew above them all.

Still, in the lowering clouds over Kham Rinpoche could soon see only the sun. After three long years' wait, the time had come when he could go to his guru, Jamgon Kongtrul, to receive the "spiritual milk" the master had promised him.

Rinpoche wanted to follow the tenth Trungpa's example by walking to his guru's monastery at Sechen, but it was felt that he was too young for the ten-day trek and would go on horseback. Surmang's secretary Karjen was so concerned for his young charge's well-being that he decided to accompany him on the journey himself – and he had also arranged for two cows to accompany Rinpoche to ensure his nutrition. Karjen's nephew, Yonten, was also with the traveling party. He knew the way well, having made the journey several times before as Surmang's courier. He had earned a reputation as a doughty traveler, able to find his way through the mountains of northeastern Tibet to an array of destinations in the foulest weather, often while evading bands of brigands, and sometimes shepherding herds of Surmang yaks to market.

They arrived at Sechen on Rinpoche's twelfth birthday. Jamgon Kongtrul was overjoyed to see him, and looked pleased when he was told of the two cows, as this meant that Rinpoche was there for a long stay. The boy was struck by the monastery's quiet serenity. No-one was allowed to raise their voices, and the monastic drums, horns and cymbals were unusually soft-toned. Pervading the calm was an atmosphere of tremendous vitality, and although the monastery's discipline was extremely strict the monks were all very happy.

Following a month's study, Rinpoche was empowered to enter a teaching cycle that Jamgon Kongtrul was presenting on "The Treasury of the Mine of Precious Teachings" (known in Tibetan as the *Rinchen Terzöd*) – a huge collection which included all of the most profound doctrines taught by the tenth Trungpa.

For six full months, from five in the morning until eight at night, they sat and listened to the teachings. Rinpoche was the youngest of the many abbots and monks attending the Treasury Teachings, many of whom had traveled long distances to attend. Yet, while other young lamas were allowed some frivolity, he was singled out and instructed to behave correctly at all times. At the conclusion of the teachings, only one person was empowered with the authority to teach and pass on the Treasury Teachings. When Rinpoche was the one chosen he felt very shy, knowing that there were many lamas present with far greater learning than his own. The young lama was now completely happy with the work, and all his early struggles were far behind him.

One day, after about a year at Sechen, Rinpoche was out walking when a thunderstorm burst directly overhead. He ran through the storm back to the monastery, where he found a monk from Surmang waiting for him with a message. One of the senior lamas had died, and Rinpoche was to return to officiate at the funeral ceremony. Jamgon Kongtrul was unhappy to hear that he would be leaving, and told him of a dream he'd had the previous night, of a half-moon rising in the sky. Its meaning, he said, was that Rinpoche was the moon, but that his teaching was incomplete and he must return later. The boy was broken-hearted when he rode off, gazing back at the place he loved, his eyes fixed on his guru's retreat hut and the monastery's golden roof shining in the sun.

Some weeks after returning to Surmang, Rinpoche received an invitation to teach at Drolma Lhakang monastery. It lay well to the south, past the town of Chamdo, where the Communists had set up their provincial headquarters. On the way, the traveling party came to a modern road, their first such sight. Its black line sliced through mountains and gouged a straight trench across fields – a brash swordstroke through the gentle undulations and inherent dignity of the land. As they stopped at the road's edge, a Chinese truck bristling with guns roared by, its passing echoing loudly through the valley, its fumes settling foully over the landscape. The horses were terrified, as were many of the monastics. Rinpoche had dreamed of trucks years before, and as a teenager had ridden in one, but seeing and smelling one now, its explosive rumblings reverberating in flesh and bone, was utterly shocking. Everything about the the violent contraption and its straight black road seemed to negate the world they knew.

After a ten-day ride, the traveling party reached Drolma Lhakang on its high, chilly plateau. As it approached the monastery the young abbot, Akong Tulku, ceremonially greeted Rinpoche with an offering of the traditional white scarf. It was a kind of homecoming: as distant as Drolma Lhakang was from Surmang, the ties between the two monasteries were close, going back many years. The boys discovered that they were of the same age, and soon became great friends.

Also at the monastery were Akong Tulku's two brothers, Jamyang, the eldest, and Jampal, aged nine. Young Jampal was desperately unhappy at the monastery. He was there solely due to the family link, and did not really know either of his brothers, who had both left home before he was born. Nevertheless, as family he was being trained as a high official, subjected to a harsh regime of study and practice in which he had little interest; he heartily detested it all – the monastery, his studies, his confinement. Rinpoche, vividly recalling his own training, gently befriended Jampal, who felt immediately drawn to him. Before long they had developed a warm, close bond that was to last a lifetime.

A few days after Rinpoche's arrival, Akong Tulku formally requested him to present the Treasury Teachings which Rinpoche had recently received. It was a jaw-dropping challenge for a thirteen-year-old. Without a single day's break, he would be leading a program lasting six full months, each day commencing with the first rituals at 2:30 a.m. and continuing well into the evening.

Rinpoche was taken aback by the request, but after a few days consideration he agreed to go ahead. The program demanded prodigious focus and staying power from everyone, most especially from Rinpoche. But things went well, the teachings were duly completed and Rinpoche's monks were flushed with pride at their young abbot's performance. Having now experienced his teaching, and seeing that the reputation that had preceded him was not an exaggerated one, Drolma Lhakang's senior lamas asked Rinpoche if he would undertake to be Akong Tulku's guru. He declined, saying that he had first to complete his studies at Sechen. He did, though, urge the lamas to send Akong Tulku there to join him.

In the winter of 1954 Rinpoche returned to Surmang, traveling in bitter cold through heavy snowfalls. While he had been away, the Communists had been busy. Chinese shops now dotted the towns, selling Chinese crockery and the ubiquitous blue overalls, the People's uniform. At the monastery Rinpoche found that his monks were wearing different robes – machine-made and of a different style from the traditional ones. Some monks were leafing through copies of *People's Pictorial* given to them by Communist officials, who had also handed out slogan-packed posters to be plastered on the monastery's walls.

A few days after Rinpoche's return, a Communist official arrived at the monastery to see him. He had brought a roll of orange brocade, along with a sizeable portrait of Chairman Mao, which he offered. He then asked Rinpoche what he thought of their regime, but received no answer. It was Rinpoche's first face-to-face meeting with the Communists. He found them to be "quite a different sort of human being" – he could not even understand their smiles.[47]

As soon as he could manage it, Rinpoche returned to Sechen. He again found himself in a cheery, peaceful place, and a while later was delighted to see Akong Tulku, who had taken his advice and undertaken a hard journey through ice and snow to get there.

Amidst the general sunniness, though, Jamgon Kongtrul's message to Rinpoche was far more somber than before. The overall situation was, he said, very serious. From now on, the Buddha's teachings would lie in the hands of individuals alone, as the world that had supported them would soon be gone. As if to punctuate this message, soon afterwards a Communist team arrived at a nearby monastery with a movie projector which they set up in a sacred shrine hall. Curious, Rinpoche decided to attend. The officials screened a documentary – the first film any of them had seen – showing the schools and hospitals the Red Army had built, and purporting to show the enthusiastic welcome it received wherever it went.

In the early spring of 1955, Rinpoche received an urgent message from Surmang. The Dalai Lama, together with the Karmapa and other senior figures, were returning from an important visit to Beijing and wanted to share their message with the people of Kham. All the lamas of the Kagyu school were to assemble at Pepung monastery to hear it. Rinpoche could easily have borrowed horses for the journey, but the fifteen-year-old decided to walk, and he and Akong Tulku struggled through heavy spring snow, suffering intense snow blindness along the way.

When they reached Pepung, they heard that earthquakes had apparently blocked the Dalai Lama's route, and the Karmapa would be delivering his message instead. With Chinese bodyguards and officials standing close by, the Karmapa spoke of the hospitable treatment they had received in Beijing, and then instructed the assembly to keep up their religious practice and institutions. It was obvious to all that the Karmapa could not speak openly, and that Tibet's leaders were already under the Communists' tight control. Everyone clearly sensed the gathering storm.

A few weeks later, the news went out that the Dalai Lama would at last be talking in person, this time at Derge monastery nearby. No explanation was offered for why he could now suddenly make the trip. People from far and wide headed for the monastery, ebullient at the prospect of seeing their leader. They lined up along the road into town to greet him – and were crestfallen when he sped past in a closed car, invisible to all. They could not even catch a glimpse of him entering the monastery.

The next day, the Dalai Lama's Communist minders allowed him to give a short talk in the monastery's great hall. Religion should be foremost in their lives, he said, and Tibetans should try to maintain a friendly attitude towards the Chinese. Then, although intensive preparations had been made in Derge to host the nation's spiritual and political leader, it was announced that the Dalai Lama would be leaving before nightfall and he was abruptly whisked away. Rinpoche had hoped to discuss the developing crisis with the Karmapa, and to request his personal guidance, but he too was rushed off, waving a white scarf from the window as his car disappeared into the rain and mist, leaving disappointment and worry thick in the air behind.

Returning to Surmang, Rinpoche held a meeting to pass on the Dalai Lama's message to the monks and the district's leading laity. Again, Chinese officials were present, closely monitoring his every word. Unable to speak freely Rinpoche, knowing of the overwhelming might of Communist military power, said that while he understood the people's feelings as loyal Tibetans, there was no choice but to accept Chinese domination.

The Communists now had the monastery firmly in their grip, and green PLA uniforms were everywhere. They had set up their headquarters in the great hall, the sacred space where Rinpoche had been enthroned all those years before. They had stripped brocades and banners from the walls and ceiling, and pushed to the side or dismantled thrones and shrines, replacing them with office desks; where brilliant banners had been, there now hung the ubiquitous red flag. Once they had settled in, the Chinese took to mocking the lamas and monks, saying that the Communist regime possessed all of Tibet – and especially the province of Qinghai, where Dudtsi-til monastery lay, which, they scoffed, was not even part of Tibet. Rinpoche reflected that while they had suffered under the heel of the warlord General Ma, it had been nothing like this.

Rinpoche took the first opportunity to returned to Sechen to continue his interrupted studies. He found the once serene place in turmoil. No-one could now avoid the dark future they faced. Jamgon Kongtrul told Rinpoche that an eminent teacher had already fled his monastery for India, where he planned to continue his work. He thought that it might be wise for them all to follow him there. It was achingly obvious to Rinpoche that his time with his teacher was quickly dwindling away, and he redoubled his efforts at study and meditation. For his last three weeks at Sechen, he moved into his guru's residence. Jamgon Kongtrul's final teaching to him was a simple one: he must continue to learn, continue to be a pupil on the path.

On returning to Surmang, Rinpoche found that the Communists were tightening the screws. They handed him an invitation to visit China, following up with a suggestion that he join the Central Committee of the Communist Party. Rinpoche politely declined both offers, saying that as his general secretary had already joined the committee, there was no need for him to do so himself. Communist commanders knew their *Art of War*, Sun Tzu's classic on strategy: aiming to avoid hardening resistance, they were advancing quietly and gradually, whenever possible co-opting those susceptible to their cause rather than confronting them. Still, it was all too clear to Rinpoche and his senior lamas that the Communists would stop at nothing to get him under their control.

The vast waves of change sweeping over Kham now swelled in strength. In April 1956, inspired by the "high tide of socialist transformation and socialist reconstruction" surging through China, Chairman Mao set up a "Preparatory Committee for the Tibetan Autonomous Region." The committee recommended wide-ranging initiatives, including the raising of between forty- and sixty thousand cadres from local Tibetans, along with the recruitment of a hundred and forty thousand Tibetans into the Chinese Communist Party and the Communist Youth League. In July, large numbers of Communist cadres flooded into East Tibet and began their work,[48] coercing people into indoctrination groups, then sending them out as spies among their own families, friends and neighbors.

The people of Kham had been straining to find a way to accommodate the onslaught, striving to hold strong to the way of non-violence. Then the Communists took a fateful step, demanding that all weapons be handed over. For most Khampas this was a demand too far. Their long Khampa knives, often beautifully embossed, were precious possessions, often heirlooms; like their old rifles and muskets, they were also essential for self-defense against robbers and brigands. Nevertheless, many people were unwilling to resist their new overlords and handed in their weapons. Many did not – including Yonten, who simply ignored the order. Yet Khampas' attempts at compliance had little effect, and the frustrated Communists grew ever more abusive and heavy-handed.

Finally, people could take it no more. A local leader pretended to turn in his weapon to a Communist official, then shot the man dead. Khampas took the act as a call to arms, and their fury overwhelmed all their best instincts. The land erupted in revolt and, in the weeks of bitter violence that followed, many Chinese were killed. Khampas began to organize into armed groups, and skirmishes with PLA troops broke out across Kham.

As the conflict intensified, news began arriving at Surmang of the capture and killing of lamas and monks, and the destruction of monasteries. Pepung, where they had recently received the Dalai Lama's message, was among them, every one of its senior lamas having being rounded up and shot. Communist troops were now doing Mao's awful bidding, washing what he saw as "poison" from the land. Communist theory dictated that the "ruling class," the Buddhist lamas, was orchestrating it all; and the Communists never grasped – or never allowed themselves to see – that the revolt had come from below, from the people.

Amid the growing turmoil Rinpoche received in secret a shocking message from Jamgon Kongtrul, saying that he had fled Sechen and was heading to Lhasa. He wanted Rinpoche to go with him, and proposed a rendezvous point. Rinpoche immediately set out, but when they met he found that his guru's views had shifted: he said that he could not take on all the responsibility for such fateful decisions, that Rinpoche's work at Surmang was very valuable and that he must make up his own mind about what to do. He reminded Rinpoche that the teacher is within us all, and that we must stand on our own feet. They parted in great sorrow, knowing that they would not see each other again.

Rinpoche returned to Surmang burdened with the bleak awareness that his life had reached a crisis-point: "I was faced with the knowledge that Eastern Tibet no longer existed as a spiritual center and everything looked very dark."[49] But he was perplexed about what to do, as were Surmang's senior lamas, who felt that his guru should have given him instructions. At the age of sixteen, for the first time in his life he was alone with critical decisions to make.

With conflict and chaos spreading across the land, awash in uncertainty himself, Rinpoche decided to embark on a major new project. The tenth Trungpa's final wish had been to construct a new seminary building, and the Karmapa had later urged Rinpoche to get it done. He was passionate about the building project, and determined to bring it to completion, but he ran head-on into grim, common-sense opposition from some senior lamas. With the Communist menace growing, and everything around them seemingly coming apart, they were reluctant to call on people to contribute to the high cost of a building. Rinpoche responded: "Even if the Communists destroy the whole place, the seeds of knowledge in our hearts cannot be destroyed."[50]

It took several months to raise the necessary funds, but work began on the new building; meanwhile, the finest silversmiths and goldsmiths, and a miscellany of other artists and craftsmen were brought in. When the golden roof went up, the tenth Trungpa's vision actualized, Surmang's monks and the surrounding community were elated.

The seminary was soon flourishing, the new building filling with monastics who had traveled from far afield to study with the seminary's head teacher, Khenpo Gangshar. A close student of Jamgon Kongtrul, he had been in charge of the Sechen seminary when Rinpoche was there. Now he had moved to Surmang and become its pre-eminent figure. Brilliant, charismatic and daring, he was venerated by all, Rinpoche chief among them.

The seminary project had been a triumph, but Rinpoche remained apprehensive. A month after the building's completion, a few dozen PLA military intelligence troops arrived at the monastery. After unsaddling their horses, they announced that they would be moving into Rinpoche's private residence, setting up home in a hall near his sleeping quarters. Rinpoche's attendant panicked, saying "They have invaded us,"[51] and that they must escape now, while there was still time. Rinpoche calmed him, saying that in such circumstances it was best not to show fear.

With the mountains of Kham aflame in conflict and the Communists breathing down their necks, Rinpoche settled down to three months' strenuous study. He was preparing for his *kyörpon* examination, a degree roughly equivalent to a Ph.D. His studies completed, on the day of the examination a small field was fenced off outside the monastery's walls; a throne was placed at one end for Khenpo Gangshar, the senior examiner, while seats were arranged around him for senior lamas and scholars. Everyone present could participate in the exam. Rinpoche stood in front of Khenpo Gangshar as a scholar posed him a question; after Rinpoche had given his answer, he could shoot back a counter-question of his own. This intense dialectic went on for three full days, at the end of which the seventeen-year-old lama was awarded the degree of *kyörpon*.

His examination over, Rinpoche caught up with the latest news. Kham was in an uproar. More monasteries had been destroyed, with many more lamas and monks brutalized or killed. Every day more peasants, men and women alike, flocked to join the fight against the Communists. Surmang's lamas took every opportunity to try to persuade people against taking up arms, appealing to simple rationality, saying that there could be no hope of success against such overwhelming odds. Many followed their teachers' advice, but in the mountains large numbers of famously brave Khampas were battling the Communists wherever they could find them.

It was an unequal contest: tens of thousands of PLA troops — many of them armed with modern U.S. weapons captured from the

Chinese republicans[52] – poured in. As the Khampas began to find themselves regularly outmanned and outgunned, they appealed to the Tibetan central government for help. None was forthcoming. Lhasa merchants, though, offered British Lee Enfield rifles acquired in India for six thousand rupees apiece, bullets for thirty rupees each – extortionate prices at any time.[53]

At Surmang, Khenpo Gangshar had been feeling ill for some time, and decided to take a break from his duties. He and Rinpoche journeyed to Mount Doti Gangkar, a sacred mountain known to be one where Padmasambhava had meditated. According to legend, during the Golden Age snow completely covered the peak's crest, and it shone like a diamond; in the following age, the crest was like a semi-precious onyx, with patches of dark and light; in the third age it would be like iron, signifying that their time in Tibet had come to an end. When they reached the summit, they found that much of the snow had melted, exposing large stretches of black rock.

By the summer of 1957, Khenpo Gangshar knew the course he had to take, and his illness disappeared. Returning to Surmang, he invited all the local people to a meeting, and spoke to them throughout the day and into the evening. He said that while Buddhism's forms and rituals would go, its essence was indestructible: quoting scripture, he told them: "Cease to do evil, do what is good, purify your minds."[54] From all around people crowded into Surmang for his utterly simple and direct teachings – ones that would previously have been kept secret from all except the most seasoned meditators. He instructed the lamas and monks to turn their attention to helping lay people; they should stress meditation and loving kindness, remember the importance of non-violence and human rights. Finally, he made a round of meditators' caves and retreat huts, telling the occupants that they must prepare for the shock of re-entry to the world, and learn how to meditate in everyday life.

Khenpo Gangshar's systematic dismantling of sacred forms and customs was breath-taking – the most radical changes in over a millennium. At first there was strong opposition, but it soon dissipated. All were coming to grasp the awful truth: they were entering a time more devastating than any in Tibet's long history. However much it went against ancient forms and tradition, the changes had to be made.

It was a sublimely brave piece of strategy. It seems that Khenpo was pre-empting the enemy, setting in motion what would soon be happening anyway, sanctifying the process with his and the lineage's authority. He was breaking open the teachings' time-hallowed container, sending its contents spilling across the landscape for all to help themselves from, empowering them all.

The Communists were now as concerned by Khenpo Gangshar's actions as they were by Rinpoche's. Surprising everyone, he said that he would be delighted to meet with Communist officials and discuss the teachings with them. This he did, but observed later that the meetings had little effect, and it was unlikely that conditions would improve. Meanwhile, he pressed the many Tibetans he met not to take up arms against the Chinese, pointing out how slim were their chances of success.

Khenpo Gangshar then decided to return to Sechen, and was accompanied by Rinpoche. A few days from the monastery, they heard that it had been attacked; although its lamas had been tortured, the monastery had suffered relatively little physical damage. Khenpo Gangshar told Rinpoche that it would be best if he returned to Surmang and continue his work there. Rinpoche was desolate: "I had had to part from my guru, Jamgon Kongtrul, and now my last support, the guru to whom he had passed me on, was to be taken from me. I was alone."[55]

At the age of eighteen, then, Rinpoche was entirely responsible for the life-and-death decisions he would have to make – not just for himself, but for many others. Returning to Surmang, he found that the Communists were pressing down ever harder. They had demanded fifty thousand Chinese silver dollars as "tax," and also that the monastics hand over all wristwatches, Indian or European goods, and any photographs of the Dalai Lama. Rinpoche's regent abbot, observing the Communists' implacable aggression, remarked to Rinpoche that he had become familiar with their brutalities in Mongolia: Rinpoche, with all the precious training and instruction he had received, should consider escaping; however, he should not do so without first consulting the Karmapa.

In the spring of 1958 Rinpoche received an invitation to conduct an enthronement at Kyere monastery, a few days' ride to the south, which he accepted. He set out from Surmang in the midst of a fierce storm, with only a small group of people gathered in the downpour to say goodbye; his mother was there, as were others Rinpoche had been especially close to. As he rode off into the driving wind and rain he was overcome by heavy-heartedness, sensing that he would not see them, or Surmang, again.

3

Razor's Edge

Leaving behind the high valley of his home monastery, Trungpa Rinpoche and his attendants rode south to Kyere. The monastery where he would be conducting the enthronement ceremony lay near Lhatok, where he was well known and had many students, while the ceremony itself would be an unusually personal one: he would be enthroning his younger brother.

The boy deeply loved Rinpoche, who in earlier years would often play with him, and it was a moving event. Afterwards he struggled to hold back his tears when Rinpoche took his leave in the traditional manner: his group and the one remaining behind rode in circles waving white scarves, as they whistled down the scale, meaning "Return soon."

Rinpoche did not return directly to Surmang. Instead, he toured widely in the area, giving teachings and conducting retreats for villagers and local people. He stopped everywhere to teach, even approaching individuals on the road, doing whatever he could to inspire and fortify people for the coming difficult times.[56]

Here and there Rinpoche took a few days to meditate. One retreat took place in a holy cave high on Kyere Shelkar (White-Faced) mountain, where he was accompanied by a disciple of the tenth Trungpa. The cave was in a striking setting near the summit; it was approached along a path which wound up a grassy slope, and – high on the mountain – crossed a narrow splinter of rock that

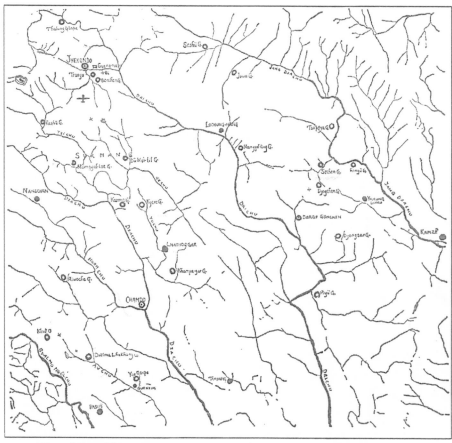

Kham/East Tibet, Surmang at upper left. (See p.315 for enlarged map)

formed a natural bridge over the abyss. By now, at his young age, Rinpoche was widely known as a *terton*, or treasure-finder; within a rock wall in the cave he discovered several *terma* – treasures hidden there by Padmasambhava twelve-hundred years earlier. Among them was a small ritual dagger with a three-sided blade made of meteoric iron; he also found strands of the hair of Yeshe Tsogyal, Padmasambhava's consort, which he distributed among his attendants.

While they were in the cave, Rinpoche had two unsettling dreams. In one he was standing on a hill above Surmang, its valley so deep in smoke that only the monastery's high golden pinnacle could be seen. In the other he looked on as Communist soldiers in their green uniforms performed some sort of rite in Surmang's main assembly hall.

Following his *terma* discoveries on Kyere Shelkar, Rinpoche paid a call on the King of Lhatok. Soon after his arrival, he was asked to officiate at the enthronement of the king's son, who was to replace a father whose mind had begun to fail. After the ceremony, Rinpoche was just about to leave Lhatok to return to Surmang when he received three invitations: the first came from Khamtrul Tulku, a highly respected Buddhist leader, who asked Rinpoche to visit him at his nearby monastery; the others were invitations to teach at Drolma Lhakang and Yag monasteries, far to the south.

Shortly afterwards another messenger arrived, bringing disquieting news from Surmang. The resident Communist officials had been highly alarmed by his sudden absence, and were accusing the monastery's monks and lamas of hiding him. It seemed very likely, the message went on, that when Rinpoche returned he would be arrested and taken into custody. Later, news came that when the lama who had been with Rinpoche on Kyere Shelkar mountain arrived back, the officials demanded to know Rinpoche's whereabouts and why he had not returned with him. The lama told them that Rinpoche had, unfortunately, broken his leg in a fall from his horse and could not possibly travel. Whether or not the officials believed the story, they seemed to relax. Perhaps other reports had arrived saying that Rinpoche had been spotted in Lhatok, traveling openly and teaching widely; the officials may have felt that it was better to wait for him to return to Surmang in his own time, rather than arousing people's ire by arresting and bringing him back.

Now Yonten arrived from Surmang, bringing provisions for Rinpoche. From this point on he would travel with his abbot. They rode with the attendants on to Khamtrul Tulku's monastery where, shortly after they arrived, Rinpoche's host invited him to join him in performing an advanced divination.

Over the centuries, Tibetans facing difficult decisions have resorted to divination after earthy fact, information and rational analysis have failed. Matters of life and death are sometimes decided this way and little is left to chance. Years of training, intricate techniques and detailed manuals, centuries of experience with a method's reliability, and precisely performed rituals – all are brought to bear to tap into the deeper reaches of mind. The materials used are often ordinary: dreams, dice, stones, rosaries, doughballs, the flame of a butter lamp, the striations in the shoulder blades of animals, and – especially among nomads – folded bootlaces.

Khamtrul Tulku wished to use a technique that employed a crystal or brass mirror. In this technique a female deity is invoked, whose image appears reflected in the mirror to offer guidance. The mirror is not usually read by the diviner himself, but by a virgin boy or girl no more than fifteen years old – Rinpoche described the reading process as allowing the mind to relax into a child-like state of openness and purity, a state not unlike meditation. It is very rare for someone to have the power to both invoke the mirror deity and to read the divination: Rinpoche could do both, and had become famous in East Tibet and beyond for the clarity and reliability of his readings.

Khamtrul Tulku was focused on the need to escape. The divination provided clear-cut directions: he should leave his monastery soon, and he should not head to Lhasa to take the traditional route, but make directly for India. Assuming that he followed these directions to the letter, the divination specified the time he would take on the journey, the obstacles he would face on the way, and the precise date he would cross the Indian border.

Khamtrul Tulku asked Trungpa Rinpoche to go with him, but he declined; he must, he said, first honor the teaching invitations he had received from Drolma Lhakang and Yag monasteries.

After Rinpoche resumed his journey, heading southwest past Chamdo, his attendant managed to get him a ride on a Chinese army truck going their way. It was Rinpoche's second such experience; the first time he had been with Khenpo Gangshar who, noticing the teenager's excitement as the vehicle raced down the road faster than any horse, had sternly warned him against becoming fascinated by the toys of materialism. This time Rinpoche sat among PLA soldiers armed with sub-machine guns – perhaps enjoying the irony of being driven speedily southward by an enemy who, further north, was on the lookout for him. Later, as the truck passed a group of mounted Tibetans, he reflected on how much happier and more comfortable they were on their horses than he was in the truck.

When Rinpoche reached Drolma Lhakang it was midsummer, the countryside aglow with wildflowers. After the welcoming ceremony he spent some time with his friend Akong Tulku, then with a sense of urgency sat down to write letters. He wrote to the Karmapa and to two other highly respected lamas, in each letter describing the grim situation in East Tibet and requesting advice. For the Karmapa, he laid out his personal dilemma: should he try to continue on at Surmang or escape to Central Tibet? He concluded almost pleadingly: "I need your guidance more than ever."[57]

It was the most acute of dilemmas. On the one hand lay Surmang, a centuries-old monastery of high renown, famed for its shining spirituality and splendid art. Its reach, its political and spiritual influence, went back hundreds of years and extended from the highest levels of the Lhasa government to the Emperor of China. It was a source of leadership and inspiration for many in East Tibet, and for generations of disciples, monks and lamas. The monastery was unlikely to survive without a Trungpa *tulku* in residence, someone who could continue it all and be capable of bringing in the funds needed for its upkeep. With Surmang's demise, everything would go, including the means of livelihood of everyone there.

On the other hand, there was the issue of Rinpoche's safety. He was the one on whom the Communist's baleful gaze had settled, the one under greatest threat. It was ultimately not a question of personal safety. His life as an individual had ended at the moment of his enthronement, when as a very young child he became the eleventh Trungpa *tulku*. From then on enormous resources had been poured his way: the finest tutors, well-stocked libraries, a disciplined training carefully tuned across many centuries, and "spiritual milk" fed him by the highest lamas in the land. Surmang's wealth and the gifts of nobles, villagers, nomads and peasant farmers had all been funneled into his long and careful nurturing.

For, as everyone knew, the teachings were not in the end to be found in books, belief or ritual, but in the minds and hearts of realized individuals, in the teacher. Rinpoche was now seen not so much as a repository or carrier of the teachings, but as their very embodiment, the teachings themselves. Many felt that guarding them – protecting him – was of paramount importance, superseding all other considerations.

As we reach this waypoint on Rinpoche's journey, with him contemplating his weighty dilemma at Drolma Lhakang, an intriguing undercurrent to the story emerges – one that he carefully omitted from his account in *Born in Tibet*. As Rinpoche told the story there, he was now on the second leg of a teaching tour and would return to Surmang when he had completed it. His decision to escape still lay some six months in the future.

The first glimpse of this undercurrent came from Akong Tulku over five decades later. He let it be known that, when he and Rinpoche were at Pepung monastery to receive the Dalai Lama's message upon his return from China three years earlier, they had crafted a contingency plan for Rinpoche's escape. It was a simple one: when the Chinese army reached Surmang, Rinpoche would make for the area of Drolma Lhakang; once there, they would together work out the route and practical details of his departure.[58]

Rinpoche had stayed at Surmang long after the PLA had arrived – even long after they had moved into his private residence. Now, finally, with the invitation Akong Tulku had sent to Rinpoche to come to Drolma Lhakang to teach, it appears that they were putting their Pepung plan into effect.

Yonten's recollections confirm that there was more to Akong Tulku's teaching invitation than met the eye, more than *Born in Tibet* had revealed. When Yonten left Surmang, he was not merely bringing provisions to Rinpoche for his ongoing teaching tour. His uncle Karjen, the general secretary, had also handed to him complete responsibility for Rinpoche's care and well-being – along with the awesome injunction to protect him during his escape.[59]

Yonten was unshakably loyal, brave to the point of bravado, physically strong, an accomplished horseman and a seasoned traveler who had journeyed as far as Lhasa. Several other attendants at Surmang could have carried supplies to Rinpoche, but only Yonten was perfectly fitted to accompany him on a long and hazardous journey. Now, for the first time in years, he was with him.

Others' memories of the time also shine light on the hidden undercurrent, and on the reality of the two lamas' secret Pepung plan. When Rinpoche was traveling in Lhatok after conducting the Kyere empowerment, his intention to escape seems to have been obvious to his fellow Tibetans. When a woman he met on the road asked if she could go with him on his escape, Rinpoche refused, saying: "There's nowhere to go. I can't even take my mother and brother with me."[60] We also know now that he had advised his family and senior lamas to flee Surmang in good time, before any violence began, and to hide among the mountains near Kyere.[61]

Akong Tulku's invitation sent to Rinpoche in Lhatok to visit Drolma Lhakang had not come out of the blue. Recent reports reveal that they had been in communication after Rinpoche left Surmang. Akong Tulku had also been kept current on Rinpoche's intentions and whereabouts, and knew where to send the invitation – the invitation that would provide innocent cover for Rinpoche's moves, and for his escape.[62]

When we look more closely at Rinpoche's narrative in *Born in Tibet*, we can see the contours of the undercurrent, and find persuasive clues that he had been preparing for an escape for some time.

When, three years before, he and Akong Tulku left Sechen to hear the Dalai Lama's message in Pepung, they walked the whole way through heavy, sludgy snow, a long and grueling journey – this in spite of the fact that horses were readily available. Rinpoche does not explain this choice as he had done with his wish a few years before to walk to his guru; and, while the two friends' trek might have similarly been an expression of devotion to the Dalai Lama and Karmapa, it may just as well have been that they were giving themselves a taste of the rigors ahead – hardening themselves as much as they could for an escape which they knew could be forced on them at any moment.

And when Rinpoche left Surmang for the last time, he did so in the middle of a raging storm, with only a handful of people to see him off. He offers no explanation in *Born in Tibet* for why he chose such an unusual, uncomfortable time to leave. But the storm proved to have been excellent cover for eluding the Communists, this at a time when he was under tight surveillance and perhaps on the verge of arrest – indirectly evidenced by the officials' swift discovery of his absence, and their highly alarmed response.

Then there are Rinpoche's movements after the enthronement ceremony at Kyere. Instead of returning to Surmang – he had no further invitations to teach in the Kyere area, and no obvious need to remain – he spent some time traveling around, giving teachings to all and sundry. While he was certainly fulfilling Khenpo Gangshar's injunction to offer people guidance for the coming dark times, he might have done that more naturally, and perhaps with greater cause, in the area of his home monastery. Rinpoche seems to have been keeping out of the PLA's clutches, while also delaying his return until Akong Tulku's vital invitation reached Lhatok.[63] It's not inconceivable that, as genuine as the Kyere empowerment was, the event had been carefully timed to expedite Rinpoche's escape – that the invitation's timing had been set not by Kyere, but by Surmang.

After all, at the very crux of things Rinpoche faced a cheerless, inescapable truth. Even if he returned to Surmang, and was not arrested on the spot, he would not be allowed to resume his traditional role. For years the Communist overlords had been maneuvering to get him under their thumbs, their demands growing ever heavier, ever more pointed and impatient. At best he might try to work around and through them in Surmang, but with these ever-watchful, hyper-paranoid men that tactic would soon be detected. The likeliest outcome of his return would be that at some point – likely sooner than later – he would have to decline to go along with some Communist dictate. Such a prominent and influential lama taking a stand against them could not be countenanced, and would mean jail for him, or worse.

By now, circumstances had spoken loudly and clearly. For eight years, ever since Rinpoche had spotted PLA troops from Dorje Khyung Dzong, and discussed escape details with Karjen, he had known that it could come to that. Now he knew that his position at Surmang was untenable, and could quite possibly turn lethal for him. Rinpoche's dilemma was a real one – in *Born in Tibet* he posed it in a chapter titled "Must We Escape?" – and he genuinely wanted advice. But there was more under way, and more to the story, than he was ready to tell in the book.

We can't say that Rinpoche had "made up his mind" to escape, but rather that events had pointed him that way. He also knew Sun Tzu's classic *Art of War*, and its notion of the general as a sage-commander. Such a general's actions are dictated by the balance of forces and the play of circumstances rather than by his personal plans, ideas or inspirations, which always take second place. In fact, Rinpoche's movements seemed to have been entirely guided by a fluid, open appraisal of events.[64] Responding to them, he had headed southwards to where escape would be easier, to where the plan he and Akong Tulku had worked out could be put into play. And, in the best Sun Tzu tradition, he masked his movements behind normal invitations and teaching activities.

So although Rinpoche had not yet settled on an escape, he had made a tactical withdrawal from Surmang, positioning himself for one. It had been inscrutably conducted, under the guise of a perfectly genuine teaching tour. In the first phase, the short leg south to Kyere, he had eluded immediate Communist surveillance at Surmang; in the second, the longer journey to Drolma Lhakang, he had put himself beyond the PLA's reach, while obscuring his whereabouts. He had arrived in an area from where he could escape, an area close to the Chamdo-Lhasa road.

From here, out of view of the Communists, he could watch events unfolding before making his decision to return to Surmang, or to leave Tibet. If there was to be any sure sign that things were lightening up, any solid indications that the Communists were relaxing their unrelenting pressure for all Tibetans to bend to their doctrine, he would likely return to his monastery.

In Surmang, Rinpoche would have kept the Pepung contingency plan secret, perhaps sharing it only with Karjen the secretary and one or two others. It might have been unnecessary to communicate it at all – the situation spoke for itself, to Surmang's senior people as much as to Rinpoche. With nothing communicated there was nothing to be denied, and no-one could be accused of conspiring in his escape.

When Rinpoche wrote his book just a few years later, he had no idea who at Surmang might still be alive. Had he written about – or even hinted at – the plan of escape, or the way it was conducted, it would surely have implicated senior people close to him, whom the Communists would accuse of conspiring in it, with deadly repurcussions.

At Drolma Lhakang, Rinpoche continued to do his best to prepare people for the coming catastrophe, stressing that they were very near the time when "our world, as we had known it, would come to an end."[65] Even as he did so, reports of the destruction of monasteries in Eastern Tibet continued to come in almost daily. He urged people to take the news as a warning, to take to heart the very live menace they faced; and he told them to always remember that, whatever the circumstances, the Buddhist teachings were their one true refuge.

For Rinpoche and other lamas, those under greatest threat from the Communists, the call to escape was ever louder, ever more pressing. In spite of this, Rinpoche's dilemma remained as sharp as ever. Then someone arrived at Drolma Lhakang who had no doubts about what Rinpoche should do, and was more than eager to let him know. Tsethar had for many years been Surmang's bursar, responsible for the monastery's finances, for balancing its accounts and distributing funds. A man in his forties, he had been a student of the tenth Trungpa and, with that austere teacher as a model, had not always been comfortable with the way the youngster had run the place. At Surmang, Tsethar had been held in check by the senior lamas, but here he was the monastery's most senior person after

Rinpoche himself and, as the older and presumably more experienced man, believed himself to be responsible for Rinpoche and his actions.

For Tsethar, there could be no question of Rinpoche's escaping. To do so would be a betrayal of the Trungpa lineage, of everything for which they had worked so hard over six centuries. With admirable assurance, he told Rinpoche that little at Surmang would change as a result of the Communist incursion and that everything would go on as before, as everyone at Surmang hoped it would; he added that the monks were growing anxious at the thought of his leaving them. Obviously, in spite of the overbearing PLA presence in Surmang, both Tsethar and the monks remained oblivious of the larger threat descending upon them. And abandoning Surmang would wipe out the meaning of Tsethar's life's work, while the prospect of an arduous escape to a strange new world could not have been too appealing at his age.

As pressures on Rinpoche mounted, a new request arrived. It came from Yag Tulku, who asked him to transmit the Treasury Teachings at his monastery. According to his vows, Rinpoche could not refuse the request even if he had wanted to – although it seems that other lamas argued against the wisdom of embarking on a six-month teaching cycle in the current turbulent, unpredictable circumstances. However, Yag Tulku, like Tsethar, was convinced that everything would be fine, and saw no reason why they should not go ahead. Yonten, who from his time at Surmang had an earthy sense of Communist intentions, was very worried by the danger that the teaching delay would impose on Rinpoche, tying him down for a lengthy period. And he was deeply irritated by Yag Tulku's approach, feeling that he was being "very pushy."[66]

With little delay, Rinpoche made the two-day ride to Yag monastery and, after a few days' preparations, was ready to begin the teaching transmission. He had a surprise for the many lamas, monks and lay people assembled: he announced that he would be giving the complete cycle, but that each day would begin a few hours earlier and end well into the night. This must have jolted many present. The Treasury Teachings cycle was famously demanding, normally going from well before dawn into the evening, with no break for six full months; now Rinpoche was adding further hours to every day. The greatest strain fell on him: while Rinpoche taught, he had to be utterly present, moment to moment, for the entire time. Before long, the various shrine attendants found that they could not keep up, and began to work in shifts. Even Yonten, although not a monk, was brought in as reinforcement: "Daily I prepared Rinpoche's clothes for the day ... [after which] I did everything, and was busy day and night ..."[67]

About a month into the cycle, Rinpoche received a confidential message from Khamtrul Tulku requesting another meeting, adding that their contact should be kept secret. These were perilous times and, as unusual as it was to do so, Rinpoche interrupted the teaching, then rode off to the undisclosed location. Khamtrul Tulku was traveling incognito, in civilian clothes, and Rinpoche was struck by how much the doffing of his monastic robes had changed his personality; still, Rinpoche felt that "it was only too clear that he was in disguise."[68]

Again Khamtrul asked Rinpoche to join him in a mirror divination, and again, its indications were clear: Khamtrul Tulku should escape without delay and, if he did so, he would reach India without undue difficulty. Again, Khamtrul Tulku implored Rinpoche to join him and, again, Rinpoche declined, saying that he must first complete the teaching cycle. When he told Khamtrul Tulku about the opposition he was facing, specifically from his bursar, Khamtrul Tulku said that he should not allow others to hold him back. Then they parted, with the hope that they would meet again in India.

Upon his return to resume teaching, Rinpoche found the monastery in a deeply unsettled state. Before leaving, he had felt that he had to tell Yag Tulku – who was not just his host but the sponsor and chief recipient of the teachings – why he had to interrupt the cycle, and had asked him to keep the information secret.[69] For reasons known only to himself, Yag Tulku had immediately leaked the news, which swept through the monastery like a brushfire. Although no one had known the reason for the meeting, many grasped that Khamtrul Tulku was planning to escape, and that he had asked Rinpoche to go with him. A number of people asked Rinpoche if they could join him when he left. Again, he had to refuse, telling them the blunt truth: that he did not know himself what he should do or where he would go.

Nevertheless, whatever their fears of the advancing menace, all were committed to completing the Treasury Teachings cycle and they soon settled back in. Finally, after a full-blown effort by everyone present, the monumental cycle was fully transmitted. It had been completed in just three months, half the normal time.

The day the teachings were concluded was doubly momentous: Rinpoche received the long-awaited replies to his letters requesting advice from the Karmapa and the two eminent teachers. Yet all the replies were noncommittal: the Karmapa simply said that it was important to carry on what spiritual work Rinpoche could do in the crisis, while the others more or less repeated that advice. One included a short poem which began: "The darkness of the barbarians sinks deeper and deeper into the heart of the country. He who would light a torch must do so from within himself."[70] For all their spiritual and worldly wisdom, none of these towering figures, starting with Rinpoche's guru, Jamgon Kongtrul, presumed to know what course he should follow in the chaotic and dangerous times.

Along with the letters, the messenger had brought terrible news. Jamgon Kongtrul had been captured by the Communists. Heedless of his personal safety, and in spite of attempts by the Karmapa and other lamas to restrain him, he had responded to a call to perform funeral rites for some of his students who had been killed by the Chinese, and made straight for the danger zone. When he was recognized and arrested, he had not helped his cause by being forthright and outspoken to his captors, as was his style. As Rinpoche listened to the news, he recalled that, one day during the recent teaching cycle, he had felt a strong sense of his guru's physical presence, and that night had had a vivid dream: Jamgon Kongtrul, riding a white horse bareback and carrying holy books and a reliquary, was heading up the rocky path of a mist-covered mountain until, in the distance, he dropped the books, which rolled down the slope, finally falling on Rinpoche.

After telling the monastery the news of Jamgon Kongtrul's capture and the gist of the replies to his letters, which everyone eagerly wanted to hear, Rinpoche consulted those around him. The senior monks thought that all would be well and Rinpoche should stay, since the Karmapa had given no indication of whether or not he should leave Tibet. A few lamas were not so sure: deeply concerned about the news of Jamgon Kongtrul, they felt that Rinpoche needed to be very careful himself. Hugely multiplying Rinpoche's sense of predicament, even though everyone knew that he had received no indication of what to do, they were all looking to him for leadership.

Yag monastery lay close to one of the main routes to Lhasa, and in the preceding weeks many reports had reached them of East Tibet's plight. Refugees fleeing the fighting told terrible stories of killings and torture as the Communists advanced, and of the widespread destruction of monasteries and villages. As the accounts flooded in, Rinpoche's monks began to worry about Surmang's prospects, while many in and around Yag monastery were growing jittery and demoralized. Their life of centuries, all that they had known, seemed to be coming apart around them; in the entirely novel chaos they were confused by the upsurge of unfamiliar emotions, not knowing what to do with them. Rinpoche gathered as many people as could attend, and passed on to them what he had been told, and what he now knew himself: nothing could stop them from meditating, and if all their external teachers were gone, they must find the guru and the teachings within themselves.

Among Rinpoche's visitors at this time was Jigme Tulku, a lama he knew and respected. Around fifty years old and a student of the tenth Trungpa, he had come specifically to speak to Rinpoche. With bracing clarity he told Rinpoche that he should escape; further, that as a large group could not be concealed, he should leave secretly so that the many people who would want to join him could not do so. He emphasized that it was not a question of protecting his personal safety; Rinpoche had received profound spiritual instruction, which he was duty-bound to pass on to others.

A few days after Jigme Tulku's visit, a close friend of Rinpoche's also arrived to speak to him. He confidently asserted that the Communists had no intention of taking over Tibet. In what Rinpoche felt to be an unusual manner from his friend, he reminded Rinpoche that Surmang was expecting his return, and implied that Rinpoche should not think only of himself. A day or so later, another lama arrived from the same monastery and, in almost identical terms, gave him the same advice.

Rinpoche realized that Tsethar had put both men up to it. The bursar had launched a multi-pronged campaign, determined to undermine any thoughts of escape that Rinpoche might hold. It also grew clear that Tsethar's campaign had just begun. During their months at Yag monastery, many devotees had brought gifts for Rinpoche, who had planned to distribute a portion of them among the poor and needy, and to convert the rest into money. Tsethar, knowing that money was portable and would be highly useful on an escape, instead bartered away all the gifts for horses, yaks and sheep, which could be used for Surmang's upkeep when they returned.

Rinpoche was upset by Tsethar's blatant disobedience, while Yonten was shocked by the disrespect to his lama; he knew as well as anyone else that, although still a teenager, Rinpoche was a highly respected teacher and the abbot – Tsethar's abbot, after all – of a renowned monastery. [71] And it is surprising to read of the bursar's near-mutinous actions, and of his stubbornness in the face of the storm engulfing East Tibet.

Yet at least some of this reaction comes from hindsight. The struggle between abbot and bursar was being played out in the councils and committees of innumerable monasteries, and in the minds and hearts of hundreds and thousands of people across Tibet. It involved the highest stakes, and the cruelest choices, pitting the violent, overwhelming threat confronting them and their religion against the desperately risky venture of leaving it all behind, of setting out for unpredictable welcomes in unknown lands.

As Rinpoche contemplated the spectrum of views and opinions on offer, and considered the frequent reports coming into Yag monastery about the conflict, the size and ferocity of the fighting growing every day, Jigme Tulku paid a second visit. Now fully aware of the immense pressures bearing down on the young lama, he told him that, although the decision was ultimately Rinpoche's to make, he himself emphatically felt that he should not return to Surmang. He went on to say that he would be making a strong case for this view at the next morning's meeting.

Before Jigme Tulku had a chance to do so, Tsethar approached Rinpoche that afternoon and "let fly."[72] He, Tsethar, was there to take care of him and Rinpoche, as head of Surmang, should listen only to advice from his own monastery; he had no right to listen to advice from interfering people who were not from Surmang. Seeing that there was no point in doing so, Rinpoche made no reply.

The following morning Rinpoche invited the bursar to continue the discussion. He assured him that he was grateful for his consideration for their monastery, adding that he himself was fully ready to give his life for Surmang; but, he went on, Tsethar must remember his place, and that the decision was not ultimately his to make. Then he said that if Tsethar wanted the responsibility, it was his for the taking. Put so painfully on the spot, the bursar went off to think things over. When he next saw Rinpoche he was quieter and more hesitant, saying that while he was convinced that they should return to Surmang, he had no wish to take the final decision which must of course be Rinpoche's alone. The bursar had been subdued, if only for the moment.

With the space pacified, everyone having fully expressed their views, at the next morning's meeting Rinpoche delivered his own decision. He said that as Surmang was his first duty, and since his monks there were awaiting his leadership, he was going to return. There was a long silence, finally broken by Tsethar who asked with some emotion: "Is that all?"[73] Rinpoche said nothing further on the subject, then or later.

Their course set, they began to prepare for departure. Now circumstances again had their say. Tsethar wanted to take with them the many horses, yaks and other animals he had acquired for Surmang in disobedience to Rinpoche's wishes. But to get the large herds and flocks there they would need to add twenty or so men to the party, to load and unload the baggage and tend the animals. Also, they would be forced to travel at the speed of the slowest yak, which meant camping along the way.

In a time of peace they would not have given this a second thought, but Rinpoche's monks – who had been looking forward very much to returning to their home monastery – were becoming increasingly nervous at the prospect. News had arrived that Tibetan government forces were heading east from Lhasa, and that they might strike at the Communist headquarters at Chamdo. If this proved true, there would be heavy fighting on their route back. Even Tsethar grasped that they could not now get the animals through to Surmang. He suggested that they abandon them, then change into civilian clothes and divide into small groups, making their separate ways back to Surmang. Rinpoche agreed with this plan, commenting that they should not try to force the issue, that this was their karma.

For at least three years – since the Dalai Lama's visit to Beijing and Jamgon Kongtrul's thoughts about escaping to India – the pressures on Rinpoche had been mounting. They had come from a range of sources: from the oppression, killing and destruction; from the legions of frightened people needing his advice and counseling; from the super-intense strain of completing the Treasury Teachings in minimal time; and from the massive pushes and pulls surrounding his great dilemma. Now it was, sometime in the fall of 1958, that events caught up, came to a crescendo, and there was a fracturing.

The evening after settling on the plan to return to Surmang, as Rinpoche was turning in he began to feel ill, then was overcome by a pain so intense that he fainted. At the same moment, in a shrine room back at Drolma Lhakang, the roof beams cracked. When they heard of the precise coincidence at Yag monastery, it was taken as a sign of the darkest sort, heralding catastrophe. Many took it to mean that Rinpoche was about to die.[74] Jigme Tulku, who was trained in medicine, was immediately sent for. He had never wanted Rinpoche to return to Surmang and, after looking him over, he prescribed rest, lots of it.

As was customary at times of illness, Tsethar the bursar sent out messages to friends and lamas, requesting that they include

Rinpoche in their prayers. One message reached a lama who held a senior post in the new Communist administration in Chamdo. He replied saying that Tsethar's message had come as a blessing, because it gave him the chance to inform Rinpoche that the local Communist committee had launched a vigorous search for him. The lama added the disturbing news that fierce fighting had been reported around Surmang itself.

It was plain that Rinpoche could not now return to his monastery. It was one thing for him to be under close surveillance by local officials in the Surmang area, quite another for orders to be issued from Communist headquarters to find him. There could be no further doubt that the Communists saw Rinpoche as a significant threat, and wanted him under their control or in custody; moreover, it seemed certain that they took his sudden disappearance from Surmang, and his long absence, as evasion and escape. Equally clearly, he could not stay at Yag monastery; local people were well aware of his presence and, with many refugees and travelers coming through, he was sure to be tracked down.

For now, though, Rinpoche was in critical need of rest and recovery, and was secluded under care, protected from all the alarms and anxieties besetting the monastery. Jigme Tulku and Yag Tulku took over the decision-making. They decided that Tsethar should return to Surmang to assess the situation. Ill as he was, Rinpoche wrote letters for Tsethar to take with him, telling the monastery of his situation and expressing the hope that they understand that he had no wish to stay away from them. He reaffirmed that they must not take up arms against the Communists however hard things became, as they would surely face extinction if they did. He concluded by saying that, if things grew unbearable for them, they should try to make their way south to Yag monastery to join him.

After arranging for their stocks of animals to be cared for at Drolma Lhakang, Tsethar, accompanied by a small group from Yag monastery, left for Surmang with the letters – together with a stern warning from Rinpoche that he not antagonize any Communists he met, as this could only have a sorry outcome. Sure as ever that all would be fine, Tsethar was looking forward to putting Rinpoche's

Surmang residence in order for his return. Two days later the Yag group returned, bringing news from travelers that the Communists were collecting all weapons in the Surmang area, even meat cleavers, and that they had posted guards at all river ferries and crossing points.

The news heightened worries for Rinpoche's well-being. If Tsethar was stopped and recognized on the way, every means would be used to extract from him the details of Rinpoche's whereabouts. Just as troubling was the news that PLA troops were flooding across East Tibet; it would not be long before they reached Yag monastery. As soon as he was well enough to travel, Rinpoche would have to leave in total secrecy and go into hiding.

Following a week's total rest Rinpoche felt strong enough to take up some duties, and called the community together for a final ceremony. After they had said prayers for their reunion, Rinpoche lit a lamp he held from the shrine candles, and then passed his light, signifying the flame of wisdom, on to lamps held by everyone in the hall. Then he tied the end of the white scarf draped around his neck to that of the lama next to him, who tied his scarf to his neighbor's, until the whole assembly sat illumined in a net of shimmering white amid the encircling gloom.

Rinpoche concluded the event by saying that, while no one knew what the future would bring, they were now spiritually joined in a union that would last many lifetimes. The hall in which they sat, he said, would soon be empty, with everything in it – shrines, thrones, decorations and sacred art – dismantled. This, and the Chinese menace to their world, should remind them of the First Noble Truth of Suffering. They must always look to the guru within. With these words the ceremony ended, and with it Rinpoche's formal role as a high lama in his homeland.

Time was growing very short now. With the Communists actively hunting him down, the monastery's senior lamas felt that, even ill as he was, Rinpoche should not stay at the monastery longer than another week. Many other monastics felt likewise, beseeching him for his own good: "Please go, please go."[75]

But he still needed rest before heading out, and he also had to find a secure place of refuge. This remained an obstacle. Although many friends and ordinary people had offered to hide him in their homes, or had suggested a place where he might go, Rinpoche felt that none of them was sufficiently safe or remote.

Closing the yellow curtains to his room, Rinpoche went into retreat, to rest and to prepare for the journey. He also performed a mirror divination for his escape, which indicated that he should seek refuge in the area of Yo, which lay to the south. He communicated this information out to people who knew the area, and they concurred: Yo was indeed a sound choice. Arrangements were made for a guide to lead him there, and for the means to keep him supplied with food through the winter.

Rinpoche's curtains remained drawn, the community considering him to be in retreat. He called in his monks, and told them that if anyone requested his blessing, they should simply say that he was in retreat and was seeing no one; if someone offered gifts, a monk should pretend to come to tell him, then return and say to the donor whatever he felt to be appropriate.[76] He then asked an elderly lama, whose own room was nearby, to ring his ritual bell and sound his drum as if they came from the curtained room.

Around midnight, Rinpoche and his two attendants quietly left the monastery. And so, his movements again masked by friends and cloaked by the elements, he slipped away from his pursuers and vanished into the enclosing dark of a winter night.

4

The Valley of Mystery

As Trungpa Rinpoche stepped beyond the warmth of the monastery walls the bitter cold struck him full on. During the weeks he had rested in seclusion, the Tibetan winter had arrived, and the air was frigid, biting at the fifteen-thousand-foot altitude. And the night was ink-black, so dark that Rinpoche and his attendants could see nothing as they picked their way forward, moving so quietly that no-one, not even the monastery dogs, noticed their going.

Jigme Tulku and his brother met them at the monastery's outskirts with the horses, some loaded with baggage and supplies secretly packed by Yonten. Rinpoche's horse would not be his own one, which had been left at the monastery to reinforce the impression that he was still there.

Trusting to his new mount's sure-footedness and their guide's knowledge, they set off into the valley's blackness. There was little snow on the ground, and the animals were able to keep to the track without even starlight to guide them. They made their way on down until they reached the broad Auchu River valley, then headed south, riding through the night. Just as the first light of dawn touched the terrain, they arrived at the house they were seeking.

Their host, who was the owner of the valley where Rinpoche would be hiding, greeted them effusively. They were frozen, and were grateful for the warmth of his welcome and for the hot milk he offered; even the landowner's ox-dung fire helped, although it gave off more smell and smoke than heat. Soon, feeling somewhat restored, and needing to keep their presence secret, the group remounted and continued on their way before the locals were up and about.

Led by the landowner, they continued southwards down the Auchu valley until, after five hours' ride, they turned off the road and began to climb towards a high pass that led over the western range.[77] The track on both sides of the pass was precipitous, the snow drifts deep, and it took them until late afternoon before they had made it down into the Yo valley. It was too late to choose a proper campsite, so they looked for a level patch of ground and settled down for the night.

Early the next morning they set out to explore their surroundings, and after a few hours found a place to their liking, a near-perfect spot in as secure a location as they could hope for. They would be making camp at the valley's far western end, from where they would get ample warning of anyone approaching them from the pass. Cut off for much of the winter at its eastern end by the snow-bound pass they had crossed, here at its western end the valley was blocked by a high, narrow gorge where the Yo-chu River left it via a series of turbulent cascades. Used for grazing during the summer months, the valley was empty now. Only the landowner and a few of his herdsmen knew of its existence – which they talked of, perhaps whimsically, as the "Valley of Mystery." He was confident that the Communists would never find Rinpoche's group here, and assured them that in an emergency he could always use yaks to plow a way over the pass.

They decided to set up their tents in a herdsman's hut. It was built up against a large boulder which would help to fend off the worst of the wintry blasts, and near to a frozen stream from which they could draw water. Although it was a primitive, shaky structure of loose stones, it was large enough to contain their tents within its walls, giving additional protection from the weather and from being spotted from afar; the roof was too low, but it proved simple enough to dismantle. There were three tents in all, two of white canvas for Rinpoche and Jigme Tulku, and a larger, traditional yak-hair tent for the attendants, which would also act as the kitchen. They were abundantly supplied: in addition to provisions sent by Akong Tulku and Yag Tulku, the landowner left them lavish amounts of butter, cheese, cakes made with butter and dried curd – fatty fare they would need over the months to come – along with flour made from a local artichoke-like vegetable.

Rinpoche's new life could hardly have been in sharper contrast to his previous one. From soon after birth he had been nurtured as the supreme abbot of a renowned monastery, comfortably ensconced in warmed rooms on brocaded chairs and thrones, his every need attended to. Yet he and the others soon settled into a cheerful routine. In the early morning, accompanied by a chorus of bird song, they roamed the valley collecting firewood. At first Rinpoche went out for firewood with the others, but this so upset his young attendant – who felt that he should do all such work for him – that he instead spent the mornings in prayer and meditation. Although Rinpoche was wrapped in a heavy sheepskin coat, and his devoted attendant strove mightily to warm him with a twig fire, as winter deepened nothing could stem the cold. Before long, the metal of his ritual bell and drum became impossible to hold.

Yet Rinpoche began to revel in his surroundings and in their raw, elemental beauty. It was the first time that he had been really isolated and free of distractions. Gone were the tutors, the swirl of monks and lamas, the stream of visitors and supplicants, the endless round of ritual and responsibility, the chanting, gongs, bells, horns and drums resounding through the monastery. Behind him were the recent years' colossal stresses and strains. Now he was in a quiet and spacious realm of bird and animal calls, of the sounds of wind, rain or falling snow – in their way more magnificent than anything the monastery could offer.

Making good use of the time, Rinpoche settled fully into meditation, then poured his insight and understanding into writing; he was working on a comprehensive text on meditation practice, describing its methods and progress from the first beginnings to full fruition, enlightenment. Between his primal surroundings, his intensified meditation and the sixty volumes of sacred texts he had brought with him, he was well equipped for the work.

In the afternoons Rinpoche and Jigme Tulku went for walks together, and in the evenings everyone would gather in Jigme's tent, which was larger than the others and had a smoke aperture. An older man, he was cheery company; he had traveled widely, including on a pilgrimage to India and, with his rollicking sense of humor and fine eye for detail, he regaled them with yarns about people he had met along the way.

By the first days of 1959 it had begun to snow heavily. One morning the valley echoed to a great rumbling which they at first took to be Chinese gunfire, until they realized that it had been an avalanche. A while later, they were almost as jolted when they spotted a dark figure heading their way from the direction of the pass. With the drifts as deep as they were – and they were much deeper near the pass – no visitors were expected. As the figure came nearer they saw that it was a horseman plowing through the drifts towards them, the snow up to the horse's stirrups. The rider turned out to be an old man who was a servant of Jigme Tulku's. He talked with some emotion of his bitterly cold journey and of the deep snow, but his horse had been sound and he seemed unscathed. He had brought them fresh butter, gladly received, along with the news that some at Yag monastery were beginning to doubt that Rinpoche was actually still there in retreat. Then, as soon as he and his animal had rested and eaten, the hardy fellow left on his return journey.

He carried with him a message from Rinpoche to Akong Tulku, inviting him to join them in their frigid refuge. Even with the fine companionship – Rinpoche's sense of humor had supplemented Jigme Tulku's – as the bleak, frozen weeks had dragged by they had begun to feel the need for fresh company. Akong Tulku wasted no time responding to the invitation, and arrived at the small encampment in early February, in good time for the Tibetan New Year's celebration. It was a relatively grand affair. A local man who knew of their presence in the Yo valley had sent in several horsemen laden with holiday gifts of food. They were so lavish that, as they enjoyed the feast the attendants created from them, they wondered whether they could eat it all.

Around the beginning of March, a familiar figure arrived in the valley: Tsethar the bursar, returned from his mission to Surmang. After resting and eating, he began to tell of a series of events that were nothing short of calamitous.

A few months earlier, he said, the Communist authorities had invited the senior lamas and political leaders in the Surmang area to an important meeting in Jyekundo, the provincial capital. Such invitations had become customary even during Rinpoche's time at Surmang, but this one was different. It came as an order, along with the disquieting instruction that everyone was to travel under armed PLA escort – for their own protection, they were told. When they arrived at the meeting hall, they saw that it was completely encircled by soldiers.

This time there were no attempts to persuade. One after another, Communist speakers loudly and forcefully asserted their sole right to rule Tibet. Everyone present understood that, from this moment on, resistance meant imprisonment or death. Deciding to act before it was too late, a local leader named Rashu Behu leapt to his feet, dashed from the hall and out through the circle of troops, then galloped for the mountains accompanied by his six bodyguards. They were eventually chased down and killed in a vicious fight, whereupon the leader's body was brought back to the meeting hall and put on display. In the meantime every Tibetan at the meeting had been arrested.

The news spread rapidly and, when the Communists intensified their search for weapons, the area rose in a new revolt. At first, the Khampa resistance made widespread gains, in a series of merciless battles pushing the Communist forces out of many areas and back towards the border. Surmang was engulfed in the violence. During the fighting, one of its outlying monasteries was destroyed, with almost every monk and lama killed.

Rinpoche's home monastery, Dudtsi-t'il, was not quite so ravaged – the PLA intended to use its buildings as a permanent base for attacks on local resistance fighters. Nevertheless, the destruction was heart-crushing. The library, stacked with the precious texts of centuries, was broken into and its volumes torn up, strewn around and fed to cattle. Sacred painted scrolls were ripped from the monastery's walls and turned into trays for the troops' meat and rice meals. Ritual shrine objects were smashed to fragments, their precious metals carefully packed up and sent off to China to be melted down. In the crowning desecration, the Communists hammered open the tenth Trungpa's tomb, leaving the embalmed remains exposed, open to the air.

Many monks and lamas, along with their families, had already made their escape, but those remaining were rounded up and placed under close guard. PLA officers interrogated them all, one by one, seeking information on Rinpoche's whereabouts, but Surmang's people knew little and gave nothing away. At the interrogation's conclusion, the senior lamas were herded off and shot. Most of the monks were spared, to be used for whatever hard labor their overlords chose. Karjen, Surmang's general secretary, who had stayed at his post to maintain a picture of normality after Rinpoche's disappearance, was jailed; the Communists no doubt thought that he had information on Rinpoche's whereabouts that they could extract later at their leisure.

A month later, in the maelstrom of Khampa onslaughts on Communist forces, the PLA received orders to evacuate Surmang and retreat to Jyekundo. After rounding up the prisoners, including many women and children, together with the area's cattle, they set off on a brutal forced march – the Chinese on horseback, everyone else on foot, pushing on day and night until they reached the safety of the provincial capital. No-one could say how many lives were lost on the march.

Tsethar's earliest information had come from travelers he had met on the way, this to be confirmed and re-confirmed as he rode on. From them he also heard that the Communists had evacuated

Surmang, so he went to see the damage for himself. What he saw matched everything he had been told. Before leaving, he arranged for a party of monks to properly cremate the tenth Trungpa's body.

While in Surmang the bursar was told that the monks who had made an early getaway had headed south towards Lhatok, where they thought they would be safer. So, before heading for Yo valley to report to Rinpoche, he went there. He found the monks, who, along with a number of Surmang families, had found refuge at Kyere monastery. Rinpoche's mother and two sisters, following his instructions, had left Surmang before things took their drastic turn, and were in a house next to their relative's, the abbot of Kyere and the younger brother Rinpoche had enthroned months before. His mother had sent a message for Rinpoche with Tsethar, saying how relieved she was that he was in a safe place. She added that if he decided to flee Tibet she would be content.

Rinpoche found Tsethar's report profoundly distressing. The ruin of the monastery, the destruction of its art and library, the desecration of its most sacred elements, was awful enough. More terrible was the fate of everyone connected to it. Surmang's pulsing, joyous reality came from its people, and from their close personal and spiritual bonds, many of them nurtured over many lives and generations. All this too had been wrecked and laid waste. His family, some lamas and many of his monks were safe for the time being, but Rinpoche now knew that many others – including Surmang's most senior people, men he was especially close to – were imprisoned or dead.

As well as he knew his bursar, Rinpoche might still have been surprised by what came next. Tsethar said that at Kyere he had called a meeting of the Surmang monks. All of them, he said, wanted Rinpoche to return there. In fact they had begged him to come back to them; all of them hoped to settle back with him back at their monastery. They had also asked Rinpoche carefully to consider the disastrous implications if, during the life of the eleventh Trungpa Tulku, Surmang were to cease functioning. These pleas were contained in a letter that Tsethar handed to Rinpoche.

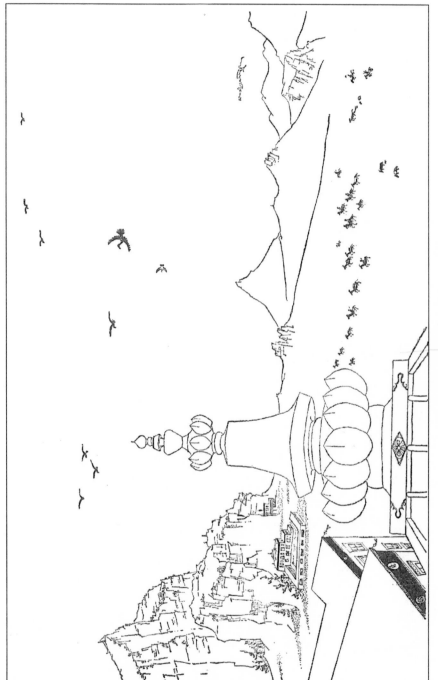

Travelers approaching monastery

It all bore the bursar's stamp – including the unsubtle insinuation of guilt should Surmang's demise happen during Rinpoche's lifetime. But he did not confront Tsethar on the letter, instead questioning him closely on its key details. How had he been able to travel to Surmang amidst the current turmoil? It turned out that a crucial ferry crossing was open only because a Khampa attack had forced PLA guards away from it, and by now they could well be back. Were other monastic communities returning to their destroyed monasteries? Tsethar said nobody else intended to do so. What were the individual opinions of Rinpoche's own monks about his return? Tsethar had to admit that they were happy with the actions he had taken to evade the Communists, and were also relieved that they would not themselves have to bear the responsibility for him in the dangerous and chaotic circumstances.

Yet even with Tsethar's stratagem exposed for what it was, even with the array of tragic news, Rinpoche still faced his awful dilemma. Indeed, it was now at its most acute: should he join his monks and family at Kyere, to be with them as their spiritual guide at this desperate time, perhaps with the hope of returning to Surmang later, or should he escape? With no-one of sufficient authority to consult, Rinpoche again resorted to mirror divination. The indications were unambiguous: not only should he not go back to Kyere, but he must leave the Yo valley soon.

Rinpoche wrote a reply to the monks' letter, trying to show them what they faced: "We should not think only of the survival of our monastery, nor of my own reputation. You must see that the whole country has been devastated." If they tried to re-establish their monastery, he wrote, the Communists would return and they would all die. What's more, if he joined them they themselves would become a prime target, and the persecution would be re-ignited. "Nothing would be more dangerous than to return to Surmang."[78] He concluded by saying that he would make no attempt to escape before he heard back from them.

Tsethar, hopeful to the end, said little. Wholly consumed by Surmang's tragedy and even now thinking of its revival, he was blind to the fact that the same fate was befalling the whole country. Even so, after leaving the Yo valley with Rinpoche's letter and arriving back at Drolma Lhakang, he set about selling the herds of animals he had brought previously, bartering them for portable items and money.

Meanwhile, around this time Yonten had set out from Yag monastery to carry provisions to Rinpoche. Accompanied by a local man as guide, he rode down the Auchu River valley until they spotted what looked like a group of horsemen in the distance, and prudently stopped to observe them. As they did so, the PLA patrol, for this was what it was, wheeled around and began to ride towards them. Yonten and his companion came to a snap decision. The guide swung his horse around and rode at a leisurely pace towards a nearby village where, as a local man, he would draw no attention. Yonten, who would be instantly recognized, both by the villagers and the PLA, as a stranger – his Nangchen clothes and dialect were unmistakable – took off at a fast trot for the mountains a few miles away. The soldiers whipped their horses into a gallop after him. Yonten kept going, confident that his fast and sturdy horse would stay well ahead of them. And so it turned out: by the time his pursuers started up the foothills behind him, their horses were flagging and they had to stop and dismount. After a while, they took up the pursuit again, with the same results. Finally, just before nightfall they gave up and headed back towards the river. Yonten waited until dark, then, feeling that it was too dangerous to go on with Chinese troops somewhere ahead of him, returned disconsolately to Yag monastery.[79]

By now it was well into March and winter was retreating from the Yo valley, the spring breezes unveiling its wealth. Rinpoche and Akong Tulku began to take long walks together, following animal tracks through the juniper scrub, enjoying the new vegetation and a rich variety of birds and animals, including wild geese, musk deer and, once or twice, Tibetan pandas. Then, on a moonlit night, they heard a fox's bark – in Tibetan lore, hearing one is a bad omen – followed by the howling of jackals, the calls echoing eerily around the valley rocks.

The next morning a rider appeared at the camp with a message for Jigme Tulku, informing him that his sister was very ill, and possibly dying. He and his brother left immediately to attend to her. Some days later another messenger arrived. He brought with him a letter from Jigme Tulku, written after his sister's cremation, inviting Rinpoche to join him at his family home – saying that, until he had experienced a warmed room he had not realized how cold they had been in their tents.

Rinpoche was most reluctant to go. He had grown fond of the valley, and warmed homes held no appeal for him now. He had also found it to be an ideal workplace, quiet and free from distraction, and had nearly completed the text on meditation that he had worked on through the winter. But he felt that he could not decline an invitation from someone who had been so kind to him; he decided to leave immediately, accompanied by Akong Tulku, and then return to the valley after a brief stay. His time there was growing short: in accordance with his recent divination, he would be leaving the valley soon; and he would have to leave anyway when the snow melted off the pass, opening it equally to herdsmen and PLA patrols.

Someone needed to take care of his possessions while he was away, and Rinpoche asked his young attendant – who liked the idea of warmed rooms, but whose meditation had made good progress in the valley – to stay behind. He would have company in the form of an elderly nun, who would be in the valley to watch over yaks.

By now the valley was largely clear of snow, but as Rinpoche and Akong Tulku climbed towards the pass the drifts grew gradually deeper until, near the top, Rinpoche had to hold on to the horse's tail to pull him up. As they reached the crest they were hit by a howling blizzard, then, as they descended the even steeper eastern slope, Rinpoche had to cling to the horse's bridle to stop from sliding down the mountain.

After reaching the Auchu River valley they rode northwards through the day, keeping their eyes peeled for any sign of Communist troops, and reached the landowner's home near nightfall. The man was surprised to see them and, fearful for Rinpoche's safety, pleaded with him to return to the valley where he was sure to be safe from PLA patrols. Rinpoche thanked him for his concern, but after dark they remounted and continued northwards, pressing on as fast as they could through the night's intense cold. Just before dawn, after a punishing journey of over twenty hours, they reached Jigme Tulku's home.

Rinpoche's and Akong Tulku's frozen hands and feet tingled painfully in the heated rooms as nerves and sinews struggled to adapt to the sudden change, but the feeling went away after a while and the two settled down to enjoy the alien comfort. Their presence in the house was a closely held secret, with Jigme Tulku now pretending to be on retreat, keeping the doors to his private residence closed to outsiders. Later, in the full light of day, they saw that it was just as well that they had hurried on through the previous night's journey: from the house's windows they could see on the far side of the river an apparently endless stream of PLA troops marching south.

Communist troops, in such large numbers this far to the south, was very ominous. What Rinpoche and the others did not yet know was that, after the initial Khampa successes in the northeast, the Chinese had counter-attacked in force, their weight of numbers, mechanized transport and automatic weapons easily wiping out whatever resistance stood in their way. By now they had largely regained control of North East Tibet and had reoccupied Surmang and, with Kham crushed, they were shifting their forces south. What the watching lamas did know was that they were all now in great danger.

In the warmed house, an abrupt and drastic change in surroundings following a very hard journey, Rinpoche began to feel ill. After a week's rest and prayer he felt no better, and Jigme Tulku, again taking on his medical role, decided that Rinpoche was too ill to undertake the arduous return journey to the Yo valley. He also felt that before Rinpoche's presence became known he would have to move. The house was fairly close to Drolma Lhakang, and they discussed potential hiding places near the monastery. Rinpoche remembered a cave on Mount Kulha he had long wanted to visit, and Akong Tulku and Jigme Tulku both felt it would suit his purposes well. That decided, Akong Tulku left for Drolma Lhakang to make arrangements.

Rinpoche wasted no time: "I left with my attendant for the cave, starting at midnight: our guide was an elderly nun from one of the Drolma Lhakang nunneries."[80] This was his third night ride. Few people in Tibet, not even brigands, traveled at night. For a start it was cold, even in summer, and often well below freezing. More challenging were the roads, usually little more than dirt tracks winding through, and up and down, the terrain, a rough surface of ruts, troughs, hollows and undulations, littered with stones and the occasional rock or boulder. A moon, or starlight, might illuminate the landscape, or reveal the outlines of peaks against the sky, but in poor weather there was no light at all. On Rinpoche's journey from Yag monastery to the Yo valley, they rode for hours without a scintilla of light to guide their way, yet covered a good distance and arrived without mishap at their destination. For both horse and rider, the journeys were feats of earthy knowledge, awareness and skill. And now, apparently to no-one's surprise, Rinpoche was being led through the bone-chilling night to a cave high on a great mountain by an elderly nun.

When they reached Mount Kulha it was close to dawn. They could not hope to reach their cave before daybreak and, after climbing as high up the slope as they safely could, they took refuge in a lower cave for the day. A fire would have been welcome, but they could not afford to light one for fear of discovery; Jigme Tulku had, though, packed them a generous supply of dried meat and cheese along with warm saddle rugs, and they rested comfortably throughout the day.

At nightfall they resumed their journey and reached their chosen cave, where, thanks to Akong Tulku's monks from Drolma Lhakang monastery, they were welcomed by a lit fire and laid-out bedding. It was a first class cave, easily warmed with underbrush collected from the nearby mountainside and with a stream nearby for water. Above them rose the great peak of Mount Kulha, covered in its "crystal tent" of snow, and sacred to the memory of the legendary King Gesar of Ling, Tibet's "King Arthur."[81]

Rinpoche quickly settled down to work on the meditation text that he had aimed to complete in the Yo valley. To do so he needed long blocks of uninterrupted time to meditate and work, but it was soon clear that these were going to be denied him. The nun who had led them to the cave had stayed on to cook but, maternally concerned for Rinpoche's well-being after his illness, she would hardly leave him alone. As he put it, "I found the constant ministrations of the good nun somewhat distracting."[82] He decided to move to another cave he knew of, about three hours' journey further along the mountain. Rinpoche makes no further comment on this decision, but it seems clear that, rather than asking the nun to go – which could have been a shattering blow to the highly devoted woman – he opted to make a move himself.

When Rinpoche and his attendant reached the new cave, they found its mouth blocked by fallen earth and large rocks that were far too heavy to dig through. They needed some form of shelter, and the attendant made his way down to the valley, where he was quietly able to borrow a black tent, which he then set up on the only available spot, a large stone ledge high on the mountainside.

It was barely workable. While the tent's dark covering absorbed some of the sun's radiant heat, the slope was in shadow for much of the day; and nights, this early in the year and this high – around sixteen thousand feet – were intensely cold. In spite of his sheepskin coat and several rugs, Rinpoche could not get warm, but was able to resume work on his text. And there was a large, frozen waterfall nearby, with a narrow passage behind the ice that Rinpoche could clamber along and then climb the rocks for exercise.

Although they had arrived at night and were far too high to be seen from the valley, rumors that Rinpoche was on the mountain began circulating among people in the nearby village. The excitement grew until the headman, who had been unable to contain the villagers' curiosity, climbed up to the ledge to see for himself. When his eyes lit on Rinpoche he said, using the traditional image: "a golden rock has fallen on our doorstep."[83] He assured Rinpoche that he would be completely safe where he was, that the villagers would keep his presence secret and would take care of him.

Rinpoche returned to his meditation and writing, but next day the headman returned – this time accompanied by a few of his relatives. He also brought food supplies, and the news that the Communists in Chamdo were intensifying their repression of the local population. Loudspeakers blared out announcements throughout the day, announcing that the Dalai Lama had been abducted by Tibetan guerillas, and that the Communist authorities had, regrettably, caused some minor damage to his Summer Palace to quell the unrest. Trenches had been dug around Chamdo and troops were everywhere; townspeople were frightened and miserable, living in dread of spies and informants. Outside the town, the Communists had established a concentration camp.

Rinpoche continued to meditate and write on the frigid ledge. Then, at dawn on April 11, they heard the sound of horses neighing in the valley below. A few hours later, one of Rinpoche's monks arrived at the ledge. He brought the news that Tsethar – who was still at Drolma Lhakang, busily selling the herds of animals he had purchased – had become deeply anxious about the developing situation. Communist troops had been seen in the area, and were reportedly heading their way, apparently coming in from all directions. Wherever they went, they proclaimed that their forces had captured Lhasa. With danger looming so close, the monk became edgy, worried that disaster may have befallen Akong Tulku and Drolma Lhakang.

Rinpoche considered the Communists' possible moves based on the information he had, then turned again to mirror divination. The reading indicated that while the danger was increasing, there was no immediate cause for alarm. Even so, Rinpoche knew that finding refuge at either Drolma Lhakang or Yag monasteries was now out of the question.

Nine years earlier at Surmang, shortly after Chinese Communists appeared on the Tibetan scene, Rinpoche and his advisors – among them the lama who had seen them in action in Mongolia – had rightly assessed their full nature and intent. From then on, Rinpoche had known that at some point he would probably have to escape. Everything since had confirmed that first appraisal, and now the moment was upon him. Like being marooned on a strip of land as the flood rose around, the space and time for an escape was dwindling by the hour. And amid the ebb and flow of news, rumors and vague information, one thing was certain: when the Communist flood came upon them, Rinpoche's flame would be among the first to be snuffed out.

Rinpoche mentions no thought or reflection at this point: all was being overwhelmed by events. Without mentioning the word 'escape,' he sent the monk back to Drolma Lhakang to pack his luggage and prepare his horses, saying that he should be ready to leave by the next full moon day, April 23, 1959. In spite of the increasing peril, the rapidly shrinking window for an escape, Rinpoche chose to wait for an auspicious time to leave.

Some time later, another monk hiked up to the ledge, this time with the news that Drolma Lhakang remained peaceful and undisturbed, with no sign of imminent attack. Hearing this, Rinpoche decided to move down to the headman's village at the foot of the mountain, to wait there until the full moon day. There was no need to spend more time on the icy ledge: he had completed his work on meditation, which came to a full thousand Tibetan pages, while the villagers nearby were thoroughly aware of his presence.

After dusk, Rinpoche and his attendant climbed down towards the village, again using night to cloak their movements. For over a year secrecy had served him well, keeping him out of his pursuer's reach, hiding his identity, his whereabouts and his movements. He had left Surmang in the midst of a raging storm to elude the resident officials, then headed towards the planned area of escape under the benign cover of a teaching tour; after hearing of Communist headquarters' active search for him, he had left Yag monastery for the Yo valley in the dead of night; and from then on he had lived hidden and, whenever possible, had traveled in the dark. Each phase was triggered as the Communists closed in on him, his departure delayed until the last possible moment, until there was no option but to go.

Now, as Rinpoche was about to begin the most perilous phase of all, his escape from East Tibet, secrecy was more crucial than ever. While the Communists had been preoccupied in quelling Khampa resistance, the problem of a missing lama was secondary; now their push to find Tibetan leaders would resume with redoubled ferocity and determination. From the moment of Rinpoche's departure from Surmang he had been aided by friends, monastics and ordinary people alike, who had risked their own safety to protect him. Down in the village, secrecy would be maintained under the leadership of the headman, who planned to host Rinpoche covertly in a series of family homes, moving him under cover of darkness from one to the other.

Then there was the escape itself. Months before at Yag monastery, Jigme Tulku had emphasized that Rinpoche must leave secretly and alone. From Rinpoche's own experience, he knew this to be the safest approach – it was in a way just common sense. As long as he had traveled alone, with only a few people in the know, it had been possible to keep things tight and secrecy had been almost flawlessly maintained; alone, he could choose the most auspicious time to leave based on circumstances, rather than on others' agendas; alone, he could travel fast and inconspicuously. As soon as anyone else joined him, things would become more complicated and unpredictable, more dangerous.

A few days after Rinpoche moved down to the village, Yag Tulku arrived to see him. The older lama had previously been relaxed and sanguine about their prospects under the Communists: he had requested Rinpoche to transmit the Treasury Teachings at the most inopportune of times, and confidently assured him that there was nothing to be worried about. Now he appeared to Rinpoche to be more nervous than he was himself. So, in spite of his concerns for secrecy, Rinpoche felt that he could not withhold his decision to escape from someone who had been so generous to him: after they had chatted and exchanged news, he mentioned that he was leaving, along with his date of departure and proposed route.

Yag Tulku immediately asked to join Rinpoche's escape party – adding that he would be bringing with him a number of his senior monks and a sizeable amount of baggage. Rinpoche tried to convey to him that this journey would be quite unlike their safe and leisurely travels of times past, that it would be a desperate, life-and-death venture. If they were to have any hope of success, they would have to keep their group small, their baggage minimal. Yag Tulku thought about this for a while, then said he would still like to join Rinpoche, and that he could possibly manage with a few monks, along with a few mules for personal baggage and the monastery's precious objects. He doubted, though, that arrangements could be completed by the 23rd. Before he left to return to his monastery, Rinpoche stressed again that "the party must be kept as small as possible, or there would be no chance for any of us."[84]

Following Yag Tulku's visit, Rinpoche dispatched a letter to Akong Tulku, also informing him of his escape, and that he was leaving on the day of the full moon. He wrote that there was very little prospect of Drolma Lhakang's being left in peace, and if Akong Tulku wanted to join him he should discuss it with his monks, then come to a quick, firm decision. He added that the departure date was fixed, and he would be holding to it. In a message presumably meant to be read later, Rinpoche assured the monks and lamas of Drolma Lhakang that, although the journey was likely to be a perilous one, if their abbot joined him he would do his best to protect him. Again, he emphasized to Akong Tulku that they must keep their group small. Every additional person would increase the danger to everyone else, while also adding to Rinpoche's burden of responsibility. In addition, if their group was a large one, others they met along the way might feel freer to join, multiplying everyone's danger.

Even though news of the escape would probably soon be leaking out, secrecy still had to be observed. From experience Rinpoche knew that there was little chance that Yag Tulku would be able to keep things confidential, but his monastery lay far enough to the southeast and what happened there in the short time remaining would be unlikely to impact Rinpoche's departure. More critically, secrecy must be maintained at Drolma Lhakang. For this, the departure details had to be kept to a small circle of Akong Tulku's monks, and preparations made surreptitiously. It would also be necessary for Rinpoche to arrive at Drolma Lhakang before dawn, while most of the monastery slept, when he, Akong Tulku and their attendants stood the best chance of leaving quietly and unnoticed.

On the night of April 22, Rinpoche set off for Drolma Lhakang with his attendant and a guide. In daylight and fine weather, it would have been a short journey across the broad Auchu valley. But, although it was well into spring, they rode through much of the night in a blinding snowstorm, following a circuitous route around villages to avoid being spotted by local people or PLA patrols billeted there. As much as they tried to speed the pace, storm and route combined to slow them down and, after a harrowing ride, they reached Drolma Lhakang some time after dawn.

The monastery was fully awake, and a large crowd awaited him. As hard as Akong Tulku had tried to keep the departure secret, it had proved impossible. He had decided to join Rinpoche on the escape, accompanied by his two brothers and several monks, and the rushed preparation of the horses and baggage train had been especially hard to conceal.

Some would not be going with Rinpoche. His bursar, Tsethar, unable to relinquish Surmang, its treasures or his hopes of return, had changed his mind and decided to stay. And there was no sign of Yag Tulku or of Yonten, who had been assigned to pack and bring

Rinpoche's possessions from Yag monastery, nor any message from them. The traveling party would leave without them.

Once news of the escape leaked out it swept through the area, and large numbers of anxious monks and lay people showed up to seek Rinpoche's blessing. Many were desperate for his individual advice, but there was no time for that now, and people were gathered in the large assembly hall where he could address them together. He warned them against taking up arms, saying that it was useless to resist the Communists' overwhelming power. He told them that he could offer no concrete advice on what to do or where to go; apart from a general notion of heading for Central Tibet, he had no idea himself where he was going. Then, after giving his blessing to them all, one by one, Rinpoche hurried from the hall, fearing that the people still flocking to the monastery to see him would further hinder their departure, if not block it altogether.

When the moment of departure came, it was a profoundly wrenching, tearful experience for Akong Tulku, for the senior people who had cared for him throughout his life, and for Drolma Lhakang's monks and lay people. They were losing someone to whom they were deeply devoted, and whom they dearly loved. After centuries with their lama at the heart center of their world, he was disappearing in front of their eyes.

Rinpoche's own people at Surmang had been largely spared such an abrupt separation, the sudden raw pain. Yet earlier that morning, having had no reply to the letter he had written months before to his monks and family in Kyere, he wrote a last message telling them of his departure. He never heard if either letter reached them.

PART II

5

Lhasa-bound

With the farewells behind them, they rode north west up the Auchu River valley. They did not plan to cover any great distance that day and, as soon as they had gone beyond Drolma Lhakang's environs, they looked for a place of shelter where they could regroup and take stock of their situation. They also needed to prepare some food for Rinpoche, who had eaten nothing since before his arduous ride the previous night: the crowds at the monastery had made it impossible to find time to eat there and, although his attendants had packed provisions for the road, they could not stop to find and prepare them.

Near nightfall, the party arrived at Drolma Lhakang's northern nunnery. They found the nuns calm and composed; they well understood the dire situation, but were resigned to whatever fate would bring – indeed, were more concerned for Rinpoche's plight than their own. They asked his advice, as did local villagers who had arrived after hearing of his presence. He spent an hour with them all, talking things through, preparing them as best he could. When a gap eventually occurred, the nuns served him up a most welcome meal.

Then they turned to the situation at hand, while the attendants set about repacking their baggage, which had been hastily and surreptitiously done at Drolma Lhakang. In all, there were eleven lamas and monks in the traveling party. Rinpoche's group consisted of his personal attendant, an older man, and the two young monks who had been with him in the Valley of Mystery. Yonten, who had stayed behind at Yag monastery to take care of Rinpoche's possessions, would join them later. Moving fast with his small baggage train, he would catch up soon, and when he arrived he would be taking over as bursar, Tsethar's old job. Akong Tulku had with him Jamyang Chogyal, his older brother, and Jampal Drakpa, his younger one; also with his group were a lama from his monastery, a young novice and an older monk who was "a very spiritual man, prepared to face any difficulties and dangers"[85] For transport, they had thirty horses and fifty baggage mules. The yaks had been left behind; useful as they were for baggage-carrying, milk and, if necessary, food and clothing, their ambling pace would have unacceptably slowed them down.

The lamas talked late into the night, discussing the journey ahead. Any thoughts of an ultimate destination faded in the glare of the immediate hazards. With Communist forces gaining control of Eastern Tibet, and now marching south in large numbers, the group's immediate objective was to get across the Shabye Bridge over the Gyalmo Ngulchu River, about a week's ride away. Beyond the river, the country remained in Tibetan hands, guarded by resistance forces. If they could get across the bridge they would be safe for the time being, but it was a major crossing-point and there was likely to be a Communist detachment stationed there, keeping refugees in and Tibetan fighters out.

The first few days would be the most harrowing. They would be riding directly towards danger – towards the main Chamdo-Lhasa road, which lay about fourteen miles ahead, just beyond a small range of mountains. By now the Communists would undoubtedly hold the road, and would be using it to move troops, weapons and supplies. At any time the traveling party could run into PLA patrols probing south from the road, seeking resistance positions, hunting down lamas and political leaders.

After an early breakfast, they continued up the Auchu Valley. On a normal spring day, it would have been an agreeable ride; it was anything but that. Ever since he had left Surmang, Rinpoche had moved in a fog of concealment, cloaking his identity and movements, later living in total secrecy while traveling under cover of darkness. Now their sizeable party was traveling up the broad valley in the bright sun of morning, visible from many miles away, highly vulnerable to attack or capture.

But they had taken precautions. Like military commanders deploying scouts and reconnaissance patrols to prevent surprise attacks from front and flanks, messengers had been sent to the surrounding villages with requests to report immediately to the traveling party any sightings of Chinese troops. Now, as they rode along the valley, they were guarded on all sides by a circle of watching villagers, forming a perimeter around them, protectors guarding the fringes of their moving mandala.

Near dusk they made their way to the home of a celebrated doctor, who received them warmly and served up a sumptuous meal. Then he gave them a crash course on the route ahead, the foods to eat or avoid, where drinkable water was to be found and how to find medicinal herbs. Grateful for the doctor's hospitality, but looking to making a good start to the journey, they left early the next morning. Almost immediately, they were waylaid by villagers who had heard of Rinpoche's presence and wanted his blessing and advice. It took some time until the people were calmed and satisfied with what they had received, so that the party could go on its way.

Further along the valley they came to a lake encircled by mountains known as the Five Mothers, held to be sacred by Tibet's old Bon religion. There Rinpoche faced the moment he had known was coming, and which he may have been quietly dreading: he would be removing his lama's robes to disguise his identity. Rinpoche recalled, from the previous year, the "bad psychological effect"[86] that changing from robes into ordinary clothes had had on Khamtrul Tulku. Now it was his turn. From early childhood, Rinpoche had worn only one garment, his robes. In their rich blend of saffron, maroon and gold brocade, the robes had a powerful but simple splendor to them, the colors vibrant with meaning and symbolism going back twenty-five-hundred years to the time of the Buddha. For monastics, as for many Tibetans, they were the vestments of true nobility – higher in meaning, held in deeper esteem, than the garb of any king or aristocrat, and worn with a quiet, deep pride. It was not an outfit Rinpoche was doffing. More than his skin, perhaps even more than his flesh and muscle, the robes were the outward manifestation of who he was. As he took them off, then donned ordinary brown lay clothes and a European-style felt hat of a style popular in Tibet, he felt "a sense of desolation."[87]

From the lake, they continued up the Auchu River valley until their route turned westwards – away from Kham, away from Surmang. Rinpoche wrote simply that the "track now led us over heights, with the land sloping down to a distant river."[88] The river was the Gyalmo Ngulchu, their first, vital objective. The track went in their direction, but only for a while; then it began to snake up and down mountains, and meander sinuously along valleys. Just as they were straining to get beyond the Communists' shadow and across the Shabye Bridge, the landscape seemed to conspire against them, slowing them down. And they had also left their protective circle of watching villagers behind; now, around every bend, beyond each ridge, they might stumble into a PLA patrol.

They had sent a message on to Kino monastery, situated some miles short of the river, to announce their imminent arrival. When they arrived they were met by a small procession of monks, then received at the monastery with full, traditional ceremonial. Rinpoche felt ashamed at having to appear in drab civilian clothes, but he was warmly welcomed by all, including the abbot, Kino Tulku, who was married and lived outside the monastery's precincts. Then, as people flocked in from the surrounding countryside to see him, Rinpoche settled down for three days' teaching and personal interviews. They remained vigilant, though, knowing that in an area of such strategic importance Communist soldiers could be upon them any moment.

While Rinpoche was teaching, Yonten arrived with his small baggage train of mules and a few extra horses he had acquired. On the way he'd had a real scare as he rode past Drolma Lhakang: from afar it seemed that the monastery was in flames, with large plumes of smoke pouring into the sky. As he rode closer, though, a nun assured him that it was just lamas and monks burning offerings to the protector deities. Later, as he neared Kino monastery, he met throngs of people heading his way: "I wondered what was going on here. People told me 'Oh, Trungpa Rinpoche is giving teachings, so we're going to go to see him.' " Arriving at the crowded monastery, Yonten was tickled by the irony of the situation: "Trungpa Rinpoche was very busy with dharma activity, and the Chinese army was very busy trying to catch Trungpa Rinpoche."[89]

During the teaching, Kino Tulku asked Rinpoche if he and his wife – who were great friends of Akong Tulku's – could join the escape, saying that he was quite happy to abandon all his possessions to do so. With the Communist menace looming, and their lama friend leaving, it seemed time to go; they would bring along two attendants, five horses and eleven mules for baggage. A local man with his wife and small daughter also asked to join; so eager was he to leave that he had already sold their home and bought three horses to augment the two he had owned.

The journey had hardly begun, yet the traveling party had already swelled in size. The simple truth was that Rinpoche could not refuse those who asked to join him. As Yonten put it, he had little choice; people were in fear for their lives, desperately wanting to escape.[90] And so Rinpoche simply said "yes" to the requests, even though it was grimly clear that each additional person and animal made everyone more vulnerable.

After three days at Kino monastery, the enlarged group set out for Shabye Bridge. They had heard from passing travelers that there were now no Communist soldiers guarding it, but the bridge was a key choke-point, and things could quickly change. As they approached the river, they found that the track they had followed was not quite done with them. Instead of inclining downwards to the river banks, the track wound up towards a mountain pass, aptly named Preta Pass. In Buddhist cosmology, a *preta* is a being whose desires can never be satisfied; climbing up to and over the pass was strenuous work that brought on intense thirst and hunger, but travelers had to keep going, unable to stop to eat or drink.[91] At the top of the pass the track conjured up a final flourish, becoming very narrow before taking a zig-zag route down the mountain's vertiginous rock face, a full two thousand feet to the river below.

When they reached the banks of the Gyalwa Ngulchu, the travelers slaked their thirst, then headed upstream. As the Shabye Bridge came into view, no PLA soldiers could be seen. The group crossed the bridge, happily recalling the origins of its name. When one of the early Karmapas had arrived at the river, there was no way across; while his attendants pondered the problem, the Karmapa removed his right boot – *shabye* meaning "right leg" – and hurled it into the middle of the current. The boot became wedged between some rocks, whereupon people set about building a bridge there using the rocks for supports, and the bridge had stood there ever since.[92]

As they stepped onto the river's western bank, a wave of relief swept through them. They were out of immediate danger and, for the first time in years, beyond the reach of the Communists. Yonten felt that crossing the bridge was like passing from one spiritual realm to another: "I felt a small liberation …"[93] They were greeted by a cheerful guard of the Tibetan resistance forces, who checked for weapons – finally allowing Yonten's cherished Khampa knife to pass, also a rolled-up sacred scroll which, with its rifle-like shape, had aroused a momentary suspicion – then issued passports for their onward journey, and waved them on.

They spent the night in a nearby village, and before dawn began their climb up another serpentine track, this one so steep that they had to stop repeatedly to rest their breathless horses. At the crest they came across their first group of Tibetan resistance soldiers, who were manning stone defenses built on both sides of the road. Although most of the men were volunteers – including a doctor whom Rinpoche had known in Lhatok – he was impressed by their soldierly bearing: "All the soldiers were tall, well set up men and looked very warlike."[94] They too were very cheerful and enthusiastic, especially the younger men, who proudly wore medallions, dangling from yellow ribbons, with the words "National Resistance Volunteers."

Although many had rifles, some carried only ancient muskets. For all their high and stalwart spirits, they would be no match for the battle-hardened troops of the PLA with their modern weaponry, nor would their small stone forts last long under mortar or artillery fire, which would shatter the rocks into deadly shrapnel. However, most in the traveling party were unshakably confident of Tibetan success. One of these was the oldest of Rinpoche's attendants; a kindly, simple man, he reasoned that since Tibet had never molested other countries, by the law of karma it would surely merit victory.

From the pass they rode on across a range of jumbled mountains until, near twilight, they left the foothills behind and could set up their tents for the night. Early next morning they reached the small town of Lhodzong, where they stopped to talk to other travelers and local people, and to weigh their options.

Heading for Lhasa seemed their best plan. Resistance fighters had repeated to them what they had heard in Kham – the Communists' claim that they held Lhasa, now augmented with one that the Dalai Lama was being held by Tibetan guerillas – but they did not believe it. Even if Lhasa was in fact under Chinese control, they might still want to head for Central Tibet. There they could wait, watching developments while keeping open the possibility of returning to Kham if the situation allowed. And if it did come to making for India, the traditional road went south from Lhasa, and they could always skirt the city to pick up the road nearer the border.

It was a reasonable objective, although Rinpoche himself may have held severe doubts. For years he had watched the Communists at work, gauged their determined ideology, and knew well their ambitions for all of Tibet; and he had a well-grounded idea of what the outcome of the conflict would be. Nevertheless, with most of the group still not fully reconciled to leaving their homeland, for now it did seem best to keep things open and make for Lhasa.

They were back in Tibetan-held territory, but it was not the Tibet they knew. Resistance fighters and weaponry were everywhere, the atmosphere thick with war's strange mix of pride, exuberance and foreboding. With fighters pouring along the road from Lhasa, bound for the front line on the Gyalwa Ngulchu River, food prices had shot up along the route and there would be little grazing for their animals.

Realizing that it would be impossible to make headway against the warlike current, they decided to bypass the main road and take a circuitous route across the rolling mountains to the north. It would take longer and be harder going, but there was no alternative. They set off up the track and, after a few days' ride, stopped at the home of a friend of Kino Tulku.

While they rested and talked, a young abbot who had been a student of Rinpoche's at Surmang arrived in a state of great excitement and asked if he could join the escape. Rinpoche accepted him, but warned that the escape would be "a difficult business."[95] He also told the young man that he would have to inform his monks that they could not join him, as the group could not afford to get any larger. When the abbot returned from the dismal mission to his monastery, he brought with him twenty mules with his baggage.

After a few further days' ride, they came upon a young monk, Urgyan-tendzin, who had been making a pilgrimage to Lhasa. He too asked to join Rinpoche's group and was accepted, whereupon Kino Tulku gave him one of his mules for his baggage. Urgyan-tendzin would turn out to be a brilliant recruit. Intelligent, resourceful and courageous, he was extremely useful in the daily tasks of loading and unloading baggage from the mules. Later, at crucial points of the escape – and in its moments of high crisis – his presence and expertise were to prove critical, both to Rinpoche as leader and to the group as a whole.

"These early weeks" Rinpoche wrote, "were really enjoyable."[96] The immediate danger of the Chinese army was far behind and the country lay open and resplendent before them – always mountainous, but far more spacious than the pile of peaks and deep, meandering valleys around the Gyalwa Ngulchu River. It was spring and the weather sublime, with flowers blooming through the valleys and up the mountainsides. Everyone was cheery, looking forward to visiting Lhasa, chatting happily about the day when the Tibetan resistance forces would overcome the Communists and the country would return to peace and normalcy. Happily, too, no-one they met had recognized Rinpoche as a lama, with many taking him for an official of the resistance.

Still, even the brightest and most sun-drenched days had their dark edge. On the track they came across numbers of travelers who, like them, had been forced away from the main road and over the mountains. Most were from East Tibet, and Rinpoche and the others listened eagerly to their news and information. It was almost uniformly bad. One man told of the Communists' arrival at his monastery: when the abbot tried to explain that they had no weapons there, and that they had always taught the practice of non-violence, the Communist official – apparently seeing no reason to put off something he would be getting to anyway – stepped forward and shot him in the forehead.

Even where they were, on a secondary track among the mountains, they could not forget that the country was on a war footing. On May 21 the group entered an area where they would need passports from the local resistance commander before they could continue. As he issued the documents, his eyes settled on the young abbot who had recently joined them, then refused to give him a passport. Wholly uninterested in his religious status, the commander insisted that everyone from the district must stay to fight. No amount of pleading or reasoning would change his mind, and the hapless young man had to be left behind.

On the whole, though, the spring days passed pleasantly and uneventfully, punctuated only by the passes they had to cross on their mountainous detour. They rode on until there were no further tracks across the ranges ahead, and they had to regain the main road. Although the military traffic against them on the road was still quite heavy, the group could at least enjoy the easier going on more level ground.

After stopping briefly at a small temple which held a famous image of Padmasambhava, they continued on until they came to a broad valley. As they entered it, they saw at its far end, straddling their way like a massive barricade, a range of mountains that they would have to cross.

The Sharkong La range was high, the pass over it unusually steep and tricky; and the weather had turned stormy, with a violent wind and rain blowing in their faces. As they climbed up the rocky, slippery and uneven track, the mules struggled to hold their footing and their baggage repeatedly fell off, forcing everyone to stop to replace and secure the loads. Some way up, they came upon a small detachment of resistance fighters armed with ancient muskets, who were guarding the pass; they were very keen, but extremely hungry, and the travelers gave them food before moving on.

After camping overnight, they resumed the climb in the morning with the weather still stormy. Higher up they met three young deserters from the resistance forces heading down from the pass, who told them that the Communists were very strong in Lhasa and Central Tibet; they went on to say that, being themselves only three in number, they had managed to travel without drawing attention, but they doubted that such a large group as Rinpoche's could stay concealed.

At around eighteen thousand feet, the group reached the crest of the pass. Rinpoche, Akong Tulku and Kino Tulku dismounted, added a flag to the cairn there, and gave the traditional shout of victory – "*Lha Gyal Lo!*" – "Victory to the deities." On the downward slope they were met by waves of brisk wind and heavy rain, and the track was covered with a fine slate dust, so slippery in the wet that they had to dismount and lead their animals. After laboring some way down they decided to stop and set up camp.

Over a warming cup of tea, they talked things over. While some felt that the young deserters may have exaggerated the hopelessness of the situation in Central Tibet out of a feeling of guilt, what they had said had been unsettling. Making everyone more uneasy, they recalled that back on the main road they had noticed that no-one else was heading their way, towards Lhasa.

With the rain pelting down even more heavily, they remained in camp through the next day. As they sat waiting for the weather to lift, a group of men, some armed with rifles, was seen coming down from the pass towards them. To everyone's surprise, and Rinpoche's delight, it turned out to be Yag Tulku and a small group from his monastery. Over tea, Yag Tulku passed on his news: although the violence and tumult in East Tibet continued unabated, both Drolma Lhakang and Yag monastery were still safe and unaffected.

As Yag Tulku continued, Rinpoche's pleasure at seeing his friend began to wane. His small group, Yag Tulku said, was being followed by his personal baggage train of sixty mules; he had clearly disregarded Rinpoche's request to travel light. Then he announced that he had ridden ahead to find Rinpoche, and that his group was just the vanguard of a much larger body of people following behind.

When Yag Tulku left his monastery he had done so very publicly, in broad daylight. As lamas, monks and villagers had witnessed the departure of their teacher, they had panicked, with many deciding to leave on the spot. Then Yag Tulku told Rinpoche that much of the main party's baggage had been loaded onto slow-moving yaks; and, to round things off, he asked Rinpoche to wait several days until they could all catch up.

We don't know why Yag Tulku chose so blithely to ignore Rinpoche's earlier, fervently-made requests to travel light and to maintain secrecy; Rinpoche makes no comment in his account. But it's hard to avoid the feeling that, apart from other issues Yag Tulku may have had to address, like Tsethar the bursar before him, he did not yet consider the young lama's views worthy of serious consideration.

Whatever the reasons, suddenly, in a brisk flurry of blows, every factor that Rinpoche knew would advance their chances of escape had been overthrown or undermined, everyone's hopes diminished. From here on, their group would be huge and highly conspicuous, easily spotted from miles away. It would also be achingly slow.

Moving at a yak's pace, clumsy and ponderous, they would stand little hope of evading an approaching threat, or of getting through tricky or treacherous terrain. And the logistical problems had been greatly multiplied; for so large a group with so many animals, food and grazing would hard, if not impossible, to come by.[97]

It was all a far cry from the year before, when Khamtrul Tulku had implored Rinpoche to quietly leave with him for India, or when Jigme Tulku had urged him to escape secretly and alone. It was as if he had been forced to change his mount from an agile and relatively invisible steed of some speed and stamina to a bulky, shambling yak in need of constant care and feeding. From here on, everything would be slower, more difficult, more dangerous.

When the main Yag party eventually came over the pass, Rinpoche was stunned by its size. He did not take a roll call, and offered no figure in his account, but the newcomers may have numbered over a hundred people, perhaps as many as fifty more than that. With their horses, mules and yaks, their group was now enormous, probably over a thousand beings in all. It was not just their numbers, or the much reduced pace at which they would be traveling from here on. Rinpoche saw that many of the newly arrived families included elderly people, small children, and mothers with babies. As he gazed at the throng of people and animals spread around Sharkong La's slopes, and at the endless series of peaks and ranges ahead, he wrote: "I wondered how we would ever manage to escape with so many men and animals."[98]

They took a few days to talk through and revise their plans, while the Yag people rested and sorted themselves out. Then they resumed the journey, making their slow way down Sharkong La's steep and difficult track before following a broad valley westwards. After a few days they came to the village of Langtso Kha, where they decided to set up camp. They chose a site away from the main road, in a small valley surrounded by rocky mountains and near a lake that they could use for water.

As soon as people were settled in, Rinpoche sought out the local military commander for his overview of the situation. It was quickly plain that they had already hit a major obstacle – one largely created by the group's newly-bloated size and weight. Langtso Kha was located near the higher reaches of the Alado River, the main road westwards following its course downstream. Just a few miles along the near bank the river disappeared into a deep gorge, with sheer, near-perpendicular rock cliffs on either side. At this point travelers had to cross the gorge on a narrow, precarious bridge before continuing along the north bank.

The bridge was a primitive but remarkable structure. Logs and rough-hewn planks, placed one atop another for support, had somehow been wedged into the cliff faces, positioned to jut out over the chasm; where they joined in the middle, only a single plank bore the traveler's weight. There were no ropes or hand guides, just the bare, slim wood. And the paths traversing the cliff face to the bridge were very narrow; one misstep would be fatal. In places, small rough-hewn platforms, supported by planks, circumvented obstacles. Children and elderly people could be coaxed over – or carried if need be – while the animals were sure-footed. But the yaks posed a real problem: they could probably handle the track, platforms and bridge, but a fully laden animal weighed well over half a ton; it seemed very doubtful that the simple wooden structure would stand the strain.

An additional problem appeared insurmountable: the time that they would need to cross the bridge. It had been built by locals for their own use and for occasional travelers heading to Lhasa, not for the weight of traffic it was bearing now. As Rinpoche and the others watched, an endless stream of resistance fighters poured past them, heading east towards the front lines. With their original small group it would have been possible to get across without much difficulty, even with the current traffic; they might have waited for the occasional lull or tried late at night – and anyway the oncoming fighters would have happily made way for a small group of venerable lamas. But with their newly ponderous bulk, and the time it would take for them all to negotiate the approach paths and the bridge itself, there seemed little if any chance of a successful crossing.

They could not go on, nor could they stay where they were. There was scant grazing in their small valley and what little there was must, as far as possible, be preserved for the horses of passing resistance fighters. But it seemed that nothing could be done about it: for the time being the party was stuck in their small valley.

Rinpoche turned the time to good use, unpacking books from his baggage and starting a study group. While Yonten headed down to the village of Langtso Kha for provisions, Rinpoche went climbing in the fair weather among the wildflowers on the nearby mountains. He was often accompanied by Akong Tulku and his younger brother Jampal, with whom Rinpoche continued to share a warm, close friendship. Occasionally, Rinpoche and other senior lamas would enjoy meals with a local landowner, who also extended his hospitality to their animals, allowing them to graze on his land.

With his text on meditation completed, Rinpoche began a new work. It was a vision of Shambhala, the enlightened kingdom whose ruler would liberate humanity from the depths of the coming Dark Age. It described the kingdom's coming into being, arising as a dazzling space of stainless purity, and told of its kings, queens, princes and princesses, ministers and warriors. Glittering, opulent and luminous, it is a realm where grain does not grow and structures are not fabricated, and where there is neither creation nor evolution; instead, all arises spontaneously from a state beyond both evil and good, from a ground of unconditional basic goodness.[99]

The days dragged by, enjoyable but not entirely relaxed. As they waited, Rinpoche met a man he had known at Surmang who had left to join the Tibetan resistance. He and his comrades were returning from Lhasa, which they had fled after its fall to the Communists; he told Rinpoche that there were not only fighters streaming down the road from Lhasa, but now also many refugees. Later, as these began to arrive in ever-growing numbers, the place became awash in rumors: the Communists were just behind them, nearing the area; the Dalai Lama had returned to the capital; and so on. No-one could offer a clear and balanced view of what was going on in Central Tibet.

Bridge over the Alado Gorge

Amid the blizzard of rumors at Langtso Kha, though, a few key realities stood out. With the growing flood of humanity coming their way, whatever tiny chance that Rinpoche's group had of crossing the bridge was gone. And, as refugees and animals surged in, food was running out and grazing land was disappearing fast – so fast that even their hospitable landowner had grown jittery.

While chatting with local people, Rinpoche had heard of an alternative route, a great, looping detour over the high ranges to the north. He had hesitated to take what would be an arduous trek for people and animals alike, but now it was choiceless. And so, near the end of May, they thanked their generous host and struck camp.

At first they headed eastwards, retracing the way they had come, but before long they spotted the entrance to the valley they were looking for, and took the rough track that ran up it. As they climbed, the valley gradually veered around until it headed north west. At its head they came to their first pass; from then on, as Rinpoche wrote, "each day we had to cross a high pass"[100] The continual climbs and descents at altitudes of around nineteen thousand feet were tough on them all – remembered by Yonten fifty years later, who spoke with simple understatement of "many, many passes, one after the other."[101]

On the desolate heights they came across a man standing near the trail. He told Rinpoche that he had come from the Lhatok area, having fled with nine nomad families who had brought everything with them, all their possessions and animals. Rinpoche followed him to his camp to meet the Lhatok people. One of the families was headed by a man named Tserge Washutsong, who had brought his extended family of thirty with him – among them his fifteen-year-old daughter Palya, twelve-year-old son Drupju and a five-year-old daughter. The family had sometimes camped near Surmang; Tserge was a long-time student of Rinpoche's and the entire family had become devotees. Tserge now begged Rinpoche for permission for his family and relatives to join the escaping party, which Rinpoche gave.

From then on Tserge met regularly with Rinpoche, then returned and told the family what he had said. Many years later, Palya vividly recalled the more colorful details of what her father had passed on, especially those relating to Rinpoche's mirror divinations, in which the family had great faith. Indeed, it appears that many who joined Rinpoche's escape did so less because of his status as a high lama of a famous lineage, than through his renown as a potent adept of mirror divination. During the escape, in place of the traditional brass or crystal mirror he employed a small, square one,[102] but apparently his mastery was such that, in tight situations, he simply licked his thumbnail and gazed into its glistening reflections.

Lhasa was topmost in many refugees' minds, and one morning Tserge Washutsong asked Rinpoche to perform a divination about conditions in the capital. The mirror deity normally appears astride a horse, holding in her right hand an arrow adorned with ribbons of five colors, and in her left a white silver mirror. But in the Lhasa divination, she arose in the mirror surrounded by smoke, her horse's legs bleeding profusely. The smoke, Rinpoche said, indicated that Lhasa was in flames and in the process of being destroyed, while the bleeding showed that much blood was being shed in the capital on both sides. The deity then communicated that the Dalai Lama was now at Bodhgaya in India,[103] the place of the Buddha's enlightenment, where he was conducting an offering feast – and that, as she planned to attend the feast herself, she could not spend any more time on the divination. With that, in one of history's few examples of a deity on a tight schedule, she abruptly disappeared.[104]

After the divination, and as they heard news from other travelers, their hopes of finding refuge in Central Tibet – or even of reaching the old road from Lhasa to India – faded fast. They met three Tibetan soldiers who had fled the Norbulingka, the Dalai Lama's Summer Palace, then watched it being shelled by the Communists before the guns were turned on the Potala. Other travelers told of being spotted on their way to Lhasa by PLA aircraft, and then attacked by its patrols. The Communists seemed to be everywhere, and no-one knew where to go. Around this time, Kino Tulku remarked that he knew the area of the Powo valley far to the south, and wondered whether they should not perhaps head there before trying to reach India, while Rinpoche heard that an eminent lama from East Tibet was leading a group of refugees towards India.

Then momentous news arrived. The Karmapa, accompanied by high teachers of the Kagyu and Nyingma lineages, along with many lamas and monks, had fled his monastery near Lhasa several weeks before the capital's fall, making for India via Bhutan. Rinpoche's attendants' were bewildered: how was it that the Karmapa had escaped to India himself, but had declined to offer advice to their abbot when he had so urgently requested it? Rinpoche explained that, in the situation in which they all found themselves, no-one could confidently offer advice. He himself was in the same predicament: in the chaotic, fast-changing situation, it had been nearly impossible to gain a sure view of what was going on.

Nevertheless, by now the larger picture was sharply etched for Rinpoche. He had heard the Communists' claims to own all of Tibet, seen them in action in Surmang, knew of their ruthless response to any opposition to their rule. He recalled Jamgon Kongtrul's somber remarks on their own future, had seen the igniting effect on Khenpo Gangshar of the mountain omen signifying that their time in their homeland was at an end, had joined in Khamtrul Tulku's divinations indicating that he should make for India without delay, and had heard the tragic news frm Lhasa.

Like everyone else, Rinpoche would have chosen to stay in his homeland. Although he had a burning curiosity about the wider world, it paled in light of his Surmang heritage and his responsibilities as the eleventh Trungpa. He had been forced out by the PLA's relentless power – and then only leaving after talking over each move with friends and advisors and, when events swirled beyond rationality's reach, turning to divination. At each step he had waited until the eleventh hour before making his escape.

News of the Karmapa's flight dissolved the last doubts: "I decided that we must continue southwards at least for a few months, and by that time we would know more about the state of affairs in

Tibet ...."[105] That was how he explained their next course to his fellow travelers. Everyone could see the decision's good sense: they could not continue westwards to Lhasa, nor could they retreat eastwards to Kham, and to the north lay only the vast wastelands of marshes, quicksands, mountains, glaciers and deserts.

But the young lama was among the few who knew that, in turning south, they were taking their first steps towards fleeing Tibet, and that their destination would be India. With the shape and course of events clear to him, from now on, whenever the opportunity came, he would be doing the shaping.

6

Rifts Above Nyewo Valley

Shifting their course southeastwards, Trungpa Rinpoche led the
long train of refugees and animals across a range of low
mountains towards Mount Nupkong La. After a tiring climb
over the pass, they made their way into the river valley beyond. The
downhill going was easier, and before long they came to the
tributary's junction with the Alado River; from here they looked east
along the Alado's valley towards its source, and could make out the
gorges where the bridge bottleneck had delayed them for so long.

Just downstream, the river presented new challenges. Here the
valley narrowed again, with a series of tricky bridges to be crossed.
After looking over the first one, Rinpoche doubted that his people
and animals could make it across, and decided to camp in a small
field to review the situation. After a while, through Russian
binoculars he had carried from Surmang, he saw a man leading
baggage mules across the bridge without any apparent trouble;
encouragingly, he also noted that the general traffic was clearly going
their way. With the assistance of local villagers the refugees
negotiated the bridges without mishap, while the animals had no
difficulty when left alone to make their own way over.

With the bridges behind them, they camped for the night. Here
they met a group of monks from Khamtrul Tulku's monastery,
including one who had assisted Rinpoche at Yag monastery during
his presentation of the Treasury Teachings. They told of the terrible
happenings at their monastery when the Communists arrived. All the
lamas were shot out of hand and the monks herded into captivity –

although a few managed to get away on a secret path known only to them.[106] There was no doubt that, if Khamtrul Tulku had not left when he did, he would have shared the lamas' fate. The monks, shocked as they were at the fate of their fellow monastics and the shattering of their peaceful life, were much eased by the knowledge that their abbot was safely in India.

Rinpoche's party continued on along the main road next to the Alado River. The river first swung eastwards then, at the village of Alado, where another tributary joined, it turned south. Now they began to see ever larger numbers of other travelers, all heading in the same southerly direction. When Rinpoche asked them where they were going, no-one seemed to know. They were, they said, just following the people in front of them.

Further on the valley narrowed again, here funneled between enormous mountains. As it did so the road became more and more congested, until it was so crammed with people and animals that it was hard to move forward at all. Far more troubling, the many thousands of animals in the cramped valley had chewed the grazing down to bare earth; starving animals were everywhere, dead yaks blocked the road, and the valley floor was littered with carcasses baking in the summer heat. Little wind reached the valley's deep trough and the putrid reek of rotting flesh was overwhelming, penetrating deep into clothes and nostrils.

If they had been a small, disciplined and relatively fast-moving group, they might have been able to steel themselves to push on through the stench and carnage before resuming their journey down the Alado valley. But with their group's new bulk it was out of the question, and Rinpoche led the refugees away from the road and into a valley on the Alado's western side. Here everything was green, the terrain covered in holly trees and bamboo, all quite unlike the vegetation of East Tibet. In other times it would have been a lovely place to camp, but the small valley was also packed with people and animals; few clean campsites remained, and the space was so crowded that they barely had room to stretch out the tent ropes.

People soon learned of Rinpoche's presence, and began to approach him for advice: he simply told them that he had "no clearer idea than themselves" about what to do or where to go.[107] Whatever his own views on their objective may have been at this stage, events were moving quickly, there were many unknowns, and he did not feel that he could advise anyone to follow whatever course he might be considering.

If they could not continue down the foul and congested Alado valley, they would have to make their third major detour to go above and around it. And so, after a short rest, they folded their tents, gathered themselves together, and followed Rinpoche out of the valley and up towards a pass that would take them over the mountains. The higher they climbed the steeper the track became until, several thousand feet above the valley, they slogged through drifts that were unusually deep for the time of year. Many other refugees had chosen the same route and, as they neared the top, Rinpoche found it "a strange sight to watch the stream of people looking like a black ribbon stretched out over the white landscape of the pass."[108]

From the crest they descended into a series of valleys, with further passes to be climbed ahead. For a few days they continued in a generally southerly direction, looking for a place to camp. They found a surprising number of people on the heights, but there was space for camping, and up here the air was fresh and clean. Just when they thought that they would find a campsite, they came to another pass, this one far more precipitous than any they had faced so far. The track was narrow, with the ground so tricky that one of their baggage horses lost its footing, struggled for a moment, then tumbled into the abyss below. Yonten noted that the cliff face was so sheer that they could not see where the unfortunate beast had landed, and its entire load was lost.[109]

When they reached the top of the pass they saw ahead of them a broad plateau. Although it already held the campsites of hundreds of refugees, it was large enough to accommodate their group, and they decided to make camp there. The plateau lay at over seventeen thousand feet, and still had occasional patches of snow. It would be cold at night, but in daytime it lay open to the unfiltered summer sun and was warm, with enough fresh vegetation nearby to feed the animals.

Perhaps none present thought it then, but the tableau spread out before them was a profoundly stirring one, a moment in time that resonated through the centuries. Here on this high plateau, under the commanding sun and azure sky, among the array of tents – some of snowy white cotton with brilliant appliquéd designs, others of dark brown yak wool – was a last drawing together of Tibet's full fabric, a whole and unbroken gathering of spiritual masters and monastics, aristocrats and political leaders, villagers and herdsmen, old and young. People were in high spirits, and the sound of songs, joking and laughter filled the air, merging with chanting, drums and horns as lamas and monks continued with their devotions. It was a fleeting spectacle which, along with others like it, would not be seen again.

There was a far echo to it all. Just as, aeons ago, their land had been driven heavenwards by a collision of vast landmasses, so the refugees had been forced up here, a full mile above the Tibetan plateau, by a mighty clash between a powerful spirituality and a ruthless materialism. As East Tibet was overcome, its people had fled westwards towards their capital; as Lhasa had fallen and Central Tibet overrun, thousands headed eastwards towards Kham, the ancient refuge of Buddhism. Now many were gathered here atop this mountain range, their ancient "house of stone that came from nowhere" dwindled down to a small refuge high above it.

People were adrift, disoriented, not knowing what had happened to the family, friends and homes they had left behind, or what lay in store for them. They had no idea what to do, or where to go. They knew only that food and grazing were running out; and that while they could not tell when or from which direction the enemy would come, come he would. Although they were cheerful and unbowed, their fears came up in a flurry of rumors swirling through the plateau's rarified air.

There were some, though, who were quite relaxed about it all, feeling that things would still work out for the best – or that at least they had ample time to decide what to do. Among them was the highly venerated teacher, Lama Urgyan Rinpoche.[110] Although Rinpoche had not met him before, Lama Urgyan had been a student of the tenth Trungpa, and their bonds were spiritually close. Lama Urgyan was now an esteemed master of both the Kagyu and Nyingma lineages, of the stature of Jamgon Kongtrul or Khenpo Gangshar; a close friend of, and advisor to, the Karmapa, he could have gone with him to India, but had chosen not to.

Shortly after arriving on the plateau, Rinpoche heard of Lama Urgyan's presence, and a meeting was arranged. As they talked he soon realized that the senior lama considered himself to be his advisor. For a start, Lama Urgyan could not understand why Rinpoche's following was such a large one; nor, when Rinpoche told him of his evolving ideas, did he approve of his plan to escape to India. Instead, he said, Rinpoche must stay just where he was. And in case there was any doubt in the young lama's mind about his views on the matter, Lama Urgyan informed him that what he had said was not a request but an order.

The venerable lama was serenely confident that there was no immediate danger from the Communists. Instead of embarking on hazardous schemes of escape, he said, everyone should join him on pilgrimages to the many holy sites to be found both on the plateau and in the surrounding valleys. There was one such holy place in the nearby valley, he went on, and named the date when Rinpoche's group would be expected to join him on a pilgrimage there.

Apart from any other reservations Rinpoche may have had, when he considered Lama Urgyan's plans, he was doubtful that they could get over the high pass into the holy site's valley. Rather than offend Lama Urgyan by flatly declining to bring his whole traveling party along, he decided that it would be best if only he, Akong Tulku and a monk should go on the pilgrimage. When the threesome appeared at the stipulated time and place, Lama Urgyan was surprised that they were alone, and asked where the rest of the party was; he had been, as Rinpoche wrote "very excited at the prospect of conducting our whole group, animals included."[111] Small though the group was, they set off, but when they reached the pass they found that the snow was far too deep to get through and had to turn back.

The passing days brought new waves of refugees to the plateau, some setting up camp there, some moving on in search of other sites. One of these groups, which carried little baggage and had traveled fast, told Rinpoche that they had passed a large group of people camped at Lhodzong, west of the Shabye Bridge. The group was from both Drolma Lhakang and Yag monasteries, and had brought all their baggage with them loaded on yaks. It had two leaders: Rinpoche's friend Jigme Tulku and his bursar, Tsethar. Apparently they had fled Drolma Lhakang and Yag in fear of the imminent arrival of the Communists. Now, though, with things apparently quiet at both monasteries, the group's leaders were teetering, uncertain whether to continue westwards to try to make contact with Rinpoche, or to return to East Tibet.

After hearing this news, some in Rinpoche's group grew restless, with doubts stirring about him, about his leadership and his decisions. If senior lamas like Jigme Tulku and Tsethar were seriously thinking of returning home, and if Rinpoche's views and plans – on everything from the general course of events in Tibet to the practicalities of pilgrimage – differed so starkly from those of the highly regarded Lama Urgyan, there seemed to be much room for doubt. And if the older, more senior lama was so obviously trying to direct Rinpoche, urging him to radically alter his course, perhaps their young leader was misguided, his decisions headstrong or mistaken. Perhaps, after all, their brave leap into the unknown had been unnecessary; maybe Lama Urgyan was right, and that for now at least they should just stay where they were.

Rinpoche's attempts to shed light on their course by sending messengers out for information did not help to instill confidence. Local people were unanimous in saying that at this time of the year, with all the rivers in full spate from snowmelt, it would be impossible to get across the mountains towards India. Rinpoche, though, was unshaken: "I myself was quite determined that as soon as it was possible we should carry out our plan to escape."[112]

Before making a move, though, he wanted to tell the group at Lhodzong of his intentions. Akong Tulku's older brother, Jamyang, volunteered to carry the message to them. Rinpoche's words were firm and forthright: he was heading for India, and there could be no question of his turning back. Apart from declaring his intentions, such a resolute message from Rinpoche would have lent weight to anyone favoring an escape, perhaps helping to dissuade those wanting to turn back. If the group at Lhodzong was in fact trapped by indecision – suspended between going on and returning – it might have reflected a stalemate between the two leaders, Jigme Tulku and Tsethar. The previous year, Jigme Tulku had strongly encouraged Rinpoche's escape, and it is likely that, as events unfolded, he had realized that it was time to go himself. Tsethar was very likely still yearning for Surmang.

Around this time Yonten left the plateau with baggage mules and drivers in search of provisions. After riding south until they reached the peaks over the Nyewo Valley, they made the steep, day-long descent to the villages below. He found the valley packed with refugees who had poured in from across Tibet, and food was already extremely scarce. Unable to find sufficient provisions, he decided to stay in the valley until he could obtain more, and sent a message up to the plateau to inform them of the situation. When the message arrived, Rinpoche advised the refugees to ration themselves to *tsampa* and wild vegetables until Yonten could lay his hands on a good stock of supplies.

In spite of their remote, semi-besieged location, they were hearing news from the outside world. A resistance leader camped nearby owned a battery radio, and Rinpoche and others occasionally joined him to listen to broadcasts from Beijing and Delhi. The Chinese poured out propaganda about how evil the Tibetan uprising had been, especially considering that the Communists had come only to liberate the people from oppression, and assured the world that everything was now well under control. The Beijing broadcasts were quiet on their earlier line that the Dalai Lama had been kidnapped by Tibetan guerillas; Delhi radio, meanwhile, reported his daily doings in Mussoorie, India.

One morning several senior lamas arrived on the plateau. Lama Urgyan wasted no time in suggesting to Rinpoche that they all join forces and set out on a new pilgrimage. Rinpoche would have liked to go, and would have also enjoyed the opportunity to talk things over with him and other lamas on the trip. However, the pilgrimage meant crossing a mountain to the valley beyond and, after asking around, Rinpoche felt that the valley would be too small to hold them all. Again not wanting to offend Lama Urgyan, Rinpoche sent a message to say that he would follow him there in a while if he could. A while later they heard that the valley was too small even for those who had gone, and so dangerous that several horses had been killed by falling stones and rocks.

If some had been unsettled by Rinpoche's disagreements with Lama Urgyan, their confidence in his leadership shaken, he himself felt drained by the confrontations. He too held the older lama in high esteem, and was pained by their differences. When he wrote of their disagreements, and of the outcomes of Lama Ugyan's proposed pilgrimages, he did so simply, passing on his account as best he knew it, although perhaps with a sense of regret. But the confrontations – coming as they did after a strenuous, obstacle-strewn journey, and with the daily pressures of leading and caring for a large group of people – had taken their toll. He was tired out.

Rinpoche felt that he must renew his strength in retreat. But the plateau was far too crowded and busy to provide the seclusion he needed. He decided to find a more peaceful spot, while also moving the group further south, nearer the Nyewo Valley. After breaking camp, they shortly came to the next mountain pass. This one was especially difficult, up a very steep zig-zag path, dangerously slippery from the white, slimy mud that coated everything. If an animal lost its footing here, it would plummet onto those following below. They reached the top without mishap, though, only to find that the crest was like a knife edge, very tricky to traverse and very slippery from those who had gone before. In the end all made it over, finding to their relief that the downward slope was much easier, and before long they arrived in the Lawa Valley. Relatively small, it was surrounded by trees and undergrowth with ample vegetation for the animals. It seemed quiet enough, and they chose a campsite and settled down.

The valley's peace was short-lived. A group of refugees arrived and, seeing Rinpoche's group, decided to make camp nearby. They were soon followed by more people, but these were passing through; they brought the news that Tsethar's group had left Lhodzong and was following hard on their heels. Shortly afterwards, Rinpoche and Akong Tulku set out to explore the surrounding area for a retreat site. They found a wooded nook which seemed ideal, not far from their camp but well away from the track. Rinpoche knew that there would be far too much happening, far too much business to attend to, for his retreat to be in total seclusion, and scheduled daily times for visitors – an hour in the morning and two in the afternoon, when his food could also be delivered.

He settled down to rest and meditate, to prepare himself for what lay ahead. The surroundings were pleasant and it was quite warm, with a far greater variety of plants, birds and animals than he was used to in East Tibet. That night some of the local fauna came to investigate the new arrival. The noises were strange and unfamiliar, and at first Rinpoche was uneasy, but "I soon found that these visitors were not dangerous."[113]

One morning soon afterwards, an attendant came to the tent in a highly excited state. He said that large brown bears had killed one of their horses and mauled several mules, and, after the first attack, the marauders had been coming back every night. A few days later, the attendant returned – this time spotting bear prints around Rinpoche's tent; having already met these locals, Rinpoche remained at ease and unconcerned.

After the attendant returned to camp, though, a small procession of people began arriving at the tent, imploring Rinpoche to leave. Then a few visitors spotted what they thought were the tracks of *drewo*, supernatural obstacle-makers, among the bear prints. One of the tracks, like a human footprint but much larger, was supposedly seen just outside Rinpoche's tent.[114] Before long much of the camp had trooped over to see the *drewo* tracks – including a number of excited children, who were disappointed to find that it had all been so trodden over by previous sightseers that the tracks were obliterated.[115] Meanwhile, inside the tent, Rinpoche continued with his devotions and meditation.

A few days later, Yonten sent a message up from the Nyewo Valley that did alarm Rinpoche: Communist troops had broken through the wall of resistance fighters guarding the pass at the end of the valley, and were heading their way. Before Rinpoche could get word to his group, the news was out. Panic swept through the refugees, with families frantically packing their possessions, intending to flee into the mountains to hide. Rinpoche sent a message advising everyone to stay where they were for at least another day: if the news was accurate, and the Communists were indeed heading their way, there was little that could be done about it. On the following day, another message came from Yonten saying that it had all been a false alarm – anxious villagers had mistaken a group of resistance fighters for PLA soldiers.

False though the alarm was, there may have been a new edge to Rinpoche's retreat. From all he had learned, it was clear that the Communists now held much, maybe most, of the country. At any moment, day or night, the PLA could descend on them from any direction.

Rinpoche was now getting daily reports from Yonten down in the Nyewo Valley. When the time came to leave the heights to begin their journey south they would have to travel along it. At the valley's western end lay the high pass where resistance fighters were holding back the Communists. Under the relentless onslaughts, the fighters' situation grew shakier by the day, and they had been reduced to obtaining desperately-needed weapons, ammunition and food through daring attacks on enemy positions and supply columns. Sheer weight of numbers and weaponry must soon overwhelm them. When that happened, the Communists would pour into the valley, and Rinpoche's group would inevitably be rounded up – with summary executions probably beginning soon afterwards. Further darkening their prospects, Yonten reported that the Nyewo Valley was now congested with refugees and animals, with all places of shelter already taken up. What's more, movement along the valley had become very restricted, boxed in by rivers swollen with snowmelt.

As concerned as Rinpoche was about the situation, he knew that if he returned to camp he "would be caught up in a ferment of agitation,"[116] and he decided to spend a few more weeks in intensive retreat. There he could build up his strength while also bringing his full focus to bear on the problems ahead. During this time, he had a dream which made a dark, lasting impression. He was leading pilgrims to a holy place when they came to a river whose waters were tinged with blood; they managed to get across on a log bridge, but as Rinpoche lay resting on the far bank he heard that some pilgrims following behind had fallen into the river.

The retreat was soon disturbed again. Tsethar the bursar had arrived in camp, and shortly afterwards appeared at Rinpoche's tent, wanting to talk. As Rinpoche noted drily, he was "in a complaining mood."[117] He grumbled about the camp's organization; he was shocked that they had allowed bears to get at their animals; on the whole, he found their campsite to be quite unsuitable, and told Rinpoche that his entire group must retrace their steps and join him in his own camp, situated on the far side of the slippery and dangerous pass. As always, he was quite confident that the Communists posed no immediate danger.

Before answering, Rinpoche asked the bursar a series of pointed questions, the approach he had employed with him before. It was soon plain that Tsethar's camp was densely crowded, that they had lost many animals through lack of grazing, and that the refugees themselves were very short of food. No-one in Tsethar's group had made any attempt to acquire the latest news, and they had little sense of the larger picture – and no idea at all about where to go from where they were. It was obvious that the general conditions in Tsethar's camp were worse than those in Rinpoche's.

In spite of his patently weak, almost delusional, case, Tsethar was insistent: everyone should pack up and go back to his camp. Rinpoche was unmoved. Having failed to sway his abbot, Tsethar went across to the camp to try to persuade Yag Tulku and Kino Tulku to join him. When they balked at his aggressive approach and showed no interest in going along with him, he huffed that they could do as they liked, but that his own abbot, Rinpoche, must absolutely come back with him to his camp. No-one responded, and Tsethar left the camp for his own.

Still, questions about Rinpoche's leadership burned in many people's minds. They knew that their prospects for a safe and successful journey were bleak, even frightening, and they had noted that Rinpoche's differences of opinion with both Lama Urgyan and Tsethar had been fundamental ones. Was it not prudent to follow the counsel of the older men with their many years of experience, rather than follow their young lama, however much they venerated him or trusted his divinatory powers?

In later years, Rinpoche outlined Padmasambhava's approach to leadership. The great teacher would, he said, sometimes just "let the phenomena play... Let the phenomena make fools of themselves by themselves."[118] Rather than try to persuade someone, or strive to prove some case, Padmasambhava allowed the totality of the logic of the situation to speak for itself – to let events play out until their implications were too obvious to be missed.

There is reason to feel that, up to around this point of the journey, Rinpoche had himself been following this strategy. For some time – maybe years – he may have been clear that India must be their destination. Yet he had left things open, waiting to see how things unfolded, entertaining all options, allowing the space for others to voice their views without imposing his own – all the while waiting for the full, implacable logic of events to make itself known.

Now, with Tibet's fate bleakly obvious, and the news that the Karmapa and many other leading lamas had fled to India, the logic of events was inescapable. With Rinpoche's own view now luminously clear, his style of leadership shifted: from being open and receptive to all opinions, he was firmly asserting his views and position. He would continue to consult his fellow lamas, but from now on he held the reins firmly in his grasp, guiding their course as he thought best.

Tsethar, though, remained asleep to the dangers, and good sense and rationality had fled. Unshakably confident in his view of things, he had failed to see both the inexorable logic of events and the shift in Rinpoche's approach to them. But rather than pulling rank on Tsethar, overriding him as his abbot and the heir to the Trungpa Lineage, Rinpoche spent the next three days talking and debating with him, sometimes heatedly. He pointed out that he himself had already traveled across a large part of the country and had a good sense of what they were up against. Going back to Tsethar's camp was out of the question; he would instead be leading his people southwards, down to the Nyewo Valley where there would be food and supplies. Ultimately, he concluded, their best hope lay in heading for India. At the end, Rinpoche rejected all of Tsethar's arguments out of hand.

The debate over, Rinpoche instructed Tsethar to take steps to rid himself of all useless baggage, and to keep only small and portable items. Yet, still stubbornly holding his ground in his area of monastic responsibility, the bursar argued that all the other groups had managed to bring with them all their baggage and animals, and flatly refused to follow his abbot's instructions,.

Yonten, just back from the Nyewo Valley, overheard this exchange. Although Tsethar was by far his senior in the Surmang hierarchy, Yonten told him how shocked he was by his flagrant disobedience and chided him for his treatment of his abbot. He went on to say that, whatever the bursar did, and even if the chances of getting to India were very small, come what may he himself would do all he could to get Rinpoche there safely.[119] Others then chimed in on Rinpoche's behalf, and Tsethar apparently capitulated, saying that he would do what he could with the baggage, then left for his own camp. Events were to show that, even now, he had no real intention of carrying out his abbot's instructions.

Tsethar had left, but his baleful influence hung in the air. A few days later, Akong Tulku's older brother Jamyang arrived at Rinpoche's tent with his own criticisms of Rinpoche's leadership. His doubts had likely been fueled not only by Tsethar's overbearing views – Jamyang appears to have travelled back with him from Lhodzong – but by hearing of the disagreements between Rinpoche and Lama Urgyan. Jamyang said that, compared to Tsethar, Rinpoche was always changing his mind about the route, and even now had no real practical plan of how to proceed; Tsethar, on the other hand, showed decisive leadership, had taken a direct route and traveled fast along the main road to their current camp. Taking all this into account, Jamyang went on, he had no choice but to remove his brothers Akong Tulku and Jampal from Rinpoche's group, and to take them back to join Tsethar. He added that if Rinpoche settled on a definite plan for the route, he would reconsider his decision; at that point, after consulting with Tsethar, he might rejoin Rinpoche.

While understanding Jamyang's concerns for his younger brothers' well-being, it's hard to take his judgement on Tsethar seriously. After all, when Tsethar took the direct route he did, he would have known, either from Jamyang himself, from Rinpoche's message or from passing travelers, where his abbot was. He would not have had to weigh options, assess alternative routes or deal with large and unforeseen events, as Rinpoche had had to do. Moreover, much had changed in the two tumultuous months since Rinpoche's group made the journey. With Tibetan resistance collapsing across the land, the fighters that had flooded eastwards along the main road would have slowed to a trickle, perhaps stopped altogether. Tsethar would not have needed to make the long detours that Rinpoche was compelled to undertake. It's possible that Jamyang did not know of the bursar's long-term serial obstructionism, or of his wavering about whether or not to escape. Still, it seems hard to credit that Tsethar could be taken to be a crisp decision-maker.

However murky Jamyang's reasoning may have been, he voiced his reality: he was under Tsethar's sway. Rinpoche did not respond to Jamyang's criticisms or to the thinking behind them. Instead, he reminded Jamyang that Akong Tulku had chosen to join his escape, and that at Drolma Lhakang he had promised Akong Tulku's people that he would do his best to assure his safety. If Akong now joined Tsethar's group, Rinpoche continued, he would raise no objection, but his own responsibility for his well-being would be at an end.

As Jamyang realized where his reasoning had taken him, his argument came to a standstill. By taking his brother Akong away from Rinpoche's group he would himself be taking on the responsibility for his safety. With Jamyang thus put on the spot – and in an echo of Rinpoche's tactic with Tsethar the previous year, when the bursar was pushing him to return to Surmang – there was a long pause; then Jamyang said that he would need to talk things over with Akong Tulku. A while later, when he returned to Rinpoche's tent, his position had shifted: he would still be taking his brothers to join Tsethar's group, but he would first attempt to persuade Tsethar to discard the heavy baggage, and then he would try to bring everyone to rejoin Rinpoche.

In his narrative Rinpoche simply describes events and moves on, saying nothing about Tsethar's motives. But it seems almost certain that, even at this late stage, the bursar had no intention of leaving Tibet, and was still nurturing dreams of returning to Surmang. Yonten, for one, was sure that this remained his objective.[120]

This ambition underlay much of his fractious behavior. For over a year, as Rinpoche's self-appointed guardian, the bursar had accorded himself power well beyond his authority, trying to undermine Rinpoche's plans to escape, persuading others to talk him out of it, then subverting his wishes to convert Surmang's wealth into portable money. Now he had apparently launched a desperate, last-ditch power play, bringing Jamyang under his wing while trying to convert the other lamas to his views – in the process flagrantly criticizing his young abbot to his face. Tsethar could have thought that his maneuvers had succeeded, if only partially. He had not diverted Rinpoche from his plans, but he had managed to prise Akong Tulku away from him while keeping Jigme Tulku, Rinpoche's advisor and faithful companion, in his own camp.

At the same time, it made good sense for Akong Tulku and Jigme Tulku to go along with Tsethar, if only for the time being. That way they could take on responsibility for the Drolma Lhakang and Yag groups in Tsethar's camp, relieving Rinpoche of the need to lead and care for hundreds of additional people and animals. Not only that, but together they could face down Tsethar, also removing that burden. Rinpoche was silent on this centrifugal turn of events, but the departure of Akong Tulku, his dear friend and close support, must have been a blow.

By now they had been on the heights for about a month, first on the plateau, then in Lawa Valley. It had been a period of anxieties and alarms, disagreements and disputes, power plays and rifts – in its way no less stressful than their previous hard journeys had been. Now food and grazing were running out, both in the camp and in the valley below. Looming over all, the Communist forces dammed up at the end of Nyewo Valley could break through at any moment.

In the first week of July, Rinpoche felt that they could wait no longer. He left his much-interrupted retreat and called a meeting. He says little about what transpired at the meeting or how his retreat may have clarified his view of their impending journey. But Yonten got wind of the fact that Rinpoche and a few senior lamas had conducted a secret divination. It had favored India as their destination, but only marginally.[121] The lamas may have wondered at the ambivalence – maybe their objective, India, was the wrong one; maybe the divination's muted support for it reflected the sheer riskiness of the venture. Young Palya Washutsong recalled that around this time Rinpoche told a few trusted people, including her father, that very few of the traveling party's group of refugees would actually reach India. The remark sent a chill of anxiety through her large family.[122]

What is clear is that at the post-retreat meeting, all agreed that they should immediately head down to the Nyewo Valley. With the decision made, the refugees packed up their possessions, rounded up their herds and followed Rinpoche southwards out of the Lawa Valley. As they neared the point where they had thought they would begin the descent to Nyewo, they came to an unusually high mountain that had to be crossed. The hike to the ridge line was gradual and innocuous, but then the slope fell off steeply down to the valley, a difficult descent of nine thousand feet, a day-long trial that left both people and animals exhausted. When they finally reached the valley floor, they camped as soon as they could find a spot, close to the Nyewo River and to a bridge that crossed it to the southern bank.

At the much lower altitude they sweltered in the midsummer heat, plagued by clouds of flies. Somewhat making up for the physical torment, after nearby villagers heard that Rinpoche was the group's leader they did everything they could to make the group welcome. As throughout the journey, they also invited Rinpoche into their homes for meals, requesting him to perform devotional ceremonies and asking his advice on the dire situation. When Yonten went looking for supplies he had to conceal whom he was buying them for, otherwise the villagers would invariably have undercharged him.

In the midst of this new busyness, Rinpoche sent a message to Lama Urgyan up on the plateau, telling him of his changed location; upon receiving it he would know that Rinpoche would not be joining him on his pilgrimage to the holy valley. It was the last contact Rinpoche had with the venerable lama, and never learned of his fate.

Within a few days more disconcerting news arrived, further darkening the picture. Throughout the country, areas held by resistance forces were disappearing, the last holdouts crumbling under the Communist onslaught. As if to underline the precarious situation, the group could hear aircraft flying overhead at night. Meanwhile, although anxiety festered among the villagers in the valley, they felt a natural sympathy for Rinpoche's party and their escape, and extended themselves towards them in every way they could, including passing on all they knew of possible routes across the mountains.

Much was learned and, as Rinpoche contemplated the flow of advice along with the intelligence on Communist movements he had received, three alternative plans took shape for him. They could take a southerly route over the mountains, more or less directly towards the region of Kongpo and the great Brahmaputra River (named Upper Kongpo in that region of Tibet), but the route had drawbacks: it meant crossing the very high Lochen La Pass, and further on they might run into the Communist forces that probably controlled that part of the country. Secondly, they could join forces with a guerilla leader who planned to fight his way through to the southwest, then head for Central Tibet before pushing on to India, Bhutan or Nepal.

Rinpoche settled on a third plan, which seemed the least risky. If they continued eastwards along the Nyewo Valley, taking a narrow track that wound along the river's ravine, they had reach a point from which they could head southeastwards to Kongpo. It would be a difficult route, and they would need to find a guide to lead them across the mountains to Kongpo, but from there they could reach the Brahmaputra. After crossing the great river they would still have to climb the formidable Himalayas, but they would be largely beyond Communist control and within striking distance of India.

As word of Rinpoche's plan spread through the camp, the refugees' spirits lifted and doubts about their leader's abilities evaporated. Their objective was now clear – it must be India – and they knew how to get there. It was a fine plan, clear and simple, and had been related to Rinpoche by someone who had made the journey himself.

In all, their prospects seemed promising. It was early summer, the weather was warm and fair, and there could be months more of the same to come. They had surmounted without major mishap the challenges they had faced so far, and had every reason to believe that they could overcome the greater ones that they knew lay ahead.

7

The Bridge to Rigong Kha

The journey's challenges would start soon, and they were serious ones. To head eastwards along the Nyewo Valley, they would have to use the track that ran along the river's north bank. This meant crossing the river after its junction with the Alado River, which presented real difficulties. There were no bridges or ferry boats, while both rivers were in full flow from snowmelt, and their merging multiplied their power. Villagers said that no-one had made it across since early spring.

Rinpoche and his advisors inspected the river and noted that, although the current ran strong and fast, there were no waves. He thought that the horses could probably swim across, perhaps towing people behind.

A more worrying challenge faced them further down the valley. There, where the track ran along a cliffside, it was completely blocked by fallen boulders, which Rinpoche wrote was due to a 1950 earthquake. Years later, Yonten amended this: the fall had in fact been precipitated by local villagers aiming to block Communist troop movements, a fact that Rinpoche would have omitted from his account.[123] Whatever its cause, while people should be able to clamber over the rockfall, none of the animals – not even the nimbler and more sure-footed mules – would be able to get past.

This was deeply dismaying. Leaving the animals behind meant losing their means of transport, for themselves and for their extensive baggage; in the case of the yaks, it also meant abandoning a mobile source of food and clothing. They would be on foot, carrying everything they would need on their backs – food, clothing, blankets, tents, books, precious possessions and, in many cases, young children and babies. From now on they would, as Rinpoche described it, be traveling the hard way

Although Rinpoche and the others had recently climbed some steep, high passes, they'd had little exercise since. And, when he considered his role as leader, he was especially apprehensive about his own capacity to walk so far. From the time of his enthronement as a high lama, his life had been a largely sedentary one and he had, with only a few exceptions, traveled everywhere on horseback. Could he withstand the journey's rigors? All the monastics, lamas and monks had led mostly sedentary lives, immersed in endless hours of study, chants and meditation; how would they manage? And what about mothers with babies, the elderly, children?

Yet in spite of the stunning new obstacle, their plan still seemed the best available. They were sharply aware of its drawbacks, and were not wedded to it, knowing that events could always overtake it. But no-one disputed the choice, or thought of dropping out.

To Rinpoche's surprise, around this time a group of families arrived from the heights above the valley. Feeling that their best hope lay with Rinpoche, they had decided to leave Tsethar's and Jigme Tulku's groups, and asked if they could join him. Shortly afterwards, a group of eighty people, students of some other lama, arrived and attached themselves to the group – taking for granted that Rinpoche would assume responsibility for them. Acutely aware of what the added burden would mean, he took on both groups.

Again, time was growing short. Every day, much effort was spent talking to villagers, fellow travelers and local resistance leaders about routes, weather and, above all, the latest news on the Communists. It was not always easy to separate rumor from reality, but what they heard was invariably dark, and darkening. Communist forces had subdued most of the country, and were doubtless determined to overrun it all. Troops were massing in the northeast while others were advancing from the northwest. They were apparently also present in force in the south and in Kongpo, the area that the travelers would have to go through if they were to stand any chance of reaching the Brahmaputra and freedom.

Abruptly, the time for the weighing of options evaporated. Information arrived that the Communists had finally broken through the Tibetan forces defending the pass. Although they were being opposed every inch of the way, they were apparently already in the upper part of the Nyewo Valley. Chaos and panic erupted as refugees rushed down the valley, soon jamming the bridge near Rinpoche's camp. Meanwhile, locals hurriedly armed themselves. They had no rifles, but intended defending their villages with axes, knives and anything else that might serve as a weapon.

Rinpoche had been busy with funeral rites in a nearby village, and when he returned to camp he found it in a state of near-panic. He heard that all the recently-arrived families from Tsethar's and Jigme Tulku's groups had fled, along with the eighty strangers he had just accepted. Rinpoche made no immediate move; he wanted to confirm for himself the accuracy of the news of the breakthrough. Asking around, he could find no-one who had actually heard the sound of fighting or gunfire. Then he sent a messenger to the lieutenant of a nearby resistance group to ask what he knew. The officer replied that he too was doing his best to find out for himself, but had heard nothing definite, and did not know of an eyewitness who could confirm the PLA breakthrough.

Rinpoche chose the prudent course: "After waiting for a couple of hours, I decided that we must move."[124] Traveling by night, while keeping everyone quiet so that they could hear the sound of any gunfire, he led the group eastwards along the southern bank. After passing the turgid waters at the junction of the Nyewo and Alado rivers they arrived at a small valley Rinpoche had heard of, close to the point where they would have to cross the river to the north bank. The valley's entrance was narrow, but it opened into a space just large enough for them all, with fresh grazing for the animals. To keep up with developments, Rinpoche had left a man behind in the Nyewo valley with instructions to warn him if he heard any gunfire or to bring any definite news; the next day he turned up to say that nothing had occurred, and that the previously packed valley around the village of Nyewo was now entirely deserted.

Later that day Rinpoche received a message from the local resistance headquarters: Communist forces had set out north from Kongpo and were heading their way, obviously bent on subduing Nyewo's small pocket of Tibetan resistance. Underlining the impending threat, they could hear Communist reconnaissance aircraft droning overhead at night. The news from resistance headquarters confirmed the wisdom of their earlier rejection of one of the three plans they had considered. And the other remaining option – to join resistance forces in their attempt to fight their way through to the southwest – must now have seemed doomed at the outset.

For Rinpoche, the only question now was when to set out on their chosen route. Even though the scare had turned out to be another false alarm, Rinpoche took its suddenness, and people's hair-trigger reaction to it, as ominous, and felt that they must move soon. He talked things over with the other lamas, and there was consensus. They must move without delay, and the only route that gave them any realistic hope at all was the one they had chosen: they would continue eastwards along the valley until they could take the track towards Kongpo.

With everything settled and prepared, they still had to find a way to get across the river. At this point, Urgyan-tendzin – the monk who had joined the group after they crossed the Shabye Bridge – stepped forward. He had already proven himself to be a highly energetic and resourceful man, and now announced that he would do what he could to get everyone across in coracles.

Urgyan-tendzin had earlier suggested to Rinpoche that they acquire several large yak hides. Now, after soaking them in the river to make them pliable, then finding the appropriate tree trunks and saplings, he set about constructing the first coracle. After several hours' work, he had made a craft large enough to carry eight people with their baggage. He first tested it on the river himself. After tying one end of a long safety rope to a rock on the bank and the other to the coracle, he climbed in and began paddling. He found that he had no difficulty getting to the far bank and back. Once safely ashore, he set about making another coracle.

Now the unsettling moment arrived when they would be leaving their animals behind and starting out on foot. Few were physically prepared for it and few, if any, had planned on it. They faced the immediate problem of how to carry their food, clothing and possessions. All they had, apart from the yak-skin bags they used for personal items, were the large baggage packs normally slung over the backs of mules and yaks. So they settled down to convert them, cutting them down, fabricating straps and doing their best to come up with serviceable backpacks.

Although Rinpoche's attendants highly disapproved of their abbot carrying anything at all, he insisted on sharing the load, saying that everyone must do their bit. He would carry sacred texts, with his food and personal items distributed among two or three attendants. Yonten carried his tent, food and boots as well as his own possessions; on his person he held the sacred Trungpa seals and statues with which Rinpoche specially entrusted him. As they organized themselves, the sturdily-built Kino Tulku took it upon himself to shoulder the heaviest load of all, an act of generosity that would shortly have a grievous outcome.

They were ready to leave, and it was time to send off the animals. Rinpoche dispatched a small herd, together with a selection of his Surmang baggage, to Tsethar's camp on the heights. He also sent a message to Akong Tulku informing him of their plans. Being more up to date on Chinese troop movements than Akong could be, Rinpoche advised him to follow the same route that he was taking; knowing that Tsethar would pay it little heed, Rinpoche did not communicate the plan to him. He then sent the remainder of the animals and baggage, which included many sacred texts and ritual objects, to Lama Urgyan. He also sent him a letter, which began: "The wind of *karma* is blowing in this direction; there is no indication that we should do otherwise than attempt this way of escape. Events are changing so suddenly, one cannot afford to ignore the dangers … "[125]

People in the Nyewo Valley remained edgy, on high-strung alert for any sign of danger and quickly aware of any hint of a way to escape the approaching menace. As Rinpoche's group made their final preparations, it had been impossible to conceal the building and testing of coracles, or the sending away of baggage and animals. Everyone in the area was conscious that something was afoot. Word spread and the details of the plan leaked out, and shortly afterwards the newcomers from Tsethar's and Jigme Tulku's groups, along with the eighty strangers – all of whom had dashed off down the valley after the recent scare – reappeared at the camp. Without waiting for Rinpoche's permission, they crammed themselves into the small valley, again expecting him to take responsibility for them all.

Rinpoche could now turn his attention to the practicalities ahead. He sent out word that porters were needed to carry their possessions and to prepare their way along the track. Before long, a hundred local men arrived at the camp, ready to go. Along with the information on the rockfalls on the track, caused by locals to impede the Chinese advance along the valley, Rinpoche had heard that the bridges had also been pulled down. Unless the rock debris was removed and the bridges replaced, if only crudely, their escape would be stillborn. Volunteers were called for from among the porters – especially strong, able and agile men who could not only repair the track and bridges, but perhaps help people across – who were then sent off ahead to do the work. As with the rockfalls, Rinpoche said nothing in his narrative about the bridge repairs or why they were needed.

Rinpoche still lacked one vital piece of intelligence. He had heard nothing about whether or not there were PLA forces on the north bank downstream. Having exhausted all other means of finding out, he performed a mirror divination. The indications were unambiguous: there were no Communists along their immediate route.

Finally, they were ready to go, and news of their imminent departure spread through the valley. People well understood that Rinpoche's group was beginning a journey of unusual peril, one that would require courage and endurance of the highest order if they were to have any hope of reaching India. Messages from lamas, villagers and fellow-refugees poured into the camp, wishing them well.

As they left the small valley and headed down to the river, Rinpoche experienced "a great feeling of happiness that we were starting at last."[126] Behind him were the unending calls for his personal advice and ritual presence, the daily hunt for accurate information, the discussions and disputes, politics and power plays, and the rumors, false alarms and general tumult of the past month. Perhaps shining most brightly for him was the reality that now, finally – well over a year since he had left Surmang, perhaps four years since the idea of escape had taken shape – they were starting. And they were heading for India, the birthplace of the Buddha. At the last moment, a horseman galloped up with a message from a resistance leader, urging Rinpoche to join forces with him. Rinpoche replied that it was too late, and they were on their way.

It took a lot of paddling and a number of trips before Urgyan-tendzin, and a man he had trained to work the other coracle, got everyone across to the northern bank. There they dismantled the craft, organized themselves and set out along the narrow track along the bank. They knew the river well, having first met it as the Alado on its early westwards journey, when they were forced into a long detour by its narrow, rickety bridge. They had met it again on its southern journey, when they crossed a series of tricky bridges before coming up with the mass of refugees and their dead or dying animals. Now heading eastwards, they were again following the river, at this point renamed the Yigong after its waters joined the Nyewo's. It had fresh challenges in store, ones that would give the refugees a fearsome baptism into the rigors ahead.

This first leg of the journey would be down the Yigong Valley to the village of Rigong Kha. It was much warmer and damper in the valley, the vegetation far more luxuriant. Its track was rough and primitive, rarely used by anyone except locals. Rinpoche ensured that their first day on foot was an easy one, leading them at a leisurely pace to allow everyone time to adapt to walking with heavy loads, taking frequent rests to recuperate and to make adjustments to their newly-contrived packs. Before long they reached a small village, to which Rinpoche had earlier sent word of the unprecedented number of people about to pass through.

Beyond the village the track snaked higher up the mountain, and became narrower and more precarious. And the further they went, the more the mountain encroached on the river and the steeper the slope became. At several hundred feet above the water, the track became so narrow that at night it was only wide enough for one person to lie down, and too cramped to allow for any but the most rudimentary bedding arrangement. Sleepily losing one's bearings, or just rolling over, meant certain death in the roiling torrent below.

Further along, the track plummeted down and through a rocky gorge, where they came to a number of deep crevices. Some had to be crossed on rough pine logs, laid across by the porters who had set out ahead. Without safety ropes or hand guides it was a scary traverse, but one that everyone had to make. The porters, men who lived among these mountains and had the sureness and agility of mountain goats, gave much help. Then they reached the rockfalls they had heard about, the track blocked by large boulders which they had to squeeze around or clamber over, with the porters carefully assisting the children and elderly. It was obvious to everyone that their animals could not possibly have come this way.

Crossing the rocks and crevices had been nerve-wracking, but worse was to come. The further they went, the more difficult the track became until, just as they began to think that they must surely be nearing the village of Rigong Kha, they came to a sheer cliff which plunged all the way down to the river. Here the track more or less disappeared; as Rinpoche wrote:

I was horrified when I looked at a very sketchy zig-zag path going up this cliff. I had expected a track, but there appeared to be nothing more than a broken chain dangling at intervals, beside what appeared to be little cracks in the rock. One of the porters told me to watch the first of their men going up; he had a load on his back and never seemed to hold on to anything, but just jumped to the footholds cut in the rock; I thought I could never do it.[127]

The young men were the first refugees to try the cliff ascent: one by one, however, they found that it was beyond their courage and agility, and had to pass their baggage to the porters to get up. Then came the turn of the older men: porters offered to carry some of them up, but the this was felt to be far too dangerous, and they instead went up very slowly, roped to porters above and below.

Everyone then followed that method, including the women and children. Some got part way up and then stopped where they were, frozen in fear. People who had gone before coaxed them on, calling down that the porters simply could not hold on to a stationary person: they had no choice but to pull themselves together and climb on up. No-one could ignore the result of missing their grab at the dangling chains, or of slipping off one of the steps: a tumble down to the fast-running river far below, to be swiftly pulled under by their heavy clothing, bags and boots.

It seemed to take forever to get everyone up, until Rinpoche's turn finally came. The porters told him that they had selected their best men to carry him up. He thanked them, but said that he would rather go alone. He had been closely watching how others had done it and felt that he should have no problem, but as he started the climb he was alarmed to find that the shallow footholds in the cliff had become coated in slippery mud, left there by the boots of everyone who had gone before. Then he found that the rubber soles of his modern boots did not grip nearly as well as the traditional Tibetan soft leather ones, making the footholds even more slippery.

In all, though, he did not find the climb as hard as he had expected. But this was just the first part.

> When I reached the top of this hazardous ascent I found myself on a very narrow ledge with a sheer drop beneath it. I asked the porters, "What do I do next?" They told me that there was a long ladder from this ledge down to a rock in the middle of the river; from this rock there was a line of bridges made of pine trunks which crossed a series of rocks to the further bank. The porter looked very cheerful and said, "It's only a ladder; just follow me."[128]

Only when Rinpoche reached the top of the ladder did he see how enormously long it was, the ledge so high that people below seemed like dwarves. And it took a certain flair to call what he was to climb down "a ladder." It was in fact just a single pine log with shallow notches cut into it – the notches now also slippery with mud from the many who had gone before. The bottom end of the topmost log was lashed to the top of another log below it, and so down to the rock in the middle of the river. The porters had had some frightening moments with some of the older men, who had come close to fainting from fear. Young Drupju Washutsong had been carried down on a porter's back, his eyes pressed tightly closed in a state of sheer terror. Now all eyes were anxiously fixed on Rinpoche as he began his descent.

> When I climbed down the first few notches I could see the swirling green waters of the river underneath; a few more steps, and I felt I was poised over an expanse of water. There was a cold wind coming up from a large cave under the rock into which the river was pouring; worst of all, the ladder shook in a terrifying way with the weight of the many porters who were there trying to help me.[129]

As Rinpoche stepped on to the rock in mid-river, there was rejoicing from the refugees, all now safe on the Yigong's southern

The perilous route to Rigong Kha

bank. Almost miraculously, no-one had been lost. With everyone on dry land, drained from what they had gone through, they made camp where they were. That night, gathered together around the fires again after the constraints of the meager mountain track, the talk would have been about the trials they had faced and overcome – no doubt with much of the humor that Rinpoche had reflected, more drily, in his account.

The next few days brought new challenges, but none were as frightening as the first crossing to the south bank had been. They were beginning to take them, sheer cliffs and all, in their stride and began to make good progress, even when they found that they had to remove debris or rebuild the track. Rinpoche himself felt that he was adapting smoothly to the physical strain, and that both walking and sleeping had become far easier.

But they'd had little success in finding streams for drinking water and were all very thirsty. And they now suffered their first casualty when Kino Tulku's eyesight began quite suddenly to fail. The very heavy loads he had chosen to carry had proved too much for him, and he'd had some sort of hemorrhage. But there was nowhere to stop on the trail and, even though Kino Tulku's condition was rapidly deteriorating, the best they could do was to share out his load and push on. Adding to the growing stress, the track wound upwards again, climbing hundreds of feet above the river. But in the distance, along the gorge they began to make out small farms. They must be nearing their objective, Rigong Kha, and Rinpoche sent a porter ahead to inform the villagers of their arrival.

With everyone exhausted and Kino Tulku's condition dire, Rinpoche chose the first possible campsite they came to near the village, a small field about half a mile away. While a group of refugees went on to the village to buy food, people set up their tents and turned to caring for the ill lama. His condition worried everyone, and could affect their plans.

Meanwhile, a group of Rigong Kha's villagers had grown very nervous about the throng of new arrivals. Seeing none of the usual maroon and saffron robes, they were most unsure that the strangers were who they said they were. Yonten, though, had gone to the village in search of water, and at a mountain stream met a young woman he had known – perhaps romantically – from his earlier travels. Once she had recognized him, and told her friends and family, everyone relaxed. Before long a delegation of curious villagers arrived at the camp. They had never seen so many people together nor, apart from a few pilgrims or passing teachers, had they met anyone from as far off as East Tibet. For their part, dressed as they were in hairy goatskin outerwear, the women bedecked in jewelry and wearing boots embroidered in bright colors, the villagers were just as interesting to the refugees.

Rigong Kha was gloriously situated, on a triangular fold of land about fifteen hundred feet above the Yigong River, enclosed to the east and west by mountains which swooped up to meet in snowy peaks many thousands of feet above. To the south, directly across the river, was the Tsophu Valley which ran southwards before disappearing upwards into the glistening heights. Rinpoche decided to spend two weeks camped near the village, to give people time to recover from their recent trials. No other refugees had come this way and the villagers had ample food supplies, which they generously shared with the new arrivals. In all, the group could hardly have hoped for finer surroundings in which to rest.

With the refugees settled in, Rinpoche released the porters. He warmly thanked them for their help – the group owed them much – and wished them well on their return journey to Nyewo. He had grown extremely fond of these kindly, brave and high-spirited men. Although they modestly tried to turn down everything offered them, the porters left laden with jewelry and other gifts, wishing Rinpoche and his group all good fortune on their escape.

8

Tsophu Valley

While the group rested, Rinpoche talked to Rigong Kha's villagers, gathering from them whatever they knew of routes and of Communist movements and whereabouts. He also put out word that their group needed a guide to lead them over the mountains to Kongpo and the Brahmaputra.

What he heard was much as he had feared. Passing traders had reported that the entire area as far as Chamdo in East Tibet was in Communist hands. Not only that, but PLA patrols had been spotted further down the Yigong Valley. This was especially disheartening news. As the group had neared Rigong Kha, a sense of their options had opened up and Rinpoche had been contemplating a change of plan: they would continue along the Yigong valley, following it downwards as it curved southeast to meet the Brahmaputra – an easier and more straightforward route than their current plan of going across the mountains. Now it seemed that, somewhere downstream, they would walk straight into Communists heading their way. Worse, as Rinpoche listened to further reports, it became clear that it would only be a matter of time before PLA troops occupied the Tong-gyug Valley to their south, cutting off their primary route across the mountains to the Brahmaputra. When that happened, their last hope of escape would be gone.

The passing days brought mounting worries. Critically, Rinpoche could find no-one to lead them across the mountains, or even someone one who knew of a possible route. Their entire plan hung on finding a guide familiar with the mountain wilderness and the way to Kongpo – it would be near-madness to attempt the journey without one. The villagers' helpful suggestions held little promise: Rinpoche's group, they said, might join with local resistance fighters to fight their way through to India or, if all else failed, hide in the mountains above the village.

At the end of August, after a fortnight at Rigong Kha, Rinpoche decided to move across the river into the Tsophu Valley. If Communists were indeed advancing up the Yigong from the east, they could be upon them at any moment. Then everyone, including the villagers who had so generously hosted them, would be in grave jeopardy. From the Tsophu Valley, Rinpoche's party could, if it came to it, make a run for the southern mountains. And they would be better positioned for their onward journey: at the valley's end was a pass they would cross before heading southwards. This had been his original plan, and was now their only option.

He issued instructions that everyone should exchange their possessions, especially heavier goods such as rugs, for food for the journey. They must focus on high-energy items like cheese, butter, dried meat and pork fat, and, of course, their beloved *tsampa*, roasted barley flour. After a few days everyone had stocked up with ample supplies and was ready to go – everyone, that is, except the eighty refugees who had joined them in the Nyewo Valley, vanished at the rumor of approaching PLA troops, and then just as abruptly reappeared. Now, deeply apprehensive about the mountain journey ahead, they announced that they would be staying at Rigong Kha. But, they informed Rinpoche, they might decide to follow him later.

Getting across to the Tsophu Valley was anything but straightforward; a river that they had first come to know as the Alado had one last trick up its sleeve. At the crossing point, the current was so turbulent that no bridge could be built across it. Instead there was a thick hemp rope secured to large rocks on either bank; on the rope was a pulley with a belt attached, with two lighter ropes tied to the pulley that allowed it to be hauled across from either bank. One by one passengers were securely belted in, then just took a step into space. Gravity carried them to the torrent's midpoint, when men on the opposite bank hauled them up and on to the bank. Once everyone was across, Rinpoche made ready to go himself – but, just as he was about to tighten the belt, an excited messenger rushed up and announced that Communists had been seen coming their way. It was another false alarm, and none appeared, but Rinpoche wrote that, if they had done so, "we were resolved to cut the rope."[130]

Shortly after they entered the Tsophu Valley, Kino Tulku's condition sharply deteriorated. Although his eyes had responded well to rest and treatment, his legs had given way, and he could only walk very slowly; he felt that his condition was incurable. His wife, frantic with worry, begged Rinpoche not to leave him behind. He was acutely torn about what to do – but, generous and self-sacrificing to the end, Kino Tulku resolved the issue. He told Rinpoche that he should not wait for him, and that he would take his leave of the party and move to a village in a small valley nearby to recuperate. Rinpoche had grown fond of the doughty lama: it was "a sorrowful parting for us all."[131]

At their new camp a short way up the valley, Rinpoche met a newly-arrived lama who had followed their route along the Yigong River. He told Rinpoche that, back in the Nyewo Valley, everyone was saying that Trungpa Rinpoche had shown the way to escape. Many were setting out to follow, while others, hearing of the terrors of the track to Rigong Kha, had sadly concluded that it was beyond them. No-one in Nyewo knew where Rinpoche was going from Rigong Kha. Most thought that he would be taking the easier route down the Yigong Valley to the Brahmaputra, and planned to take that route themselves. Hearing this, Rinpoche minced no words, saying that as the Communists were known to be further down the Yigong, anyone heading that way must be insane. The lama then told Rinpoche that the fickle group of eighty refugees who had decided to stay behind at Rigong Kha had instead chosen to go eastwards down the Yigong Valley. Rinpoche never learned of their fate.

In early September, Rinpoche led the group further up the Tsophu Valley. He wanted to get nearer the pass at its southern end, close to their point of departure. From there, he would be better able to examine its approaches and decide on the best route. It took them about five days' travel up the deep trough of valley until they reached a point high enough to properly survey the terrain. Near its head, the valley split into two branches, the one leading southeastwards, the other southwestwards. Both led to the pass, but which would be better at this time of the year? After some discussion, they decided that the southeasterly branch looked easier, and was the one to follow. That settled, Rinpoche sent an advance party up towards the pass to examine the conditions.

Fall had arrived, and the weather was beginning to break up, with more frequent storms and rain showers. They knew that the pass was a high one and would already be covered in snow, the drifts deepening with every storm. More than likely the track would be blocked by snow, perhaps mixed with the rain, making it soft and intractable. When the advance party returned they said that they had got only a quarter of the way up before they had been driven back by a sudden, severe storm. They had, though, seen enough of the conditions higher up to report that while the snow on the pass would in fact be very deep, it was mostly fresh, light and soft. They thought that a few days' good weather should melt off enough of it to make the going workable. Shortly afterwards, as if on cue, the weather cleared.

The traveling party was positioned and ready to go, but they had still not found a guide. The journey would be hazardous enough as it was; to undertake it without someone to show them the way across the mountains was almost inconceivable. With nothing that could be done about it, they stayed where they were.

Rinpoche put the time to good use, instructing people to replenish their supplies when they could and to attend to any final repairs of clothing or boots. He also told the monk Urgyan-tendzin to train a small group of men to make coracles and to teach them how to paddle them. Yonten too put the time to good use. He had found that carrying his makeshift pack, with its extra load of Rinpoche's food and possessions, had been "unbearable." After making enquiries among some locals, he was able to replace it with a purpose-built Kongpo backpack which, with its strong bamboo frame, leather pouch and straps, was to serve him – and his abbot – well.

With the work and training under way, Rinpoche, Yag Tulku and a few monks entered a brief retreat, to gather their energy for what lay ahead. The spot they chose was strikingly beautiful, near a blue lake surrounded by pine trees and towering mountains, their peaks glittering high above the clouds. Their small paradise was soon punctured, and the group reminded of their predicament, when one night a Communist aircraft flew overhead. Although it would have been too high to spot them even in daylight, Rinpoche took the opportunity to instruct the group on how to act in time of war. He told the monks to cover their campfires, and sent a message back to the refugees to do the same, explaining how important it was not to show fire at night, which would immediately reveal their presence to the enemy.

There was still preparation to be done and, after a short retreat, Rinpoche returned to the camp. As he cast his eye over it, he realized just how large it was, how many people there were. One of his attendants said that he would take a head count and organize people into groups, each under its own leader. Crucially, there would be no time to train them, or to delegate proper authority and responsibilities. When the attendant returned with his list, Rinpoche wrote that "I was shocked at the numbers: about one hundred and seventy and among them men and women seventy and eighty years old as well as babies in arms, but very few able bodied men."[132] A venture that was always going to be a perilous one may have seemed to enter the realm of impossibility.

Still, Rinpoche was unwilling to turn anyone away, or to actively discourage any individual from coming. But he decided to explain to the refugees, as starkly and vividly as he could, just what lay in store for them, how hard the journey would be. He told them that they would have to cross many high passes and fast-running rivers and, as they could not carry tents, they would have to sleep in the snow. They might well be captured and imprisoned by the Chinese, who were somewhere in the area they would be going through. They would have to carry all the food they would need for the entire journey, as they could not visit villages to replenish their supplies; with the Communists in control of vast swathes of the country, anyone they met could be in their pay or under their control. Most forbidding of all, Rinpoche told them that the group could not afford to stop to care for anyone who faltered or collapsed by the wayside. They would be left where they were while everyone moved on.

He ended by saying that he wanted people to fully realize what they were undertaking. If anyone thought that the coming hardships would be too much for them, now was the time to drop out. Then he quickly added that he did not want to hear any definite answers for a few days; he knew that if someone, moved by the moment, shouted that they would come with him come what may, the others would follow – like sheep, as he put it.

Rinpoche let three days go by for the ordeal ahead to sink in, and for people to talk things through among themselves. On the fourth day, everyone without exception told him that they still wanted to come with him, and that they "would rather fall by the wayside than fall into Communist hands, then at least they'd feel that they had made all possible effort."[133]

It is staggering to reflect on what these ordinary people were taking on. They had already had a thorough taste of hard travel and harrowing obstacles, and had a solid sense of what lay ahead. And the rigors of the coming journey paled beside the prospect of the unknown. No-one, apparently not even Rinpoche and the lamas, personally knew anyone who had actually been to India. Jampal, Akong Tulku's younger brother, joked later about how little they knew of the wider world, how extraordinarily ignorant of it they were.[134] They had no maps, no means of navigation, not even a simple compass.

For all they knew, once they went beyond their land's walls, the Himalayas, they would fall off the earth's edge and into the void.[135] All that they really knew, or believed they knew, was that India lay somewhere to the south, where the sun moved in winter; that it was the birthplace of the Buddha, and that their leaders had fled there. Yet they desperately wanted to reach this legendary place and to follow their teachers there, to escape the dark materialist gloom that was lowering upon their land,. For this, even at the cost of their own lives, they were ready to take a giant leap into the unknown.

They had all now committed themselves to the life-and-death journey, but there was one last portal to pass through. Rinpoche called a meeting to lay out the rules and discipline that everyone would have to observe, and to which they must promise to adhere. If they were attacked by Communists, none of their attackers could be hurt or killed. No matter how hungry they felt, they could not kill animals for food. There could be no stealing of goods or property from anyone along the way. There must be no disunity, no disputes or dissension, whatever the cause. And if anything went wrong, or if anyone was experiencing difficulties, Rinpoche must be immediately informed.

The rules did not go down well with everyone. Not all of them were devout practitioners; many may have paid little attention to the religious life beyond a basic belief that they were Buddhists. And almost all were from East Tibet, from Kham, whose wild and bandit-infested countryside made carrying a weapon essential. Many had brought muskets and rifles of various vintages. And most men would have worn the long, beautifully adorned Khampa knife of the type Yonten carried; women also carried knives, but they were shorter and lighter. To promise not to use their cherished knives or other weapons to defend themselves, just as they began the really dangerous part of the journey, ran rough against the Khampa grain. In particular, some among the Lhatok families were much troubled by the non-fighting clause. Yet in the end, recognizing that they had little choice, they all gave in.

In accord with circumstances, Rinpoche had gently taken sole and undisputed command of the group. He had instructed the refugees on discipline and vigilance and delivered his standing orders, the code of conduct. Next he issued his orders of the day. Although there was still no news of a guide, people should make their final food purchases from villagers down the valley, and must barter away their tents and heavy material to do so – even now, many were loath to let go of household items like pots and kettles, and would be trying to carry far more than they could manage. As much as it distressed him, Rinpoche would be leaving behind almost all of his books.

Rinpoche then firmly instructed everyone to train themselves to ration their food: from this moment, they must learn to eat far less than they were used to. And in each group, the strongest man should be assigned extra bags of the subsistence food, *tsampa*, to guard and carry for the others. Some of the sturdiest were also handed bags of money, gold and jewelry, on the understanding that, when they reached India, they would keep half for themselves. The same arrangement was also made with the precious *tsampa* – Rinpoche's personal reserve supply being entrusted to one stalwart.

At this point a message arrived from Kino Tulku, still ailing in the small village near Rigong Kha. It could hardly have been more cheering: he had found them a guide. His name was Tsepa, a hunter who made his living deep in the mountains that Rinpoche's group would be passing through. Even more heartening, he was familiar with Lower Kongpo, the area abutting the Brahmaputra. He was willing to give up his home and hunting life to lead them there, and would be arriving on September 13. His sole condition was that his wife accompany him, to which Rinpoche readily agreed.

With a guide apparently due to arrive soon, the final, key element was in place, and Rinpoche sent a group of men up to clear the pass of snow. They returned to say that much of the snow had melted away, and that the pass would be in fine condition for their crossing.

There was no sign of the guide on the 13th, nor on the following day. There had also been no message from Akong Tulku, Tsethar and Jigme Tulku, whom Rinpoche had expected to join him when they had seen how things were developing. Rather than wait any longer where they were, on the afternoon of the 14th, Rinpoche led the refugees up to the snow line.

Since they had entered the Tsophu Valley and made their way southwards along it, they had gradually ascended several thousand feet. Now their camp lay high among the peaks, with only a few thousand foot climb remaining before they reached the pass itself. It was cold, but the sky was brilliant and cloud-free. They were high enough to see the mountains around Nyewo, and the heights where they had spent most of June – a dispiriting reminder that, ten weeks since they left it, they could still see the place they had started from.

While they waited for the guide, Rinpoche toured the groups to see how they were doing. It was soon clear to him that people were eating far too much food, apparently paying minimal attention to the rationing he had urged. He sternly told them that, if they continued like this, they would have a very slim chance of surviving the journey. He also noticed that, in spite of his instructions about covering fires, people were freely lighting them out in the open whenever they were needed, just as they had always done.

Rinpoche firmly reiterated his words on the need for vigilance, telling the refugees that they must pay more attention to concealing themselves – a skill they would soon have to put into practice. They should pay special attention to fires, as their smoke gave away their presence by day, their light revealing them by night; they should not be lit unless they were well screened from view. Later on the journey, he said, no fires at all would be allowed without his explicit permission.

Few could have missed the change in Rinpoche's manner and in what he was asking of them, the shift in his leadership style. In the early part of their journey he had been low-key and collegial, open to all views, talking things through until a consensus was reached. But from June, when they had turned south, he had been firm on their objective, India. He had meanwhile exerted himself to gather knowledge on routes and to keep up with the latest intelligence on the Communists' moves, ever alert to the nuanced shifts in the developing situation. And, while he remained open to others' views, debating them when necessary, once he had reached a decision he was unshakeable. He had fully taken on the leader's mantle.

Now that the group was camped just below the Tsophu Pass, on the threshold of the most dangerous part of their journey, Rinpoche's style had tightened, become more rigorous. Ahead of them lay weeks of hard climbs and treks, their lives entirely dependent on themselves and the food they carried. Somewhere along the way – on the far side of the pass, among the mountains, or at the Brahmaputra – were the Communists. Also ahead, awaiting them with as much ferocity as any human foe, was the Tibetan winter. Every last person, men and women, old and young, would have to reach deep into their physical endurance and courage, and their personal sense of discipline.

Such a trial demanded singleness of purpose and a unified command. Rinpoche's role had effectively become that of a general of his small non-violent army. He would be responsible for the appraisal of terrain and choice of routes, for assessment of the enemy's position and movements, for strategy and tactics, and for the discipline and care of his people. In a real sense they were entering a battleground, a field of action that would push them all to the edge, and which would require the spirit and discipline of a warrior.

Rinpoche had done what he could to guide the refugees to this view. He had laid out in the bleakest terms the challenges they would face and instituted the strict code of non-violence they would have to observe; and he had urged on them the need to be ever-vigilant, always aware of the threat facing them, of the need for stealth and concealment. Yet there had been scant time fully to prepare people for what lay ahead. There was no chain of command, and the group leaders had no real authority. People who saw Rinpoche as their teacher would strive to do as he had instructed, but the rest were a largely unknown quantity. Many had joined mainly because of his reputation as a practitioner of mirror divination, some had shown up simply because he had a coherent escape plan.

Already there had been good reason to doubt many people's capacity to act as required: to ration their food, guard their fires, stay quiet and remain concealed. Rinpoche could rely on the lamas and monks, who had been intensively trained and were used to authority, but the refugees were largely unprepared for the journey's demands. As soon as they crossed into the valley beyond the pass, the world they had known would dissolve. No longer could they rely on fellow Tibetans for food and hospitality, news and information; instead, they would have to take them as a threat. Could they adapt to the rugged, ruthless world that awaited them, and would they keep it all together when pushed to the edge, when the crisis point neared?

With their departure imminent, Rinpoche gathered the refugees together for a final meeting. He said that they must think of their journey as a pilgrimage, one that very few Tibetans before them had been able to make. They were going to India, the land of the Buddha's birth, where he attained enlightenment, where he taught and where his blessings remained powerful. And they should see themselves as fortunate that their journey would be hard – far harder than those experienced by the pilgrims of the past – for in this way their pilgrimage would be more beneficial. He concluded:

> We should not be thinking only about the enemies threatening us from without. Each moment we should be aware of ourselves and of the forces of destruction that threaten each man from within ... each step along the way should be holy and precious to us.[136]

People returned cheerfully to their campfires; with little sense of the overall picture, most remained oblivious of the impending dangers. But Rinpoche and the lamas knew that time and space were rapidly shrinking, their small island of safety dwindling away with each passing hour. They knew that they could not retreat to the north, that the Communists were advancing from east and west, and that they were present in force in the south, the way they were heading. As far as they knew, once they crossed the Tsophu Pass they would be in enemy territory, where any moment a PLA patrol could fall upon them.

Rinpoche himself felt no doubt or trepidation. All, or almost all, the delays were behind them, along with the tumult, confusion, and dissension. Now, over eighteen months since he had left Surmang, they were finally on their way. Their view was clear and open; they had a truly inspiring goal and a sound plan for reaching it: "For the first time I felt a conviction that we were going the right way and would reach India; I was aware of an inner strength guiding me and felt that I was not alone."[137]

Camped high among the snow peaks they waited for the guide through September 15, but there was no sign of him, nor any message. The skies were clear, the weather perfect for traveling, and Rinpoche decided that they could wait no longer. If the guide did not show up by the next day, they would leave without him.

9

Strange Land

When Tsepa the guide finally arrived at dusk, accompanied by his wife and carrying his hunting rifle, he was profusely apologetic. It had taken him far longer than he had thought to sell all his possessions, and to equip and supply themselves for the journey. He had also spent considerable time trying to find the Kongpo clothing that Rinpoche had asked him to acquire for everyone, but had been unable to do so. Tsepa and his wife both wore Kongpo attire and, with all the refugees dressed that way, they would draw less attention when they neared the Brahmaputra.

Rinpoche took an immediate liking to the guide, and found him an intelligent man. Tsepa had traveled widely across the region they would be going through, and knew it well; and when Rinpoche described to him their intended route he thought it very feasible, and believed that the group's prospects for making a successful escape that way were good.

Early on the morning of September 16, the traveling party packed up their food and remaining possessions and set out for the Tsophu Pass. The weather was fine, with only a light scattering of snow. And the climb was not nearly as steep as they had thought it would be, while towards the ridgeline the snow had turned to ice, making the going far less taxing than they had expected. When they reached the crest they all shouted the traditional "*Lha Gyal Lo!*" There, under a radiant sky, they gazed over a panoramic expanse of snow-capped peaks spreading away to the south, towards India.

Their moment of elation soon faded. As they made their way down the steep slope to the Tong-gyug Valley a bitterly cold wind blew into them, and not even the brilliant sun was warming. In their dark clothes they were highly conspicuous against the brilliant snow, and even a casual watcher would have spotted them from down the valley. Rinpoche was apprehensive "lest some Communists might be lurking there," but all they could do was keep going and get below the snow line as soon as they could.[138] Again Rinpoche cautioned people about noise, urging them to keep talking to a minimum and to move as quietly as they could. Even if they were, in reality, unlikely to meet people this high up the valley, everyone needed the training.

Still, many of the refugees had experienced the Communists at first hand, and had heard the dozens of reports of the wreck of monasteries and the brisk elimination of monks and lamas. Young Palya Washutsong feared capture and desperately wanted to escape; hers was one of the leading Lhatok families, and she knew they would all be singled out for special punishment and humiliation. Yonten too was driven by deep anxiety – not for himself but for Rinpoche. In Surmang he had seen how tightly focused the new overlords had been on his abbot, had noted their heavy-handed attempts to have him bow to their ideology. He, along with everyone else, had heard of other lamas' fates and had not the slightest doubt that, if captured, Rinpoche would be killed rather than imprisoned.[139]

When they reached the foot of the pass, they found a fairly concealed spot to camp and take stock. In their now more menacing land, they had no information about the area ahead of them, where the PLA might be. Nor could they approach travelers or villagers for news or food: the refugees' presence could endanger local people, especially if they received help from them; on the other hand, their countrymen and women could easily turn out to be informers, made so by choice or intimidation. From this point on they had to hide from their fellow Tibetans.

Before going further, Rinpoche sent out a small group of men to scout the area ahead. On their return they told Rinpoche that they had seen no-one, neither Tibetan nor Chinese. The only sign that people had ever been here were some old footprints, plainly those of a Tibetan. With the terrain ahead clear and safe for travel, Rinpoche led them on into the Tong-gyug Valley. His plan was to continue down its broad trough as it curved away to the southwest, trekking on until they reached a pass the guide knew that would take them up to the mountain highlands. From there they would head southeast, making for Kongpo and the Brahmaputra.

For several days they enjoyed a pleasant journey down the valley, glad to be out of the cold and wind higher up, their spirits soaring now that they were well and truly on their way. And they were getting used to traveling on foot, carrying everything they needed in yakskin bags slung around their necks, or in makeshift packs that were often used as pillows at night.

Except for the guide and his wife in their Kongpo attire, they wore typical East Tibetan clothes. Their main garment was a woolen or sheepskin *chuba*, a long, warm and wind-resistant coat tied around the waist with a sash, with extra-long sleeves for added warmth – and capacious enough to carry bags or a child inside, or to be used as a quilt at night. Some of the lamas had in addition small, light cotton tents. Mothers generally carried babies or very young children, while fathers bore most of the family's food and possessions. Some of the older children, like Palya, hefted fairly heavy packs – food, sheepskin blankets, sleeping bags and small tents – while younger ones like Drupju carried small packs of their own. Occasionally, when his five-year-old sister was too tired to walk, he took his turn in lifting her onto his shoulders before carrying her as far as he could.

Although they had seen no-one in the valley, Rinpoche remained vigilant lest they found themselves in an ambush, or walked into a PLA patrol heading their way. If that happened, little could be done with their large and unwieldy group. But, as they hiked on, they recognized that the high lands they were moving through were used mainly for summer grazing, and that in late September there would be few, if any, people around. Nevertheless, every evening Rinpoche took the precaution of finding a small valley branching off the main one, preferably with herdsmen's huts for shelter. Here they would be secluded and inconspicuous, out of the way of villagers or of PLA patrols probing up towards the Nyewo Valley, and they could relax for the night.

Once they had settled down in camp around a fire, Yonten bustled around at his various tasks. He was not enjoying them much at the moment. His duties were demanding: along with the heavy pack he carried through the day, hefting his own food and possessions and much of Rinpoche's, it was Yonten's job to select a campsite and set up his abbot's tent; he would then find wood, make the fire and cook the food. But lately, after his work was done and he had sat down to eat and relax, a few lamas, used to having people wait on them and jump to their instructions, had taken to bossing him around: "Yonten do this, Yonten do that, Yonten … Yonten … Yonten … ". The pattern had emerged over the previous months, but had become more irksome with the journey's new strains. He thought it most unfair, especially considering the little these lamas did and the relatively light loads they carried and – and, crucially, the fact that he wasn't their attendant at all. Although Yonten's resentment towards these "big shots" continued to simmer, he kept calm, added this burden to his others, and carried on.[140]

For the group as a whole, a daily routine took shape. They would start early, usually just after dawn, and then walk throughout the day, going on until they camped near sunset. The lamas' group led the way and set the pace. Individuals or families would take rest breaks when they needed to, catching up when they could. Rinpoche did not try to organize rest periods for everyone. The full group was far too bulky to manage, and anyway people differed widely in their stamina and how fast they could walk.

While Rinpoche did sometimes slow the pace to allow everyone to keep up, he could not risk everyone's lives by walking at the pace of the feeblest and slowest, stopping when they needed to stop.

Moreover, with their scanty provisions dwindling by the day, they could not afford to take time off to rest. So, as they traveled on, each day the long column of refugees tended to become more strung out and fragmented. Only in the evenings, when the last stragglers came in, was the entire group together. For the time being, this daily routine worked well enough.

As they continued down the valley's gentle slope, the weather warmed and vegetation grew more abundant, while the traveling was most enjoyable. Along the banks of the Tong-gyug River they began to find small yellow berries growing on trees that were acidic but quite edible, and supplemented their sparse diet.

One afternoon they came to an area where fir trees filled the valley. There they spotted their first fresh footprints, and Rinpoche thought it prudent to stop where they were. They set up camp among the scrub under the trees, where they would be relatively well concealed, while Tsepa went out ahead to reconnoiter. In his Kongpo dress, the guide would raise few suspicions if he met anyone – when his cover story would be that he was a messenger sent by relatives of someone in the area. When he returned, he reported that he had found a village where people had no suspicion of him and talked freely. They gave him gloom-laden accounts of the situation in Lower Kongpo, where people were living in a state of terror under intense persecution, not knowing what would be next. The wealthy had been singled out for especially rough treatment, while anyone who displeased the Communists had been sent to labor camps, many soon to die there from starvation, fatigue and punishment.

Tsepa had also procured a small amount of food, and managed to learned more about the lay of the land ahead. With the route's details clearer, Rinpoche felt more confident about the way they were going, and sent a messenger back towards the Tsophu Pass: if he met Akong Tulku, Jigme Tulku or Tsethar the bursar, he was to give them Rinpoche's location and his intended route.

After making a wide detour around the village, they continued on. Late one afternoon, they came to a lake that Rinpoche found so beautiful that, in spite of the heightened danger from its exposed position out in the valley, he could not resist camping there for the night. It would be their last such experience for some time.

The next day the weather grew colder and the valley narrower, while the track rose gradually upwards into rockier ground where there was little vegetation. Over the following days, the weather stayed frigid, the terrain bare. One morning, a man's voice was clearly heard from somewhere behind them. Panic surged through the refugees, a few men grabbing their guns and hurrying back to a small bridge they had just crossed to defend it, their recently-made promise to Rinpoche quite forgotten.

It had in fact been a man's voice, that of the bursar Tsethar, who was accompanied by a monk. He told Rinpoche that Akong Tulku's group was following some way behind. He went on to say that, in accordance with the instructions Rinpoche had given him many months before, he had sold most of the heavy possessions and the animals – glossing over the fact that, when their exhausted group had reached the confines of Rigong Kha, he'd had no choice. Then he passed on disconcerting news: a group of a hundred and twenty refugees had insisted on coming with Akong Tulku to join Rinpoche's group.

Rinpoche outlined for Tsethar the route he had decided on after weeks of enquiry and debate. The bursar listened intently, finally according it his approval – although this was heavily qualified. It was Tsethar's considered view that a rescue operation would be launched from India to save all the refugees; in light of this, he continued, it might have been better for Rinpoche and everyone else if they had just stayed where they were until the rescue operation got under way, and not put themselves through all the trouble to escape. Little could be said in response to such magical thinking.

Nor did Rinpoche comment on the large number of new people who would soon be arriving, each entrusting their life to him, all looking to him to see them to safety. From the start, he had been acutely aware that, on a journey that might push them to the very edge, every additional person, animal or piece of baggage would diminish everyone's chances of escape. The arrival of Yag Tulku's large train of people and animals on the slopes of Sharkong La had abruptly shrunk their options, drastically slowed them down and led to long delays and lengthy detours.

Rinpoche also did not mention the cold truth that Yonten knew all too well. If they were captured by Communist forces, most refugees would be released after interrogation, perhaps to a re-education camp, perhaps free to go their own way. The lamas, according to the custom of the time, would likely be shot out of hand – starting with Rinpoche himself – with the monks either suffering the same fate or being dispatched to labor camps.

Some refugees were aware of this worrisome reality, but most may have felt too desperate to care. Anyway, they felt that they had little choice, and would be entrusting their own and their families' fates to Rinpoche. Yet he knew nothing about the people about to join them, how well equipped they were, or the state of their provisions. He'd had no chance to work with them, to instill in them a sense of the journey's challenges or to lay out the rules and discipline they would have to observe. Nor had he conveyed to them the fundamentally non-violent nature of their group, or the galvanizing vision of a pilgrimage to the birthplace of the Buddha.

At this point they'd had to trek far further along the Tong-gyug Valley than Rinpoche had hoped. So, rather than wait for Akong Tulku and his group to arrive, he decided to take advantage of the good weather and keep moving. Eventually, in the fading light of dusk the guide spotted the pass he had been looking for, high on the eastern mountains. To ensure an early start in the morning, Rinpoche looked for a campsite close to the foot of the pass. As they neared the base of the mountain they spotted a group of herdsmen's huts, which they crowded into. Sheltered from outside view they lit large fires, cheering themselves before the trying days ahead.

Near dawn on a day at the end of September, they set out for the pass. Its track would take them five thousand feet up to the mountain highlands, from where they would begin their journey southeastwards to the Brahmaputra.

It was soon plain that it was going to be a very steep, stiff climb, especially difficult for the older people. Still, Rinpoche thought that with their early start and in the fair conditions they had been enjoying, they should all make it to the summit by dusk. Yet they had gone barely a quarter of the way up when snow began to fall, gradually turning into a blinding storm that forced them to take refuge in several herdsmen's shelters. The blizzard raged on for another day and night, and there was no thought of resuming the climb. Finally it lifted enough so that some men could go out to examine the track, and to see how far up they could climb. They reported that they had found the snow far deeper than any they had seen at the Tsophu Pass, and that it had been a struggle to make any progress at all.

Unless they could find some way to clear the trail and get up to the pass, they would be trapped in the snow-bound huts, and perhaps even have to return to the Tong-gyug Valley. Rinpoche selected eight of the strongest men, told them to hand their baggage to others to carry, and asked them to do whatever they could to forge a way up to the pass. The men found that they could make no headway while walking upright, and resorted to lying on the snow, one by one pressing it down with their weight – an exhausting process that could only be done five times or so before the next man took over. The other men followed behind, treading down the snow, until a track had been made all the way to the crest line.

By now the snow had quite abated, and the hard-won track stayed clear. But when Rinpoche led the refugees to the track to make their ascent, he came close to turning everyone around and returning to the huts. While the track had indeed been adequately cleared, it headed straight up the mountain's very steep slope – on such an incline, a zig-zag trail, going up by gentle increments, would usually be the only way to ascend. The slope was so steep that it was almost impossible to get a firm enough footing to propel oneself upwards. And each footstep compressed the snow into ice as it was trodden down, making it more difficult by the moment. But Rinpoche and the lamas decided to push on, pausing periodically to see how everyone else was doing below: although it was terribly tiring, people were able to make their slow way up. During one of the pauses, the lamas noticed a large group down in the valley behind them, and assumed that it would be Akong Tulku and his party.

Around midday, Rinpoche and the leaders' group made their way onto a rock-strewn plateau. As they wound their way through the boulders, they saw ahead of them an even steeper climb than the one they had just completed. This high, though, the snow was harder than further down and, in spite of the daunting incline, the going was easier. At this stage, the guide Tsepa, Yonten and a few others were leading, but the deep snow cover made it hard to follow the track. Periodically they would stray off it, hiking on until they realized their mistake, when everyone would have to turn around and retrace their steps. It was only near dusk, the sun a red glow on the horizon, that the leading group spotted a prayer flag ahead, waving from the summit.

An icy wind blew in the deepening gloom, and Rinpoche and the lamas grew increasingly anxious about the people following behind, worried that nightfall would trap them out on the exposed slopes. He was especially concerned for the older people: he felt that they had done magnificently to keep going at the pace they had, but they must have fallen far behind, and would have to sleep in the snow. Peering down, they could not see much past the rocky plateau; the mountain below seemed bereft of life and movement. The lamas checked through the family lists, and began to relax as they realized that there were enough younger people with the families to take care of the elderly.

The leaders' group could not wait where they were, exposed on the summit. In what light remained, they tried to make for a path and some level ground they had seen ahead and below them, but they were obstructed by rocky outcrops which, as they wended their way around them, broke up the group. And the footing was tricky, the track littered with stones and small rocks that often tumbled down onto the people below, accompanied by a shouted warning. In near-darkness they eventually found each other, and shortly afterwards came to a level spot where they could camp. There was an overhanging rock large enough to provide shelter for a handful of people, but the lamas insisted that Rinpoche have it while they slept outside in the snow.

They woke early, intensely concerned for the stragglers' well-being, and by sunrise were on the ridge watching for them. Before long, the first people came into view, then others appeared, singly or in small groups. They were drained from the previous day's climb and the exposed, freezing night on the mountain, but there had been no casualties, and to everyone's great relief they all finally made it to the top.

Rinpoche would have liked to allow the latecomers the complete rest they needed, but the group had to keep going. He sent a man to scout the terrain ahead, who reported that the valley ahead looked safe for traveling, with no-one to be seen and no evidence of wild animals.

In bright sunlight and a light wind, Tsepa led the refugees forward across the heights. If people had placed their faith in Rinpoche to get them to the Brahmaputra, he himself was relying on the guide. After a while they came to a plateau with a river flowing across it that was fed by streams from the small surrounding valleys. Tsepa pointed to one of the valleys which ran off to the southeast. Although he would be taking an unfamiliar route, he was emphatic that this valley was the one to take.

Just a short distance up the valley, the mountains began to press in on either side, forcing them to keep to the broken, difficult terrain along the valley floor. As they stumbled across it, the older and weaker people, still exhausted from the climb, were finding it hard to keep up, and began to fall behind. Rinpoche asked Tsepa to slow down to allow them to keep up. This was no simple or straightforward decision: with their limited food supplies, time was not on their side, and the more they paced themselves by the slowest among them the greater the ultimate risk to all.

During one of these slow-moving days, they spotted two men coming up behind. As they drew nearer they saw that it was Akong Tulku and a monk, striding strongly along well ahead of their party, clearly intent on overtaking Rinpoche's group. The two old friends were overjoyed to see each other. Akong Tulku said that thanks to the cleared and trodden-down track, his group had had a relatively easy climb up the pass, and could then travel fast to catch up. Rinpoche waited until all the newcomers arrived, then they went on together, walking until they came to a group of herdsmen's huts, where they camped. Akong Tulku had much to report since they had last seen each other, and the two friends talked well into the night.

In early July, while still on the heights above the Nyewo Valley, Akong Tulku had received Rinpoche's message telling him that he would be taking the track along the Yigong Valley to Rigong Kha, and advising him to abandon their possessions and animals and follow suit.

However, his brother Jamyang, aligned with Tsethar the bursar, had other ideas. Their group would make for Rigong Kha, but would find a way that did not force them to leave their goods and herds behind. They decided on a route that headed northeast before coming in to Rigong Kha from the north, from the towering mountains behind the village. Yonten later surmised that Tsethar had an additional reason for pushing for this route: it would put the group within reach of the road to East Tibet and Kham, keeping open the option of returning to Surmang.

It was a grindingly difficult journey over untracked mountain terrain, often having had to build their own bridges, or fell trees to get across chasms. Many horses were lost with their loads, either by falling off the rudimentary bridges or by collapsing and dying from the strain. In the end, it had proved to be a far longer, costlier and demanding route than the track along the Yigong Valley had been.

When Akong Tulku's group finally reached Rigong Kha, the villagers were astonished. Most of them had never seen horses, mules or yaks – and none had seen so many animals of any species. Their arrival spawned immediate problems. The grazing around the village was sparse, and the large herds had to be fed on the villagers' precious grain. Then the group was faced with getting the animals across the fast-running Yigong River and into the Tsophu valley.

Even Tsethar recognized that it could not be done, and dolefully made arrangements to leave his herds behind – many months after Rinpoche had first instructed him to do just that. Some refugees were still determined to take their animals with them, whatever the odds, and tried to have them swim across the Yigong, only to lose most of them to the torrent.

In the Tsophu Valley, Akong Tulku found Kino Tulku, who was still seriously ill and very lonely without Rinpoche and the lamas. But Kino was sure that, in spite of the many dangers ahead, Rinpoche's decision to head for India had been the right one. This message boosted Akong Tulku's determination to press on, and to find Rinpoche's group.

By then the tracks made by the group across the Tsophu Pass had been obliterated by snow, and some refugees – fearing that they might never find Rinpoche, and unwilling to part with the few animals that had survived the river crossing – decided to take their chances and stay behind in the valley.

When Rinpoche arose the next morning, he gazed over the camp: "I was amazed to see so many people, for Tsethar's group had added some hundred and twenty to our numbers, thus bringing the total up to nearly three hundred."[141] As they set off on the day's journey, he glanced back at the mass of people behind, and thought that it looked more like an army on the march than a group of tired and hungry refugees.

Tsepa the guide led them over an expanse of bare, rock-strewn ground punctuated by abrupt, steep slopes, trekking on until he recognized the Powo Valley-Kongpo trading road ahead of them. Here they stopped and found a place to rest, hidden among rocks, while scouts went ahead to survey the countryside. They returned to say that they had seen a man leading four loaded yaks along the road, but no-one else. After waiting two hours for the man and his animals to move out of view, two scouts crossed the road and climbed up a nearby peak to a vantage point from where they could see for three miles in either direction. After they signaled the all clear, Tsepa led the group across the road, then forded the river running beside it and made for a small valley.

There, still fairly close to the road, they again spent the night in herdsmen's huts. Few slept restfully: there was a great deal of noise from the many women and children in the newly arrived group, and in the middle of the night there was a scare when some of them thought that they heard the sounds of men approaching in the dark.

At sunrise on a morning in early October, Rinpoche sat down with Tsepa to address a pair of troubling issues. Neither of them by itself was of pressing concern, but when their effects combined a few days later they would have the gravest of consequences.

The first item they discussed was the route. During the previous day's journey, Tsepa, in spite of recognizing the Powo Valley-Kongpo trading road, had at times felt unsure of their whereabouts. In talking the issue through, though, he sounded fairly confident of the course ahead. He thought that they should leave the valley, and then cross a high pass to the south. He did not know what was on the far side of the pass, but at least they would be heading in the right direction, towards Kongpo.

Then Rinpoche mentioned his concern about the newcomers. They had no idea how to conceal themselves or how to act in an emergency, were unusually noisy, and wore bright colors that made them highly conspicuous against vegetation or dark terrain. Most of them were simple country folk who had no real sense of the threat they faced, no idea that they risked being captured by the Chinese. He decided that with such a naïve and noisy group they could not afford to take chances. They would have to abandon the easier and more direct routes that passed near villages or along open valleys.

With a smaller, more disciplined group, Rinpoche may have felt that traditional routes were worth the risks, relying on good scouting to keep out of trouble – when necessary hiding in side valleys, among trees, behind rocks or simply detouring around more populated areas. This was no longer an option. The journey over the difficult mountain terrain would be harder on them all, especially the older people, but Tsepa agreed that, in their changed circumstances, this was what they had to do.

Something still had to be done with the new arrivals. Rinpoche gathered them together to try to convey to them what they faced, and what he would be asking of them. They would soon be entering a more dangerous part of the country, more thickly populated, and where the Communists were likely to be in control. No-one could be trusted. If they happened to stumble across villagers, they should treat them courteously and say nothing at all about where the group was going. Above all, they should try to keep as quiet as possible. Rinpoche ended by saying that if anyone fell ill, he should be immediately informed of it.

Then they broke camp and left the valley, following Tsepa up to the high pass he had spotted, heading south into the mountains. The leaders were excited – the guide was confident that when they reached the top they would be able to see an area of the Lower Kongpo. From there, they would have their bearings, and could make their way to the Brahmaputra as directly as the terrain allowed. When they reached the crest, though, all they could see ahead of them was another range of rocky mountains. They had also expected to see scattered fields or villages, but there was no sign of life, no wandering sheep or yaks, not even wild animals.

Tsepa was utterly baffled: he had lost his bearings in the unfamiliar terrain, and had no clear idea where to head next. But a decision had to be made, and he led the group down into a little valley they could see directly below, thinking that it would lead them to another valley or pass from where they could resume their southerly course. They continued along the valley for a few hours, only to find themselves in a dead end. Surrounded by lofty peaks, they had no choice but to climb to a high ridge to get past them.

Again, they hoped that from the top they might fix their whereabouts, maybe glimpse the Lower Kongpo, but when they reached the ridgeline, all they saw were three more ranges to be crossed. They spent hours getting over them, only to find that the last range ended in a near-precipice, which they had somehow to descend. For the rapidly tiring people, it was hazardous. The precipice was covered in extremely slippery grass, making it almost impossible for them to keep their footing. Some of the older refugees slipped and fell, although without any serious injury.

With the three ranges behind them, they hoped that the very long day would be coming to an end, but in front of them lay another chain of mountains. As they neared it they came across wild animal tracks, which they followed up the slope. In fading light they neared the summit and found, close to the ridgeline between two tall peaks, a deep round hollow covered in trees and grass. It was well protected from the wind and large enough for them all, and Rinpoche decided to camp there for the night.

Tsepa was by now deeply distraught. There was no disguising the predicament he had led them into. Here, at high altitude among some of the world's tallest peaks and most rugged terrain, he had completely lost track of his whereabouts. The refugees were tiring badly, the older people struggling to keep up, while some were already running short of food. And winter was coming on. Even if they had the time and energy, and could successfully retrace their steps, they could not return to the Powo-Kongpo road, back to terrain that the guide recognized. Rinpoche and Tsepa had agreed that it would be far too dangerous to attempt to get their large, unruly group through that part of the country. They had no choice but to keep going, to try to reach the Brahmaputra from wherever it was that they were.

How could Tsepa's disorientation have happened – and so soon? After all, back in the Tsophu Valley he had affirmed to Rinpoche that he knew the mountains well and could guide them to Kongpo. He was not deceiving anyone. On his many hunting expeditions, he had used main roads and well-known mountain tracks whenever he could, relying on villagers and fellow travelers for food and information. Now he'd had to actively avoid them all, choosing trackless wilderness over human paths and habitations. Tsepa's Tibet had changed as much as everyone else's. His old reference points had become potential danger spots, and he had found himself adrift.

As the reality sank in, the bursar Tsethar grew irate. He loudly complained that no-one had any idea where they were going; if they had just stayed where they were, back on the heights above the Nyewo Valley, Tibetan resistance fighters would have come to their rescue; he was sure that by now those who had stayed behind would be safely under their protection. Rinpoche replied that there was no evidence of any of this, and that anyway it was he, not the Tibetan fighters, who had been entrusted to lead their party; meanwhile, everyone, including the guide, was doing their best.

Yet anger, bewilderment or wishful fantasies could not blur or soften the piercing reality they faced. Just a few days in, but already deep in the great mountain wilderness, they were lost.

10

Wilderness

Shortly after dawn, they left the snowy hollow where they had spent the night and set out the along the ridgeline, taking a route that sloped gently up and over the peak's shoulder. At first Rinpoche worried about the bare, treeless land they were crossing, where their large party was highly visible, but they could see no signs of life in any direction.

They trekked all day until, towards dusk, they approached the crest of a mountain that they'd had to climb to keep to their southerly course. From here they could see, far to the south behind a ripple of rocky mountains, unusually high snow peaks gleaming in the late sun. A few thought that these might be the mountains of the Upper Kongpo, others wondered whether the range was in Lower Kongpo, but no-one really knew. They climbed on until dusk bathed the snow around them in a soft golden light, then found an area to camp. Although the frost was very severe this high on the mountain, they could not make fires in case they were spotted. And there were no streams nearby, so after sucking on handfuls of snow for moisture, they settled down to sleep.

Most would have spent a fairly warm and comfortable night. They would have gathered any grass or small bushes they could find or dig out, and used the vegetation for makeshift mattresses to provide comfort and insulation from snow or frigid ground. Those who had to sleep on rock would use smaller rocks to chip off the rougher, sharper edges of their sleeping spot. For heat, groups of families, relatives or friends usually stripped down to their light cotton garments and slept together, body to body, under a layer of sheepskin *chubas*, which were also used as mattresses. With only a single layer of *chubas* underneath, if they slept on bare snow or rock, the cold bit through.

Daybreak brought a blunt reminder of the hazards of traveling across unknown wilderness. They saw that the route they had been following led to a snow mountain that took them away from the direction they wanted. They had no choice but to abandon the track, descending steeply into the valley below, nervously conspicuous against the slope's bright snow.

As they neared the valley floor, anxiety flared when a few men thought that a black object they had spotted next to the river was a man – in their consternation, some also imagined they heard the sound of human voices. Through his binoculars Rinpoche saw that the object was a young yak. It seemed to be entirely alone, but there could well be a herdsman nearby. They continued some way along the valley floor, passing through a grove of low willow trees before coming to a herdsman's hut, where they decided to camp. A few young men went out to look around the environs, but saw no-one. At nightfall, as many as could fit crammed themselves into the hut while the others slept outside.

In the early morning they set off on the day's journey. Tsepa had now lost all sense of the route. When he had first become perplexed several days before, he had still had a rough idea of the heading they needed – south-southeast towards Lower Kongpo, where the Brahmaputra was narrow enough to cross. Now, in the increasingly unfamiliar terrain, he had even become befuddled about that, and had no better notion of their course than anyone else.

Having lost their bearings they had lost all sense of the route, and were hiking on more or less blindly. It was a desperate situation. It was not enough to know where the sun rose and where south lay, which direction to head. The area they were in was a maze of mountains, a tumult of massive ranges, snow peaks and deep, meandering valleys. Without an experienced guide – the heir to knowledge acquired over centuries, someone who knew the landmarks, the shapes and curves of mountains, valleys and rivers, the location of tracks and passes – each morning delivered almost impossibly difficult decisions; and every day could sink into a heartbreaking saga of confusions and corrections. Valleys that had seemed promising could, after hours of hard trekking, veer away in the wrong direction, be blocked by rockfalls or impossible ravines, or lead to a dead end. A mountain pass that had looked as if it would take them in the right direction could, after hours of energy-sapping climbing, bring them to an untraversable cliff or uncrossable range, to terrain that led nowhere.

Rinpoche's account does not mention his use of mirror divination at this stage of the journey. From others' reports, though, he was resorting to it more or less daily, apparently to cast light on the day's route.[142] As always, his first recourse was to practical knowledge and guidance, or to obvious roads or tracks, including those of animals; only when all earthly guidelines failed would he turn to mirror divination. The mirror deity's traditional range of powers seems to have lain more in the realm of spiritual and human affairs than in topography, geography and navigation; still, Rinpoche was somehow employing her services now. In any event, he wrote that he felt "… a strange exhilaration traveling through such wild and unknown country; an inner strength seemed to sustain me."[143]

They trekked on, making up the route as they went, trying to maintain the south-easterly course that would bring them to the stretch of the Brahmaputra they wanted. At this point Rinpoche's account in *Born in Tibet* becomes abbreviated: he gives no specific dates, tending to mention only key or compelling events, sparing the reader a catalogue of the daily struggles and hardships, the repetitive details of the wilderness they slogged through, the ranges they climbed, the ocean of mountains they crossed.

They were heading into areas where people had never been. The terrain was rugged and chaotic, the going arduous; they made little progress, covering only a short distance each day. All the while bodies were tiring under the short rations and heavy loads, muscles and joints strained to extremes by the climbs. Even with longer rest periods, older people, the sick or weak, or mothers burdened with young children or babies, were slowing down and beginning to lag behind. Slowly, day by day, the traveling party became more fragmented. Each day it became more difficult for some to keep up, every evening harder for stragglers to find their way to campsites.

Sometime in mid-October, about a month after they left the Tsophu Valley, a small group of refugees approached Rinpoche and asked him how long it would be before they would be able to replenish their supplies. He said that it was not likely to be soon, and that they would have to ration what they had even more strictly than before.

A week later, the group approached Rinpoche again, this time asking if he could spare them any food. He had to turn them down: his own provisions were very limited, and if he gave food to one group others would follow. However hard people may have tried to ration themselves, few could have conceived how far they would have to make their provisions stretch; few would have had much experience at it, or could have known how cruel the cravings would be from undernourished, over-exerted bodies.

One afternoon, having earlier crossed several low mountain ranges, they came to a broad valley. It was invitingly open, but it lay at a relatively low altitude and the leaders thought that there would probably be herdsmen around, perhaps even villages or farms. Appealing as it was to head down the valley, it could be very risky.

Rinpoche went ahead to scout the terrain himself, accompanied by Akong Tulku, Yag Tulku, Yonten and Tsepa the guide. They came across human footprints and traces of dung, but both Yonten and Tsepa were sure that they were well over a day old. They could see no other sign of human presence, and signaled back to the group that the valley appeared empty and that they should follow along behind. Rinpoche talked the situation through with the others, but no-one came up with anything useful or insightful. Some wanted to stop where they were and make tea, but Rinpoche felt that they could not risk a fire in such open countryside, where the smoke would be quickly spotted.

They went on down the valley until, about halfway along it, they came to a mountain whose slopes were thick with pine trees. Rinpoche had a sudden intuition, certain that this was the way to go. He had already led the group about a mile up through the pines, when Tsethar the bursar suddenly objected to the whole idea. He did not approve of the fact that they had taken this route based solely on Rinpoche's intuition, and thought that it would have been better just to keep going along the valley. A few others, tired and irritable, grumbled that they were having to struggle up yet another mountain and had not even had their tea.

Rinpoche replied that from their higher viewpoint they could see that, further along, the valley began to veer away from the direction they needed. It was also very likely that, if they were to continue down it, they would run into people – they were, after all, heading towards an area they knew to be well populated and had already spotted footprints.

Reason made little impact on the stressed and edgy group. With Tsethar in full cry, they became so agitated that they started arguing with Rinpoche. He turned to his well-tried tactic, saying: "If you want to go along the valley, you had better do so; in which case I can take no further responsibility for you. I myself am going up this mountain and when we reach a more remote spot we can stop and make tea." This seemed sound enough to a few men, who shouted "Yes! That is the right thing to do."[144] After another small wave of grumbling they all fell silent and followed Rinpoche upwards.

His inspiration to climb the pine-covered mountain was plainly something more than a passing fancy. He was quite confident that this was the way they had to go, and it's conceivable that he had recognized the pine mountain from a mirror divination. Yet nothing was straightforward in the harsh terrain: as they climbed beyond the pine trees, they found themselves in scrub so dense that they repeatedly lost the track, while men had to use their swords or long Khampa knives to slash their way through.

When they finally reached the summit, they took their tea break. There, relaxing on their high vantage point, from somewhere in the south, for the first time since they left the Tsophu Valley, they heard sounds that were clearly of human origin. They were cold comfort: some thought that the noises came from truck engines, others that they were explosions or even the clamor of battle. Whatever they were, they were not reassuring, and they came from the direction in which the group was heading.

From the summit they made their way down to a dry valley below. As they reached it, Tsepa turned to Rinpoche to ask where to go next. In the wake of his firm decision to climb the pine-covered mountain, it was clear to all that the responsibility for finding the way had, at least for the time being, been transferred to Rinpoche.

Ahead of them lay a mountain with three gaps, each of which might lead out of the valley in the direction they needed. Tsepa wanted to know which one to choose. Rinpoche instantly said, "The middle one." When asked for his reasoning, he said simply that one had to be chosen, adding the Tibetan sayings that "A doubting mind will not fulfill one's wish" and "Two needles cannot sew at the same time." He would defer to Tsepa when the guide became surer of the way, but it appears that he was taking the opportunity to re-assert his overall authority – further dissent in their precarious circumstances could be disastrous.

As they reached the crest line, Rinpoche was cheered to see a stone cairn on the side of the track: people had been this way before. Emerging on the mountain's far side they felt a sudden cold wind, and found themselves high on a cliff edge. Below was a lake, vividly reflecting the red and black rocks scattered across it. As far as they could tell, their way was blocked, the cliff precipitously steep, the lake apparently unpassable.

Once they started down, however, the steep descent turned out to be simple and almost effortless, and they were easily able make their way from rock to rock across the lake. And the bare, dry valley beyond appeared to be deserted, with only the tracks of wild animals to be seen. Still, when they lit their fires after dark, they took considerable care to screen them from any distant sight. Nothing could hide them from the sky, though, and during the night an aircraft flew over which could only have been Communist.

At dawn they continued on over flat and open ground, making good progress throughout the day. Yet the route remained anything but clear, and troubles were building. Rinpoche heard that an older man was quite worn out and growing very feeble; although his baggage had been shared among others, and his relatives were supporting him as he hobbled along, things looked bad for him. And, straddling their route ahead, was a mountain range that would involve a punishing climb to the ridge. They found hoof tracks, which they followed upwards, but the closer they came to the summit, the deeper the snow became. Finally they had no choice but to turn to their last-ditch method – the team of eight robust men taking turns crushing down the snow with their bodies.

After they reached the summit and saw the view beyond, Tsepa grew more hopeful, surer of the way ahead. To the south they could see the high snow ranges they had spotted before, although nearer now; they thought that these might well be the Himalayas, on the far side of the Brahmaputra.

As they headed on, the going became more strenuous. The way first sloped down into a depression, then inclined upwards again into a steep climb over an even higher range than the one they had just crossed. Again, the eight-man team went ahead to make a track through the drifts. Rinpoche, worried about the elderly man on the brutal climbs, gave him food from his own provisions to help him along, an infusion that seemed to re-energize the struggling fellow.

Whatever hopes they may have held of an easier, more straightforward way evaporated when they reached the crest line. All around them were snow-covered ranges – and they could no longer hear the distant human sounds they had heard before. As far as they could tell, they were at the end of a range of mountains, but could see no way forward. Nevertheless, they went on downhill, heading for a series of small lakes below the snow line. There they rested while Rinpoche took his binoculars and went out to reconnoiter the valley ahead. He saw that it was broad, with a river wandering between meadows and small areas of pine trees, but it looked thoroughly devoid of people.

Tsepa did not recall the actual topography, but he felt that he was getting his bearings. They were, he thought somewhere near the village of Tsela Dzong, which lay at the junction of the Upper Kongpo and Brahmaputra Rivers. Rinpoche knew, from travelers he had talked to in the Nyewo Valley, that if this was indeed where they were, they were in dangerous territory – near a populated area that was almost certainly under Communist control. Anyone they met here could be an informer, and people and villages had to be avoided even more rigorously than before. Rinpoche talked things over with the other lamas. All agreed that if the guide was right about their whereabouts, they must change direction: they should first leave the broad, watered valley they were in, as they were certain to meet people somewhere along it, and bear further eastwards, heading for Lower Kongpo; when they reached it, they could search out a point to cross the Brahmaputra.

Early next morning they set out on their new heading, leaving the valley and climbing part of the way back up the lofty mountain they had just traversed. Continuing along its slopes, they bore due east whenever they could. It was another hugely demanding trek, beginning with a seemingly infinite expanse of heavy scrub and thick undergrowth that took several exhausting days to slog through. Beyond it they came to a series of small mountains and valleys that had to be crossed – a stage of the journey that Rinpoche described as "a matter of continually scrambling up and down hill for about a week."[145]

Sometime in late October, about six weeks after they left the Tsophu Valley, a group of refugees approached Rinpoche and told him that they had entirely run out of food. They were eating the leather of their yakskin bags to survive. After hearing this, Rinpoche visited the various groups spread out along the trail. He found that others had turned to the same desperate measure: first soaking the leather for a day or so until it swelled, then slicing it into small, bite-size pieces and boiling it for several hours until it had something like the look and consistency of meat. Although there was some nutrition in the leather – it was rough-cured, which left behind a good deal of fat – no-one could last for long on such fare.

The discovery was a severe blow, abruptly darkening everyone's prospects. Rinpoche had made it a rule, one that people had promised to obey, that he was to be told of any difficulties that came up along the way. But people who had resorted to eating leather knew that there were no extra provisions to be had – and also, aware of Rinpoche's many other worries and burdens, the starving people had not wanted to bother him with theirs.

The food emergency was not the only matter he may not have been told about. From other accounts, we know that by this point in the journey, a number of people – perhaps a dozen or two – had fallen out and disappeared.

As the weeks dragged by, some had found it ever harder to keep up, or to catch up once they had fallen behind. Individuals or families may have come to the heart-breaking realization that they could not go on, then struggled off in the hope of finding a home or village, to cast themselves on the mercy of their fellow Tibetans. Older, weaker or sicker people, worn out by the harrowing travel, might have lagged back, lost the way and never found it again. Little is known of what became of them: some might have made their way to a herdsman's hut, or found a protected spot among the rocks, or just lain down on the side of the trail, there to stay.

For those moving on with the main group, the losses could be fairly undramatic, the mourning deferred. People would not appear at a rest stop or at a camp at night, then, after a day or two, the reality would settle in that they were gone, and that they would not be seen again. Friends and family would briefly grieve before returning to the trek's all-consuming toil.

It appears that scant news of the losses reached the leaders' group. People may have been just too spent to get the news forward to Rinpoche or, again, may have simply not wanted to bother him. They had promised to tell him of any difficulties, but many likely felt that there was little point to doing so, knowing that little if anything could be done for them; and, back in the Tsophu Valley, Rinpoche had made it forbiddingly clear that, for the good of all, those who could not keep up would be left behind. It was a hard, heartbreaking rule, but a rational and compassionate one: if the party slowed or stopped to care for the weak and faltering, everyone would be lost.

Rinpoche and the lamas would have probably come to learn of the lost refugees but, as with other details in his chronicle, he chose to omit them.[146] Hardly anything was known of their fate, and if they were still alive he had to protect them, and the villagers who might have sheltered them, from persecution, leaving out all details of their identities and possible whereabouts. It was possible too that many might revive their attempt to escape later, when they had physically recovered and restocked their provisions; then, they would stand a better chance of getting through when traveling alone or in a small group.

There were, however, dramas playing out behind the leaders that they seem to have been oblivious to. Around this time, as the traveling party made its way along a narrow track high above a vertiginous precipice, one of Palya and Drupju Washutsong's extended family – a large, strong man, carrying an unusually heavy load – stumbled, lost his footing and disappeared over the edge. He fell around fifty feet before hitting a rocky outcrop, ricocheted off, and then fell another long distance before bouncing off another, and so on, several hundred feet down. After each impact, simple good fortune combined with the dead weight of his pack to rotate his body in mid-air, so that when he crashed into each outcrop the impact was absorbed by the pack. Finally, just as he was about to plummet into the river, he managed to grab onto a stout trunk, hanging on until men managed to clamber down the slope and haul him to safety. Both man and pack were scratched and shaken, but otherwise little the worse for wear.

As the party continued eastwards, Rinpoche and the leaders gradually realized that the guide's earlier view that they had been near the village of Tsela Dzong was mistaken. Now they were going too far north – away from the Brahmaputra. They had no choice but to turn around and retrace their steps, a painful journey of three long days. Then they followed a small valley that seemed to run eastwards, but before long it too veered in a northerly direction, and they had to abandon it for one that seemed to run south. This valley led to a series of mountain ranges, all of which had to be crossed if they were to maintain their course. For the first three days the ranges were fairly low, and they managed to cross two or three a day, but these were followed by far higher mountains, each of which took a day or more to get over.

In early November, they were still unsure of their whereabouts. Everyone was deeply tired, and they were all getting very lean. They could no longer find wild vegetables to supplement their diet, and a sizeable number of refugees were now eating leather. Even some in the leaders' group were boiling strips of bags for food – probably the attendants, who abhorred the idea that their lamas would be reduced to such fare, and would be saving the remaining *tsampa* for them.

As the trek got daily more harrowing, many were struck by how relaxed and friendly Rinpoche remained. Twelve-year-old Drupju felt that he could approach him whenever he wanted to, and would always be warmly received. One day he and his young chums gathered around as Rinpoche showed them his Russian binoculars, explaining how the marvel worked and giving each of them a look through the lenses – a startling experience for the boys, as the far-off scenery suddenly leapt closer, clear and vivid. Yonten emulated his abbot's openness, entrusting Drupju with one of Rinpoche's small personal articles to carry and care for, rewarding him with small bits of dried yak meat or other food. Drupju considered the small task to be a high honor and would have happily taken it on anyway.

On the whole, the refugees remained cheerful, and were disciplined about it. The rowdy group that had arrived with Akong Tulku – and which had forced them onto the perilous wilderness route – had adapted, emulating the other refugees, and settled down. When they were close to an inhabited area everyone was very quiet, but after moving on to some sufficiently remote spot they laughed, joked and sang among themselves, while the monks sat down to devotional chanting and meditation. Rinpoche observed that although the daily hardships were intense, most of the refugees seemed to have adapted to the journey and its cruel demands.

Up to this point, the weather had favored them. Since they left the Tsophu Valley it had been mostly cool but fair. But they were well into November, and the Tibetan winter was under way. They were beset by rainstorms, which often turned into snow that stayed on the ground. The walking became harder, the mountains more taxing to climb and their progress slowed. Often now, when they looked back the way they had come at the end of a day's travel, they could still see their campsite from the night before.

One storm-free day, as they reached a mountain ridgeline, the view expanded into a panoramic vista over the ranges to the south. They stopped to survey the land ahead. Although far-off winter fires shrouded the countryside in smoke, through his binoculars Rinpoche could plainly see in the distance an unusually broad river. He and the lamas were certain that this was the Brahmaputra.

What they saw next stunned them. Unmistakable even through the smoke haze, they could make out large numbers of Chinese trucks moving along a road that ran near the river. They'd had no idea that there would be a major new road running through Kongpo. But it was not just the road that was shocking – they would obviously have to find some way across that – but what it meant about Lower Kongpo, the area they would be traveling through. Not only were the Communists here, just as they had heard, but they were obviously in full and uncontested control, the countryside fully quelled. It would likely be swarming with Chinese troops and personnel. What Rinpoche and the others always knew would be an especially risky stage of the journey was suddenly laden with new menace.

From this vantage point, though, Tsepa found his bearings. He was now certain that they were near the village of Tsela Dzong. It was deeply reassuring to know finally where they were, but it brought with it a disheartening realization: for the last month or so they had been off course – heading nearly due south rather than in the more easterly direction they needed. Now they were far to the west of their objective. Here the Brahmaputra was too wide to cross and, as Rinpoche and the leaders knew, the region was fairly densely populated, with its own Communist headquarters. From here they would have to undertake a long trek eastwards, parallel to the river, heading for the legendary mountain of Namcha Barwa where the river was narrow enough to cross.

More vigilant now, and taking even greater care to stay quiet and concealed, they set out on their new course. Tsepa recognized more and more of the terrain – a curve in the Brahmaputra, a distant monastery, the shapes of peaks. At first they journeyed along secluded low-lying valleys, enjoying the relatively easy walking. On the surrounding mountains, though, they occasionally spotted tall travelers' cairns marking the topmost points of passes; around five or six feet tall, from a distance they looked much like human figures, sending small scares through the tired and jittery group.

As Tsepa's mental map came into sharper focus, he realized that they needed to bear even further east than the way they had been going, across more challenging landscape. Rinpoche and the lamas also recognized that they would have to find a shorter route. Loath to get lost again, they had been following a route that kept the Brahmaputra in sight – but its meandering course was greatly lengthening the journey. In their depleted state, in drastic need of food, they could not afford the luxury of holding to the river as a reference point. They would have to take a more difficult, but more direct, route across the mountains.

Climbing back to higher ground, they could see a number of villages beside the river and make out the light from their fires. These occasionally faded in the glare of far brighter lights, which they assumed to be the headlamps of Communist trucks. Few refugees would have missed the rough paradox of their position: each point of firelight, every spire of wood smoke was both a potential source of food, shelter and survival, and the site of possible capture and sudden death. They themselves urgently needed fires to warm their worn and shrinking bodies, and for boiling leather and making buttered tea. But they were too close to villages to risk making fires during the day, when the smoke would soon be seen, and could only light them at night by digging deep holes to screen the fire from distant eyes, burning off their precious reserves of energy to do so.

They had reached a critical juncture. It had been almost two months since they left the Tsophu Valley, and many people, even the disciplined monastics, were worryingly thin, struggling and beginning to sicken on the scant leather diet. The need for food now overwhelmed all other considerations. They had already chosen a more direct, but riskier and more difficult, route than the one they had been following. Now, in the hope of finding provisions sooner, they would have to take an even shorter one.

Tsepa had no experience of the terrain they would be passing through on their new course, and they might easily lose their way. It would be a finely-calculated risk: weighing the unnerving chance of getting lost on a more rugged and strenuous route against the desperate need for food. With the stakes so incalculably high, it was a risk they would have to take.

11

Into the Dark

Their new course soon ran into obstacles. Shortly after setting out they saw that it was taking them dangerously close to villages and farms. They would have to head further north, away from the river. Yet as they pulled back, retreating into remoter countryside, they found themselves in an area with no trees and very little bush or broken ground. The mass of refugees would be highly visible on the bare terrain, and there were still villages around. They had no alternative: from now on they would have to travel by night.

In the dark, often in mist, storm or snowfalls, the landscape was often impossible to make out, and it was not long before Tsepa again lost his bearings. But he led onwards over ridge after ridge, heading roughly eastwards.

During one especially trying night, after they had found a campsite and settled down, Rinpoche was told that the old man who had been struggling, and to whom he had given some of his own provisions, had dropped dead in his tracks. His family had done everything they could for him, his son even carrying him over the worst and highest passes, but it had not been enough. Soon afterwards, another elderly fellow hobbled up to Rinpoche to announce that he could not go on, and would try to get to a village to ask for shelter. He understood that this might put everyone in danger, and swore that he would say nothing about the escaping party.

Their night routine soon became a simple, almost a natural, one. In daylight they would get their bearings, as far as they could, and then choose a route and select waypoints to follow the coming night. Rinpoche would usually do the scouting himself, climbing to high ground or a ridgeline, accompanied by the guide Tsepa and the monk Urgyan-tendzin – who, along with his other skills, had shown a good eye for terrain; Yonten sometimes joined them. Depending on the landscape, and on people's stamina, they traveled mainly between dusk and midnight; sometimes, though, they slept until midnight, then trekked until dawn before settling down for the day. In remoter areas, where there were few signs of people, they would risk the far easier daylight traveling.

There was no wake-up call before setting out, no-one going from group to group to rouse them for the march. When Rinpoche awoke and made ready to move, Yonten, who always slept close by, did so too; then the lamas and attendants would stir and so on, down the line of sleeping refugees. It happened non-verbally, through a general awareness; only younger children usually needed to be gently shaken awake.

Everything was more difficult in the dark: finding one's footing, keeping up with the people in front, finding them again when contact was lost. As people gradually weakened, slowed and straggled behind, the long column of refugees became ever more fragmented. Losing contact could happen in an instant. One moment people were part of a large group en route to India, the next moment they were lost, falling back into the dark or storm, disappearing down a valley or behind a ridge, their fates known only to the mountains.

As earlier in the journey, some may have eventually found their way to villages. Others may have simply collapsed, observed by no-one. Sometimes, though, there was little doubt of people's fate. Young Drupju Washutsong had looked on in pity and horror as a group of three or four people, too enfeebled to go on, were helped into a small cave, walled in with rocks for protection from the elements and wild animals, and left there. Such events were not always as melancholy as they seemed: the religiously-minded could have thought themselves fortunate – have considered it excellent karma – to die on a journey to India, Buddha's birthplace, a journey that Trungpa Rinpoche had proclaimed a pilgrimage. They might have made themselves as comfortable as they could where they were, reached for their rosaries, and begun to chant and meditate for as long as they could.

There were other bright facets to the dispiriting stories. On one night trek, Drupju Washutsong's family took a rest break. Tired and cold, the twelve-year-old found himself a small hollow shielded from the wind by rocks, lay his head on his pack and went to sleep. When he awoke, the sun was high in the sky and he was quite alone. In escalating panic he looked around him, but could see no-one, no signs of life among the vast mountains. He was almost overcome by fear of the bears and wolves known to roam the area, for which a young, defenseless straggler would be quick and easy picking.

Drupju had a rough sense of the direction they had been heading in before the rest break, and he set out that way, walking as fast as he could. After what seemed like a very, very long time, in the far distance ahead he made out a few human figures. They seemed to be coming his way. As they neared, he saw that they were three men from his family's group, looking for him. When his parents had realized that the boy was missing, some time after they had left the rest stop, the men had volunteered to go back and try to find him. As relieved as Drupju and his saviors were to see each other, there was no time to waste and they immediately set out to catch up with the family. After several hours of hard hiking they found the group as it rested, and Drupju and his family were tearfully reunited.

As they journeyed on, the going remained intensely taxing, with a seemingly endless series of low ranges to be crossed. Adding to their difficulties, the land they were passing through was bare and rocky; it was almost impossible to find a campsite where they could rest comfortably and be concealed enough to light nighttime fires. And, while it was always tempting to follow the local tracks they came across, with their promise of easier routes and better rest sites, they had to avoid them all.

One morning, Tsepa announced that he recognized their surroundings. They were near the old Powo-Lhasa road, a well-traveled thoroughfare which they would have to cross. But few travelers would be out in the cold weather, and Rinpoche decided to risk the daylight journey. When the road came into view in the late afternoon they stopped to look over the terrain. It seemed best to cross the road at the very top of the pass. There the mountain was more rocky and broken up, and they could hide among the clefts, gullies and boulders, staying out of sight until the instant they crossed.

With the extreme need for food dominating their decision-making, they decided to press on and try to cross the pass that night. But there had been a heavy snowfall and progress was slow – and, more alarmingly, there was no way to avoid leaving highly conspicuous tracks in the fresh snow. Rinpoche passed back instructions for everyone to be sure to stay in single file; if they could not conceal their passing, they could at least hide their size. Hard as they pushed, though, the deep drifts and the need to walk in single file combined to slow them down, and when dawn broke they were still some way short of the pass. Even though they had seen few travelers on the road, they could not risk being spotted, so they stopped where they were, found what cover they could, and then spent a bitterly cold day huddled high on the mountain.

When twilight came the pass was brightly illumined by the late sun, and they waited until dark before moving. They set off in silence, listening carefully for the sounds of oncoming travelers. When they reached the pass they could see the tracks of a man on horseback who had gone by during the day. But no-one was out in the wintry weather now, and they moved quickly across the road and headed into the broken ground beyond. Hurrying on, still in single file, they aimed to be far from the pass by dawn. As they made their way across the mountain slope, the terrain gradually smoothed out, until there were no rocks or bushes to camouflage their passage, break up their highly visible tracks. Rinpoche asked a man to stay behind, to warn them as quickly as he could if they were spotted, and sent another man ahead to scout the way.

Still walking as fast as they could, by daybreak they were back on high ground close to the summit. Stopping to look around them, there was little to be seen; by far the most noticeable feature in the snowy landscape was the track they had made across the mountainside behind. But with growing relief they realized that the area they had reached was wild and uninhabited, devoid of travelers and villages, and even of wild animals. For a while at least, they could travel in daylight.

Towards the end of November, Rinpoche became acutely aware of the need to conserve everyone's energy for what lay ahead. To this point they'd had to press on as fast as they could, but crossing the main Communist road, and then the Brahmaputra, would take all the focus and stamina they had. Beyond that, they dared not think.

Years of monastic discipline had allowed Rinpoche and the monks and lamas to eke out their rations. Now, though, he decided that they must turn to their reserve supply of *tsampa* – the one that they had entrusted to the stalwart fellow in the Tsophu Valley, on the understanding that at the end of the journey half would be his. To their dismay, they found that the man had not only eaten up his entire share of the *tsampa*, but theirs too. Then Rinpoche learned that the same thing had happened in other groups; again, people had not told him of their difficulties, not wanting to bother him, not with something that they knew could not be helped. The discoveries must have come as a bombshell to Rinpoche and the leaders: their prospects of a successful escape – of survival itself – had suddenly, shockingly dimmed.

Rinpoche did not comment on the errant individuals or the steep decline in everyone's chances. Instead, he saluted them all, saying that even in the dire straits in which so many found themselves, not one of the many wild animals they saw along the way had been killed for food: "Such compassionate self-control displayed by a whole band of desperately hungry people moved me greatly at the time, and it remains a treasured memory of those heart-searching days."[147]

We don't know what Yonten or the other attendants might have said to the hapless individual who had devoured their food. Yonten was, though, somewhat cynical about the refugees' self-control, saying that it "sounds sweet," and adding that they would have certainly supplemented their diet with wild animal meat if they had not taken the vow with Rinpoche. To him, their situation was blindingly plain: people were starving on their feet, and it took something more than simple self-control not to kill in order to survive.[148]

Rinpoche said little in his account about people's suffering on the journey, nothing about his own, instead leaving circumstances to speak for themselves. Yet their odyssey had spawned a new dimension, a wasteland of fatigue, hunger and starvation. Deep pangs had been succeeded by sharp, ravening pains as hunger burrowed ever deeper into stomachs, bodies burning first fat, then muscle to keep going. Starvation came with a cruel twist: earlier in the journey, pain had fallen mostly on older or weaker people; now starvation hit the youngest hardest, their growing bodies in the most intense pain from stomach contractions.

Palya Washutsong dismissed her own pains, saying that fear of the Chinese and determination to reach India overcame them all. "The pain is nothing. You have to reach India."[149] She and her fellow refugees found many sources of strength to master suffering and to keep going. Simple determination to escape oppression and reach their destination drove them on. Keeping spirits high through songs, good humor and joking lifted them all. The religious among them may have meditated on the pain, seeking to embrace it as part of a luminous whole. The encouragement of others, if only by example – the knowledge that others were experiencing all that they themselves experienced, yet remained strong and in good spirits – buoyed one up. Friends, fathers, mothers and leaders all played their part. Palya cherished above all the memory that, as she put it, "Rinpoche never lost his smile."[150]

As they trekked on they came to a fresh range of forbiddingly high mountains. At Rinpoche's urging, people had been making a special effort keep up a brisk pace; worn out, they had to make do with just the occasional short rest break. They managed to get over the high range without mishap but, not long afterwards, Tsepa once again confessed that he had no idea where they were.

Lost again, they approached the next line of mountains. It grew ever more daunting the closer they came. Moreover, they could see no way past them, no gaps or passes, no human trails or animal tracks they might follow. Surrounded on all sides by seemingly insurmountable peaks, and with no idea how to extricate themselves, Rinpoche turned to mirror divination.

The reading indicated the direction to take, and that they should look for a particular rock, which they must climb. With Rinpoche and Tsepa scouting ahead, directing the people behind when they had found a way, they came to an expanse of large boulders. They could cross them only by jumping from one to another, an exhausting, jarring method. Then Rinpoche spotted what looked like the specified rock, which they clambered up. From the top they saw in front of them a high mountain with a ridge on its shoulder, which they headed for.

It was a brilliantly sunny day. The climb through the deep snow proved to be less strenuous than crossing the boulder field had been, and most of them had dark snow goggles, which saved them from being blinded by snow glare. Once they were over the ridge they found the downslope steep and tricky; with no clear idea of where to go next, Rinpoche led them down to a small lake. Past the lake they were confronted by three further mountain ranges. Although each of them involved a steep, tiring climb, beyond the last one the ground sloped gradually downwards and the going became man easier.

On a day in early December another range loomed ahead – but on this one they could clearly make out a pass. Rinpoche took his binoculars and, accompanied by Tsepa, climbed up to the crest of the pass to survey the land ahead. As they reached it they were "amazed to see the Szechuan to Lhasa main road running along the mountainside below, less than a quarter of a mile away."[151]

They had reached the main Communist road which, ever since they had spotted it weeks before when they reached Kongpo, they had known they would have to cross. Rinpoche climbed back down to where the refugees were waiting, and urged them to stay where they were and to keep very quiet until he found a good spot to conceal them. This proved to be little problem in the boulder-strewn ground and, with everyone resting under cover, he returned to the crest line to reconnoiter.

Through the binoculars they could see that the road ran up and over the Serkyem Pass, which Tsepa knew to be very close to Lower Kongpo. There had been nothing simple or leisurely about the way they had come, but – whether by chance, blind luck, or the topographical powers of the mirror deity – they had arrived at more or less the precise point for which, all those weeks before, Tsepa had been aiming.

The pass was crossed by the new main road from China, used by the PLA to move troops, supplies and ammunition from Beijing to Central Tibet. From what Rinpoche and the others could see of it when they had surveyed it before, it was likely to be busy at all hours of the day and night. Getting hundreds of refugees across without being spotted would be a huge challenge, the most dangerous they had faced so far. They would need a simple plan and firm leadership, along with considerable focus and discipline on everyone's part.

Rinpoche decided to adopt the same approach they had used to cross the Pawo-Lhasa road: concealing themselves in the broken mountain terrain near the head of the pass before rapidly crossing the road. If necessary, they could hide among the rocks nearby or, in an emergency, in the ditch that ran alongside it. On Rinpoche's word, they would all cross as one, then keep going as fast as they could until they reached cover. They would have to stay totally quiet throughout – not because there was much chance of their being heard over the trucks' cacophony, but so that everyone could hear any on-the-spot commands Rinpoche might give. Their basic tactic for swiftly crossing the road would be familiar to an infantry soldier; and it would require a high level of courage and discipline from everyone if it was to succeed.

If the tactic they had use to cross the road was the same as before, this would be by far the greater ordeal. For a start, the window for crossing would be very tight: even though it was winter, truck convoys would be passing in a more or less unbroken stream throughout the night, headlights probing broad swathes of the landscape ahead. Many would be filled with armed troops, alert for anything and prepared to act with sudden, explosive violence. The shaky refugees would have to confront at close hand the menace they had been fleeing for months, hold their nerve as the alien machines raced at them out of the dark, headlights blazing, and then act promptly and with speed.

With plan and terrain clear, Rinpoche and Tsepa climbed down to where the refugees lay concealed. They all understood what lay ahead, and many were edgy and anxious, especially the older people; they were worried that, being so spent and weak, they might collapse under the strain, which they feared would lead to everyone's discovery. Rinpoche heard them out, and then laid out his plan, stressing that if a Chinese truck approached, everyone must immediately lie down in the ditch, and keep quiet and still. He also instructed younger people to carry the elders' baggage.

With everything explained, they rested. Rinpoche's narrative continues:

> "We waited till dark before approaching the road, but when we were some twenty yards away from it we suddenly saw the headlights of a lorry. Fortunately, there were a lot of rocks close at hand behind which we all ducked. I had to be very severe with one woman who, to help herself to control her fear, was chanting *mantras* in a loud voice; I told her that she must only whisper under her breath."[152]

The road snaked up a steep slope to the pass, and they had been able to spot the truck's headlights some while before the vehicle reached them, giving them time to conceal and compose themselves. Then they lay in the dark, listening to the unearthly sounds of the roaring engine and crunching gears, fearfully watching the headlights probing and playing over the rocks where they lay.

> "We held our breaths and the minutes seemed like hours, but eventually the lorry passed out of sight and earshot. Just as we were on the point of getting to our feet for the dash across – one man was actually standing up – we heard the noise of a second lorry. As it came near we heard the Chinese talking in high-pitched and, it seemed to us, excited voices; I was afraid it was because they'd seen us; however, all was well and the lorry passed by."[153]

They waited among the rocks for another five minutes, until Rinpoche rose and led them across the road and into the rocky terrain on its far side – leaving two men behind to brush over everyone's footsteps, erasing any sign of their passage.

As they walked on, the land leveled out and the air grew warmer. Rinpoche had been delighted by the refugees' composure under stress: "The discipline observed by everyone was beyond all praise; they looked very serious and no-one spoke a word."[154] His role up to this point in the journey had been akin to a general's: leading and inspiring the group, assessing the terrain, shaping the plan. At Serkyem Pass, though, when discipline had shown signs of cracking, he had taken on a sergeant-like role, sternly keeping individuals in line. He'd had no choice: no one else had the authority, there was no hierarchy of command, and the group leaders had no training in what to do in tight situations when courage faltered.

Still watching carefully for oncoming headlights, they hurried on down the valley for a further three miles, straining to put distance between themselves and the danger zone. At this point the woman whom Rinpoche had had to quieten at the pass suffered a total physical and mental collapse.[155] She was a nun traveling with a monastic party behind the lamas' group, and Rinpoche knew both her and her father. He had to make the unavoidable decision:

" ... it would have been too dangerous for the whole party if we had stopped for her, so we gave her what little food we could spare then left her; it was a horrid decision to have to take – it left a guilty feeling – but the safety of the whole group allowed of no other alternative."[156]

They shortly came to a thickly forested valley, which they turned into, and then made for a pass at its southern end. As they climbed, the older people were just behind the leaders, while the younger ones lagged behind. The elders had apparently been conserving their energy for this most demanding part of the journey, and having their loads carried for them had helped, although tiring out the youngsters.

The traveling party was approaching the Brahmaputra now, but there were still mountains to climb, ranges to cross. Rinpoche himself was exhausted, drained by the additional stress of getting the refugees across the Serkyem Pass. Akong Tulku and Yag Tulku rallied around to cheer him up, but this turned out to be a mixed blessing: Yag Tulku, anxious about further grueling ascents, plied Rinpoche with questions about what they would find beyond the mountain they were climbing. The gently ironic answer that maybe they would find a nice, warm and secluded valley did little to interrupt the queries, and Rinpoche tried another tack: "At last to shut him up I said, 'Perhaps we will find a still higher snow mountain.' That stopped him worrying."[157]

Crossing the pass out of the forested valley, they came to another chain of mountains. After reaching the first ridge line, they hiked along it until they found a small hollow surrounded by scrub, where they decided to camp. Although the rocky ground was too broken and uneven for comfortable resting, everyone was thankful to have somewhere safe to stop and relax. They were sufficiently concealed in the hollow to light fires, but still had to carefully screen them.

People turned to gathering firewood to boil water. The lamas still had small portions of tea, along with the required salt and butter: "After the first sip of our national beverage we all felt better."[158]

While Rinpoche waited for his share of stewed leather, Yonten, the group's cook, announced that he had been saving some *tsampa* for him, and proceeded to serve him up a portion. Rinpoche protested, saying that he wanted to share everything on equal terms, but Yonten would not back down: leather, he announced, was utterly unsuitable fare for his abbot. Rinpoche was touched by this consideration, but saddened that a line had been drawn between him and everyone else – until he heard that the other attendants had made the same arrangements for their lamas. Soon everyone was relaxing in the good cheer of food and companionship.

They had been pushing hard, had made a nerve-wracking crossing of the Communist highway and were spent. The need for rest was now more urgent than finding food, and they slept in the rocky hollow through the following day. While Rinpoche relaxed, a few men took his binoculars and climbed a nearby peak to survey the landscape. They could not yet make out the Brahmaputra, but, looking back, they watched as dozens of troop transports filled with PLA soldiers streamed along the road they had crossed the night before.

Although the refugees were somewhat restored by the break, they remained seriously tired and jittery. Some were becoming careless, and were forgetting to screen their fires at night and allowing them to smoke in daylight. Once again Rinpoche had to step in, firmly reminding them of the dangers to which such practice exposed everyone.

At dusk Rinpoche led the party out of the protected hollow and into a cold and biting wind, heading south towards the next range. When they reached it they found that its slopes were covered in grass and had a gentle gradient, a most welcome change. From the crest line they saw villages in the distance and, looming massively behind them, snow peaks that had to be the Himalayas.

They rested on the mountain grass throughout the next day, then, after nightfall, continued on down its southern slope. They were plainly in Lower Kongpo now, the area so dense with villages that many spilled halfway up the slopes of the surrounding mountains.

But at this relatively low altitude the mountains were thickly clothed in holly trees, which provided excellent cover for the refugees as they made their way over the slopes.

Maybe even more encouraging, they could not see any modern roads or hear the sounds of trucks. Perhaps the Chinese weren't concerned with the area, and felt no need to station troops here. If that was so, their prospects for the Brahmaputra crossing were good; on the other hand, it could also mean that the area was so firmly in the Communist grip that Tibetan proxies might be guarding the river for their overlords.

Before they reached the river they still had a series of low hills to cross, while detouring around valleys where wood smoke signaled the presence of villages. On their circuitous route they came to a small, closed valley, its ground so rough and broken up, and so thick with brushwood, that it was almost impossible to get through. They decided to stay where they were for the night – a decision whose wisdom was quickly confirmed when men's voices and barking dogs could be heard in the vicinity.

They were close to the Brahmaputra now – so close that they could start looking for a point on the heights from where they could make their way down to its banks. Shortly after dawn Rinpoche sent two men ahead to investigate; they reported that they had found a path leading down to the water's edge, but that on the way it passed very close to villages. This was far too risky a route, and Rinpoche led the group further eastwards along the top of the range, seeking a more prudent way down.

After hours of battling through dense, thorny scrub, they came to easier ground covered by fir and holly trees, where the air was much warmer. They went on until, late in the afternoon, they smelled wood smoke. Rather than risk blundering into a village in the dark, they camped where they were, settling down among boulders. Before turning in, Rinpoche asked a few men to look around the area to make sure of their security, waited for their report, and then joined everyone in a good night's sleep.

Late next morning, when the sun had climbed high enough above the eastern peaks to touch the Brahmaputra's valley, Rinpoche took his Russian binoculars and set out with Tsepa and the monk Urgyan-tendzin to reconnoiter. The mirror deity could offer no guidance now. Everything hung on what they could see of the lay of the land in the valley several thousand feet below.

They worked their way through fir and holly trees, moving forward down a spur until they found a position that gave them the most encompassing view. This high up, in their earth-colored clothing there was little chance that they would be spotted; and from here they could see both the full width of the Brahmaputra and its far bank. At first, as they looked over the landscape, things looked promising: the spur seemed to go all the way down to the water's edge, and the going looked good, relatively free of scrub and gullies.

But they soon realised that this way would not do after all. The spur's slope, steepening and curving away below them, hid most of the near bank; and they could not see the spur's lowest section nor where it led. In the dark of night they might stumble into a village or a PLA guard post, either of which meant disaster.

Returning to the camp, Rinpoche listened to the reports from the scouts he had sent out earlier, and then gathered his companions together for a briefing. They must go a few miles further along the ridge until they found a better way down; with no villages nearby, he was confident that it was safe to make this move.

Just after sunset, again using darkness to cover their movements, they set out along the ridge. While they saw no villages, they soon came across signs that people were around. First they spotted footprints, then they came to a nearby mill whose workers had left for the night. One of the refugees, a Lhatok man whose family's provisions had run out some while back, badly wanted to break down the door, take whatever food was there, and leave money behind to cover the cost. Rinpoche reined him in, pointing out that doing so would leave clear evidence of their presence – and in the morning, when the workers returned, the news would sweep through the area.

Trudging on, they came across a horse track, then heard the bell of a passing horse. The refugees were abuzz, wondering whether it was a Chinese horseman, or a villager from whom they might obtain supplies. Rinpoche said nothing and the moment passed; this close to the river they could not take any chances.

Further along the heights, through his binoculars Rinpoche spotted a rocky slope that appeared to lead straight down to the river. They could not spend more time and effort looking for a better route down: this was the one they would take. They explored the area until they found the full-flowing mountain stream that they would need for drinking water, and for soaking the coracles' leather hides. Then they picked a campsite nearby.

Late in the evening of December 12 they settled down to get what rest they could. Even in their worn-down and depleted state, many felt a growing excitement. Everyone knew that the next few days would see the culmination of all their sacrifices and efforts, would sustain their hopes or shatter them – would be when, as Tibetans say, rock met bone.

It had been almost nine years since Rinpoche had first considered an escape, over a year and a half since he had set out from Surmang, and eight months since he and his ten companions had left Drolma Lhakang. It had been three months since the three hundred refugees left the Tsophu Valley, carrying their worlds on their backs. Now, after an astonishingly arduous trek, most of them, including the leaders, were exhausted, sickening and dreadfully thin. For an unknown number the strain had proved too much and, somewhere back in the mountains, they lay dead or dying, or perhaps recovering somewhere in hope of future escape.

At acute and ever-mounting risk to his own life, Rinpoche had without demur accepted responsibility for getting the mass of people safely to India, and had borne the lion's share of caring for them and finding the way. Over the months the pressures bearing down on the nineteen-year-old had multiplied, and were now at their peak.

Parents, too, had been under immense stress, caring for and carrying their young children. Family men had looked on as their loved ones suffered and wasted away, starved for want of the food that was a father's avowed duty to provide. At least one, the Lhatok man who had wanted to break into the mill, appears to have gone half-mad under the strain, willing to throw it all away – not just for himself, but for everyone – to get food to his family.

But here, within gunshot range of the Communists, food was secondary. Everything now hung on secrecy, on staying hidden and concealed, on maintaining discipline. From the first day of the journey – for Rinpoche for almost a year before that – secrecy had been the iron rule, dictating their routes and when they had taken them, their daily course of action, the very clothes they wore. That rule was now overstressed and bending, close to breaking-point.

They would soon undertake the most daring of ventures, one that would be a fearsome challenge for even the fittest and most well-trained group. In the dead of night and under the very noses of the Communists, Rinpoche would lead the survivors in their bid to cross the great river. Then they would begin their ascent of the Himalayas.

PART III

12

The Crossing

Early on the morning of December 13, Rinpoche announced that it was time to build the coracles. When they reached the water's edge, everything – all their hopes of escape, their very lives – would depend on these small vessels, how many of them they could make and how sound they could make them.

People gathered the yak hides they had carried from the Tsophu Valley, together with as many of the remaining yakskin bags as they felt they could spare, and sank them in the stream to soak. Then they cut wood from nearby trees, choosing sturdier, straighter branches for the rectangular frame, pliable saplings for the ribs. When the hides and leather patches had softened, they formed them around the ribs, stitched them together and sealed the joints with resin they had scraped from trees. Then, while the leather dried out, they settled down to repair their shoes and clothing.

With the work under way, Rinpoche pondered the food situation. Maybe it would be possible to find someone in a remote village who would sell them supplies? Yet the area was surely under tight Chinese control; villagers – in fear for their lives should they be caught offering help to fleeing refugees, perhaps even for simply not revealing their presence – could just as easily turn out to be informers or spies as friends. Rinpoche again concluded that any move they made to acquire provisions could give their presence away. Once they were across the river, though, their chances might improve. On the Brahmaputra's far bank, the Himalayan side, where a troop garrison would be harder to supply, Communist strength might be lower; over there, villagers might be more willing to sell them food. Here, every hour spent on the mountain increased the chances of being spotted. It was best to complete the coracles and get across the river as soon as they could.

After two days' hard but cheerful work, with everyone pitching in, they had made eight coracles. Unwilling to waste a moment, Rinpoche announced that they would be going that very night: people were to follow him down in single file, and should remember that mindfulness and silence were crucial. A thrill of anticipation swept through the refugees, sidelining the pain, hunger and fatigue.

After dusk on the evening of December 14, Rinpoche, with the guide Tsepa at his side, led the party out of the campsite and down the ravine. With only scraps of food remaining between them all, their loads were much lighter and three men were available to port each coracle; Yonten, Urgyan-tendzin and Jamyang carried Rinpoche's and Akong Tulku's craft. But the coracles proved difficult to handle on the steep and rocky terrain and, even when held high aloft, their skins made loud scraping and crackling noises against hedges and tree branches. Mothers were meanwhile struggling to keep their babies quiet and, as young and old picked their way down the steep incline, progress in the dark was painfully slow. Most disquieting by far, the distance to the water's edge was turning out to be greater than they had thought. The further they went the more obvious it was that they would not have time to cross the river and hide the coracles before dawn.

Rinpoche halted the column. They dare not go on, and they were too far down the mountain to stay where they were; no matter how hard people might try to conceal themselves behind rocks or among trees and shrubbery, so many of them – and who knows how many babies – so close to a populated area patrolled by the PLA or its proxies were sure to be discovered. They had to retreat, high enough up the mountain to be beyond sight and hearing. Rinpoche and the lamas turned and headed back up, the others trudging along behind. Coming across a path, they followed it up until they reached a hollow high enough for them to safely stop. There they hid their coracle among holly trees, and prepared a rudimentary campsite.

They'd had no choice except retreat, but the crossing's postponement was to prove costly. The first sense that all was not well came soon: as the leading group settled down to rest, they realized that very few people had followed them up to the hollow. Somewhere, as the long line of refugees had reversed course and struggled back up the mountain, the link had broken. The lamas waited, wondering if the others had simply lagged behind, but no-one appeared. Deeply worried, Rinpoche could not sleep.

At first light on December 15, Rinpoche heard the sound of someone walking on dry holly leaves, the footsteps getting nearer every moment. Everyone was awake now, nerves stretched to breaking point. With the stranger almost upon them, Tsepa grabbed his gun, ready to shoot down any threat. Rinpoche firmly stopped him, reminding him that there could be no shooting under any circumstances. Apart from the vow they had taken, the sound of a shot from high on the mountain was sure to alert the Communists, killing their chances of escape. An edgy and embarrassed Tsepa retorted that Rinpoche should not make any noise himself.

When the source of the footsteps came into view, it turned out be a messenger from the missing refugees, overjoyed to have found them. He reported that everyone else was safely hidden lower down the slope in a holly thicket – but the rest of his news was not as good. Under the general stress and strain, and the huge letdown of the aborted crossing, discipline was falling apart in the lower camp. In spite of Rinpoche's repeated reminders, some refugees were making far too much noise while others had carelessly lit fires for warmth and to cook up leather. Rinpoche asked the messenger to remind people in that the rules he had laid down to protect everyone's safety must be strictly observed.

The messenger had another piece of unsettling news. The previous night, somewhere near the point where Rinpoche had reversed course, two men who were carrying a coracle had disappeared, and had not been seen since. Especially troubling, the

missing men were from the same Lhatok family as the man who had
wanted to break into the mill in search of food. Anything could have
happened to the missing men, but it was hard to avoid the thought
that, with their families frantic for food, the men had broken away to
see what they could find. Who knew where they had gone or what
they might get up to.

For now, there was nothing to do but rest, wait for further news
and prepare for the second crossing attempt that night. Rinpoche
asked the messenger to tell the people in the lower camp that they
would be leaving for the river soon after dark, and he would join
them just before departure. He stressed that it was imperative that
everyone be packed and ready to go when he arrived.

As the day grew brighter they looked around them, and were
relieved to see that the hollow they had chosen was a fine hiding
place, well screened from view either from above or below.
However, even after a thorough exploration of the slopes in their
vicinity, they could not find a spring or brook for drinking water.
This was now an even more pressing problem than the lack of food:
everyone in the group was dehydrated and, exposed as they were on
the southern slope under a cloudless sky, their day was going to be a
warm one.

Tsepa, ever willing, offered to climb down to the lower camp to
see if he could obtain water there. He also wondered aloud whether
he might continue on down to the nearest village to see if he could
get supplies; he felt that in his native Kongpo costume, the same one
worn by locals, he would be far less likely to arouse suspicion than
anyone else in the party. Again, Rinpoche would not countenance it;
any move that increased the risks of discovery was a dangerous one.

Down in the lower camp that morning, people talked quietly
among themselves about the missing men, and the threat their
disappearance posed. But the chief topic was the stirring fact that
Rinpoche was personally leading them across the Brahmaputra.
Almost everyone had assumed that he and the lamas' group would
go first and alone, ensuring their own safe crossing of the river while
leaving the refugees to make their crossing later, perhaps the

following night. After all, the expedition had first and foremost been Rinpoche's, and his and the lamas' escape was paramount; people knew all too well that they, and Rinpoche in particular, were prime Communist targets, their chances of surviving capture very small. Indeed, almost everyone *wanted* the lamas to cross first.

Rinpoche had not announced that he would be leading them across, nor did he mention his decision in his later account. But once the coracles had dried out, he had waited a few hours until dark and then simply roused and led the refugees down the mountain. It had taken everyone by surprise; fifteen-year-old Palya was as astonished as anyone else. It was deeply heartening to know that Rinpoche would be with them.

If Palya and the refugees were surprised and happy at Rinpoche's decision, Yonten was aghast. Ever since his uncle had passed on to him the responsibility for getting Rinpoche safely to India, he had proven himself a staunch, sometimes fierce protector; Rinpoche's life was more precious to him than his own. And from his years of travel in bandit-infested Kham, Yonten had a clear and earthy grasp of the perils ahead. It was obvious to him that trying to get hundreds of refugees down the mountain, past the villages and across the river – with all the greatly multiplied chances of discovery that entailed – would put his abbot's own safety in grave jeopardy. His worry at a high flame, Yonten begged Rinpoche to reconsider: he and the other lamas must go first and go alone; any other course would be "a big mistake."[159]

Rinpoche heard Yonten out but was unmoved: he would do his utmost to lead everyone across. No-one was more aware of the risks than he: throughout the escape, the group's large numbers had made everything more difficult, more dangerous. Yet Rinpoche also well knew that if he left the refugees to make their own way across, the dangers to them would be hugely amplified. There was no authority or hierarchy of command to take over from him, and there had already been disturbing signs of the breakdown of discipline when he was not personally present. What's more, there was a good chance that, out on the broad river under a full moon, even one or two coracles might be seen by sentries on shore – and after a single coracle was spotted, everyone's chances of escape would evaporate. For Rinpoche it was choiceless: here, at the most perilous point of the journey, he would not abandon people for whom he had accepted personal responsibility and whom he had brought all this way, not even at the cost of his own life.

With Yonten's entreaties quelled and Tsepa off to find water, Rinpoche and Urgyan-tendzin left the camp and headed up the mountain, climbing until they reached a spot where they could see both banks of the river. From here they could digest the full vista of what lay ahead and work out a viable route.

They saw that they were at the end of the range, and that Rinpoche's choice of a path down to the river had been a good one. A short way upstream the river narrowed: this was where they would cross. Although the route along the bank meant first passing near several villages, that danger was outweighed by the relatively short distance they would have to paddle in the slow and ungainly coracles. Then a dismaying detail caught their attention: all the houses on their side of the river, even a temple, were flying red flags, signaling their occupants' subservience to the Communists. Rinpoche's hyper-caution about making any contact with villagers had been well founded.

On the far shore, just downstream of their crossing place and close to the southern bank, they made out a narrow strip of land covered in holly trees. If they landed there, the trees would provide cover. They could see a backwater between the strip and the bank, but there seemed to be a dry passage that they could use to get across. Once ashore, they would have to cover about a quarter of a mile before reaching the first slope of the Himalayan foothills. A short way up the slope the track passed through a village, its houses and temples all flying the red flag. They would have to find a way through it, but once beyond it and some way up the mountain, the immediate dangers would be behind them.

As the day wore on, with nothing to be done but rest, Rinpoche and Urgyan-tendzin did not move. In other circumstances, even in their dehydrated and profoundly tired state, they might have celebrated the day; for under the dazzling sun and sky, their surroundings were magnificent. Far below, the legendary Brahmaputra wound along its valley before boiling into rapids and disappearing from view behind the eastern peaks. Facing them across the river was the fierce grandeur of the Himalayas, their northern slopes towering and dark in midwinter shadow. At their eastern end, Mount Namcha Barwa, one of the range's highest peaks, soared above them, its snowy crown glistening in the sun.

An ancient Kongpo prophecy tells of a day when the mountain's great spire will topple into the gorge below, the resulting flood pushing the Brahmaputra over the Himalayas and into India.[1] Such was Rinpoche's and Urgyan-tendzin's mood that they might have felt that the catastrophe could happen that very day. They were, Rinpoche wrote, "feeling very depressed."[16] From their high vantage point, they saw all too vividly what lay ahead: however auspicious a full moon might be, however well lit their way, it was going to be a dark night.

The reality was that the crossing – indeed their whole brave venture – teetered on the edge of impossibility. Rinpoche had understood that for months, at least since their time on the plateau above the Nyewo Valley, when he had told Tserge Washutsong that very few of the refugees would reach India. His view may have come from a clear-eyed assessment of the fearful obstacles they would face, or from a mirror divination.

From this point, the obstacles were never clearer, the picture never bleaker. Again, time was the key. Running out of it had wrecked the previous night's attempt to cross, and Rinpoche now knew that – even with a supreme effort – there were hardly enough hours in the night for what they had to do. They would again have to accomplish what would normally be asked only of a fit and disciplined group. Could the exhausted refugees grasp the urgency of their plight, the need for a highly accelerated pace; did they have the energy and stamina to respond even if they dearly wanted to; could they move fast, maintain silence and stay together in the darkness? If not, when dawn broke they would be out in the open, ripe for Communist capture or attack.

And then there were the coracles. In just two days, using only what they had carried on their backs or could gather on the mountain, people with scant experience of coracle-making had crafted vessels that would be carrying up to eight adults and their baggage. It was a remarkable feat, but there was no avoiding the grim truth: the coracles were makeshift and prone to mishap. Traditional, well-founded craft were constructed of large, specially selected and tanned hides that were worked around a mainly willow framework, the seams sealed with animal fat. The refugees' coracles were a patchwork of hides, and the odds and ends of yakskin bags, formed around ribs made of whatever saplings were nearby, cobbled together using the needles and cord with which they repaired their shoes and clothes; and the tree sap they used to seal the seams was not as malleable as animal fat and, with many more joints and stitches than in a normal coracle, there was a frightening chance of leaks. Would leather that had been soaked to make it soft and pliable stay waterproof; would the framework stand up to the strain? Looming over it all, none of the refugees could swim – and anyway, their heavy clothes, bags and boots would, after a few moments' buoyancy, swiftly soak up water and drag them to the bottom.

What's more, they had far too few of the small craft. Although there had been no opportunity to take a roll call – there was little point to one – Rinpoche had a fair idea of the numbers on the mountain.[161] It was obvious that each of the eight frail coracles would have to make several trips back and forth across the river if there was to be any hope of getting everyone over. On the previous night's attempt, they had run out of time before even one could set off. How would they find time for several waves of them? They would have to start early, then move quickly, quietly and in good order downhill, along the shore and into the coracles, if they were to have any chance at all of pulling it off.

Even if everything went almost supernaturally smoothly during the descent and crossing, even if Communist troops or their proxies did not intervene, what then? Where would they find enough food for the mass of hungry people flooding ashore into the small community on the south bank? And even with replenished food supplies, there awaited the fearful challenge of a midwinter climb over the Himalayas.

It would be a desperate venture, but also a mind-stoppingly heroic and audacious one. Rinpoche best understood the odds stacked against them, yet everyone knew what they faced; he would lead the endeavor, but all of them would undertake it.

Around four o'clock in the afternoon, even now warmed by the dying sunlight, Rinpoche and Urgyan-tendzin still sat on the mountainside. At times they meditated, resting and refreshing the mind for what lay ahead. Abruptly, a small cloud of crows appeared and swirled directly overhead. In the lowering gloom, as the birds' cries rasped the air and their black wings shadowed the slopes beneath, the atmosphere felt sinister and foreboding.

With darkness near, they stood up and made their way down to their campsite. Tsepa had brought up water from the lower camp, and the two men were able to quench their powerful thirst. He had also brought a small torrent of dismaying news. Without Rinpoche's steadying hand and in spite of his strict and repeated warnings, a few people had thrown caution to the wind and gone down to a village to try to get food for their families. Although they had been able to obtain a few items, the frightened villagers who did sell the food wanted nothing further to do with them. To the lamas' growing alarm, Tsepa then told them that when the food-seekers returned, they confirmed that the two Lhatok men who had gone missing the previous night had indeed been up to no good – they had made straight for the nearest village and stolen a bullock, which they drove a short way up the mountain and slaughtered. Following the theft, the authorities had arrested two innocent villagers and hauled them away in chains.

Whether or not the people who had sold food to the refugees later informed the Communists of the presence of refugees, it was very probable that the two arrested innocents had, in pleading their case, aroused suspicions in the minds of the authorities. Perhaps there were refugees around, on the mountain; if so, they were almost certainly trying to cross the river and make for the Himalayas. Maybe all that the Communists really did not know at this point was precisely when and where the attempt would be made; maybe they were already on high alert, posting additional sentries and watchposts.

Tsepa's final piece of news was no better. The villagers who had sold the food had said that every Himalayan pass would be deep in midwinter snow, and that it would be impossible for travelers to get through. When Tsepa was done, Rinpoche said nothing. None of what he had said changed their plans in the slightest; he wrote: "There was no other solution for us but to go on."[162]

Rinpoche waited until it was quite dark before he and the lamas and attendants hefted up their packs and headed down to the lower camp. When they arrived they found that, in spite of his strict instructions, people were still busy packing. While they waited, one of Rinpoche's attendants noticed that a small bag of *tsampa* he had been saving for his abbot was missing; sure that a small boy he had seen lurking around had taken it, when he spotted him he lost his temper and hared off in hot pursuit. As people tried to prevent the angry man from beating the boy, he grew more furious. Finally, pent-up stress and emotions erupted, and before long everyone in the vicinity was shouting and arguing for one side or the other.

As the mood turned hysterical, Rinpoche stepped in. Grabbing the attendant by the arm he told him to control himself, that this was the most critical time in their escape, and that every minute was valuable. He then spoke severely to the refugees, pointing out that they were neglecting their urgent packing. The simmering attendant started to explain to Rinpoche why he had gone after the boy, but Rinpoche interrupted him, saying: "I don't think that he has done so, but in any case, let him have it. At this time we all need strength, and I hope that if he has taken the food it will help him to work all the harder."[163] He added that a greater concern was the two innocent villagers who had been punished for the bullock's theft by two of their own.

It took a while longer for the over-wrought refugees to complete the packing, but at last they were ready to go. As Rinpoche and Akong Tulku set off down the slope, everyone following behind, the two friends joked together: Rinpoche wondered aloud about the very heavy load that his friend was carrying and whether he should really be carrying that much, saying teasingly that "it might end in your collapse." Akong Tulku laughed and assured Rinpoche that on this decisive night he was more than capable of it, and that Rinpoche should "please remember that I am tougher than you."[164]

Shortly after reaching level ground and moving out onto the river bank's open terrain, they heard the sound of voices: there were villages nearby. They could also hear dogs barking, but they were somewhere off in the distance. With everyone being as quiet as they could and moving along in good order, they came to the Brahmaputra's sandy shoreline: they could see the surge of water just a few yards away, its dark surface broken by occasional glints. Beyond it, their peaks silhouetted against the brightening sky, the refugees could make out the Himalayas bulking dark and colossal above them.

As they worked their way along the bank, Rinpoche went from group to group, quietening and encouraging the frightened people, exhorting them to keep together, to move faster. At one point he had to run off into the dark after stragglers heading in the wrong direction. He was again having to combine the roles of general and sergeant, leading and inspiring people while holding them together, moving forward.

As they neared their launch point, Rinpoche spotted a man in Kongpo dress hiding behind a thorn bush. When he looked directly at him, the man disappeared. A few minutes later he saw another man, this one carrying a rifle; he was in Kongpo dress but had a lighter complexion, suggesting to Rinpoche that he might be Chinese. There was every indication that the Communists and their Tibetan proxies were on the alert and lying in wait.

Just as the full moon rose, Rinpoche wrote, his group "reached the river and were the first to embark."[165] Yonten's memories of those highly-charged minutes were strikingly different, belying the mood of a stately cruise on a sunlit afternoon. Although Rinpoche's baggage had been loaded into the lamas' coracle and they were ready to leave, he continued to walk up and down the bank among the refugees, talking to them, helping them to organize around their coracles, calming them, all the while ignoring Yonten's anxious urgings to board his coracle and leave. Finally, with Yonten pleading, "Let's go! Let's go!" – and, from the sound of it, almost physically bundling Rinpoche into the coracle – he climbed in, and they pushed away from the bank and paddled out into the broad, strong-running current.[166]

Even though they were crossing a narrow part of the river, and even with Urgyan-tendzin and Akong Tulku's older brother Jamyang, two strong and capable men, paddling as hard as they could, it seemed to take an eternity to get the small, heavily-laden craft across. But the coracle proved strong and watertight – Urgyan-tendzin had probably been careful to make it himself – and the eight of them reached their landing point without incident.

They arrived on the holly-covered strip of land near the southern shore as planned. Behind them other coracles were coming across or loading up. Just as soon as Rinpoche and his companions were disembarked, the indomitable Urgyan-tendzin set off back to the northern bank for another load of passengers.

As Rinpoche was getting his bearings, he heard a shout from mid-river, a man calling him by name. Paddling his family across, the man was panicking: his coracle may have been taking on water, or he had found the paddling too much for him, and he was yelling that he was not going to make it and that they were all going to drown. Rinpoche called out that he would be fine if he just kept going, and before long the man and his passengers were safely ashore nearby. By now, three loads of passengers had landed, and Rinpoche walked along the bank making his presence known, talking to each group, giving instructions and a brief sketch of the situation.

Out of the night Rinpoche heard the unmistakable sound of a gunshot. At first he thought that it had been fired by a refugee – then there was a second shot, immediately followed by shrill shouts, which Rinpoche recognized as Chinese, after which the shots quickly swelled into a fusillade. On the strip they could clearly hear the bullets as they whizzed and cracked by close overhead, the firing so shocking, so loud and heavy, that at first it was hard to tell which direction it was coming from. The storm of gunfire went on without pause, growing heavier by the second.

Akong Tulku's younger brother, Jampal, had been in the lamas' coracle, wrapped up in his lambskin coat against the intense cold. He had not heard gunfire before and didn't know what was happening. With no sense of a bullet's deadly power, he was calm until he saw how scared an older lama was – a man with experience of both guns and the Communists – and then became terrified.[167] About halfway across the moonlit river, young Palya was sitting behind her father, who was rowing furiously to get them to shore; listening to the percussive splash of bullets as they hit the water around the coracle she was terror-stricken. On the strip, as rounds thudded into the ground and ricocheted off rocks nearby, Rinpoche was spurred by the fear of being hit, thinking: "I will never give up ... I will go on to teach."[168]

These were clearly no warning shots – their attackers were shooting to kill.[169] In the midst of the shattering onslaught, refugees on the northern bank continued to board coracles and paddle hard for the far shore. Within a matter of minutes, about fifty people had gathered around the landing point on the strip of land.[170]

With a number of people now safely ashore, Rinpoche and a few companions ran to the end of the strip to find the small patch of dry land that he and Urgyan-tendzin had discerned, their bridge to the Brahmaputra's south bank – but after a rapid scouting of the area, no-one could find it. Maybe the river had risen late in the day from a rainstorm upstream; maybe it had been a trick of light conjured up by their binoculars and the distance. Whatever the reason, their bridge to the south bank was nowhere to be found.

Exposed and vulnerable under the storm of gunfire, they had to act fast. Rinpoche was now sure that the firing came from somewhere near their launch point on the north bank. He thought that, if the Communist presence was so heavy there, it was likely that there would also be large numbers lying in wait on their side of the river.

Unwilling to let their most cherished possessions fall into Communist hands, Rinpoche told everyone to throw their heavy baggage into the river. And so it was that the ancient Brahmaputra opened her waters to receive their wealth: coins, jewelry, sacred texts and precious relics – treasures carefully guarded and handed on for many centuries, deeply venerated ritual objects from great teachers of the past, lovingly preserved texts and treasures seen before only by the highest lamas, the thousand page volume on meditation Rinpoche had written in the Valley of Mystery, the legend of Shambhala he had composed at Langtso Kha – all of this, all that they had carried on their backs on the trek through the wilderness, was hurled without a second thought into the river.

Their heavy baggage gone, they still had to find a way across the backwater. If they could not, they would be trapped, open to an attack whenever the Communists chose to deliver it. Rinpoche, who had held onto a few selected bags of sacred texts and treasures, ran up to Jampal and a young friend of his, saying, "Get up, get up!" and, placing a bag each around their necks, grabbed them by the hand, ran into the backwater and began to wade across. It quickly proved impossible: the water was deep and was soon up to Jampal's neck – it was, he said, "absolutely terrifying cold." Rinpoche turned around and dragged the two youngsters back up onto the strip.[171]

Their only hope now was to try to use whatever coracles had been left on the strip's shoreline. A handful of men dashed off to look for them and, after a long while, returned with two abandoned craft. Heavily waterlogged, they had been a struggle to carry. This was chilling: it seemed that the coracles had indeed sprung leaks – here was a quarter of their tiny fleet. How many had gone down midriver, their passengers unheard amid the roar of guns?

Waterlogged or not, with everyone desperate to get to the relative safety of the main bank there was a sudden rush for them. Rinpoche intervened, explaining to the frightened refugees that some would have to wait while others got across.

Already, even where they were amid the storm of gunfire, several people in the leading groups had come to a certain perception, one that they would hold for a lifetime: they were sure that the two men who had sneaked off the night before and killed the bullock had given them all away – that without that betrayal they would not be in their dreadful plight, and that by now many more people would have made it over the river to safety.[172]

As the ferrying of refugees across the backwater began, a small group on the strip was focused in the opposite direction, sunk in one of the many tragedies of that night. Palya, her brother Drupju and others of her Washutsong family had landed a few minutes earlier, and now sat near the shoreline, huddled close against cold and gunfire. Her father, after disembarking them, had paddled back to fetch the rest of the family. Palya and the others waited for what seemed a lifetime, staring intently towards the north bank. Finally they made out the small, dark shape of a coracle, and a while later were overjoyed when they saw that it was the father returning with family. Then Palya was struck dumb with grief: in the maelstrom on the north bank, her father had been unable to find her beloved five-year-old sister.

It was near sunrise now, the coming day ushered in by the roar of weaponry. Time had shrunk for the refugees, with safety still some way off. Soon after reaching the main bank, a wave of panic swept through them – but this time, before Rinpoche could intervene, a few dozen people had dashed off into the gloom, not to be seen again. With others still waiting on the strip or being ferried across, this left only Rinpoche's group and a small peasant family together on the main bank. Yonten called out that he would stay behind to ferry people across the backwater in one of the coracles, telling Rinpoche that he should carry on up the mountain, where he would find him later.

With dawn upon them, they had to move quickly or they would be spotted in the open. They set off southwards, walking fast towards the Himalayan foothills. Gunfire from across the river was still heavy, but as yet there was none nearby. They had no time to consider the best route – nor, crushingly, could they try to find food. Their one remaining chance lay in finding cover quickly, as high up the mountain as they could get.

Rinpoche now had most of the lamas' group with him, including Akong Tulku, Yag Tulku, Tsethar the bursar, Tsepa the guide and his wife, his own and Yag's attendants, along with the peasant family who had joined them. There was no sign of Urgyan-tendzin, who had headed back to the north bank for refugees, nor of Akong Tulku's older brother, Jamyang. Young Jampal had also become separated in the tumult and was nowhere to be seen.

They had already gone some distance when, perhaps to no-one's surprise, Tsethar the bursar announced that he did not at all approve of the way things were going. In a rage, he harangued Rinpoche in front of the others, telling him that he had been wasting far too much time trying to save people. What was more, rather than heading up the mountain, their best course of action was to find a hiding place nearby, then bide their time until they could return to the river to retrieve whatever they could of their baggage. The bursar was adamant: whatever the others did, he himself was going back.

Rinpoche asked Tsethar to reconsider. They had climbed some way toward their first objective, the village, and it would take him a while to get back to the river bank. By then it would be light, and he would be caught in the open with nowhere to hide. But the older man, shaken to the quick by the sight of their last wealth and treasure so swiftly consigned to the river, would have none of it. He was going back and, with Yonten, would find them later on the mountain. With no time for further talk, Rinpoche told him that his own plan, once they were beyond the village, was to continue up the slopes until they found a suitable place to hide. With that the group resumed their climb, while the bursar turned and headed back down to the river.

Reaching the village was taking far longer than they had thought it would. They'd had nothing to eat or drink since early the previous evening and everyone was tired to the depths, their physical energy drained away. In the cold dawn, the clothes they had soaked trying to wade through the backwater, some up to their necks, were beginning to freeze hard and solid against their skin.

Then, as they continued upwards, young Jampal came up from behind and joined them. Having quite overcome his terror during the crossing, he had managed to salvage a brick of tea and a kettle from the river bank, which he was carrying. He had then found the lamas' route, and brought with him a nun who had become separated from her own group.

Just after dawn the small group cautiously approached the village. They could see no way around, and had no choice but to try to go through it. People were stirring: herdsmen could be seen taking their cattle out for grazing in the surrounding fields, while families were appearing on the balconies of their homes – some with the lighter skin that marked them as Chinese. Still, creeping along behind hedges, the group made their way through the village without raising the alarm, and made their way thankfully onto the open ground beyond.

A fresh danger rose in front of them: the track wound over a strip of chalky ground entirely devoid of trees, rocks or other cover. Like black brush strokes on calligraphy paper, their dark, sodden clothing would make them terribly visible against the whitish chalk. Once again, there was no option but to keep going. They spotted a herdsman further down the slope who seemed to be looking directly up at them, but they ignored him and kept climbing.

Having crossed the chalk with no sign of alarm from below, they came to higher ground that was well covered by undergrowth and bushes. Here they could relax for a moment and use the vantage point to survey the scene around the river. In the ongoing gunfire they could see no movement on the near bank, the backwater or the holly-covered strip offshore; the river was empty of coracles, and there were no signs of people trying to cross. Near their launch point on the northern bank, though, they could make out large numbers of people quietly gathered around fires, apparently resigned to the calamitous end of their great, brave venture.

This was no time for reflection and, while they all desperately needed rest, they could not stop now. The group was still only a few hundred feet up the slope, and the ground was fairly open. Anyone from the village would notice them if they looked up, while anyone with binoculars trained on the mountain would quickly spot them. After climbing a short way further up, they came to a copse of their allies, the holly trees. They knew that if they climbed any higher they would again be on open ground and, although they still felt too close to the village for comfort, they were utterly exhausted. They decided to stop and take cover among the trees, lying low until they felt ready to go on and it seemed safe to do so.

As they settled down they could see people walking around in all directions below them, obviously not busy with daily chores but on an active search: the PLA and their proxies were hunting anyone who might have got away. At one point the lamas heard the crunch of footsteps coming nearer and nearer, then veering away at the last moment in another direction. Later they heard someone walking close by, along with the thumping sound of a rifle being used as a walking stick.

There were now intermittent gaps in the gunfire. Lying in the shadow of the holly trees, it struck them that they could hear none of the usual cheerful singing as people went about their work in the nearby village or took out the cattle for grazing – herdsman merely shouted at their animals. Throughout the day the sound of gunfire rose and fell, now also coming from their side of the river. Adding to the cacophony, the Chinese were constructing a road nearby and occasional explosions shook the ground beneath them. Some in the group may have wondered whether the wrathful gods of heaven and earth had turned against them.

The threats around them were alarming, but their immediate situation was grimmer. They were at last off their feet and resting, but they were extremely thirsty and hungry, and terribly cold. Unlike their camp on the northern mountain, where the midwinter sun had warmed them, here it was blocked by the mountain at their backs. Although they had climbed only a relatively short way up, to around ten thousand feet, during the day the temperature on the shadowed slope was well below freezing.

There was no way to thaw or dry out their clothes, which were now rigid with ice. For some it had been excruciating even to lie down, the ice pressing into their legs like knives as they bent. Nor, with their hunters nearby, could they move to keep warm: they lay on a bed of dry holly leaves that crackled loudly whenever they shifted position. Although they made several attempts to open their packs in search of scraps of food, they had to give up each time when footsteps were heard nearby. For water, they moistened their lips with hoarfrost scraped from nearby rocks.

And so they lay, nearly immobile in the dark of the holly trees, encased in their suits of ice. As time crawled by, they kept up their spirits with quiet bantering and quips. At one point Rinpoche again teased Akong Rinpoche about his baggage – all of which he had jettisoned at the river – saying that he himself, being more modest, had managed to retain most of his own. At another, after Rinpoche's attendant had proposed that it was the perfect time to practice *tummo*, a Tibetan Buddhist exercise for generating inner heat, Yag Tulku pointed out jokingly that getting to the necessary sitting position would give their position away, not to mention the loud breathing that was part of the technique. Later, there was subdued laughter when an edgy Tsepa tried to quieten them, saying that he could hear someone approaching, and Rinpoche whispered: "perhaps this time, it is the spirits who are coming to protect us."[173]

For Rinpoche, the day in the holly copse seemed dreadfully long. The temperature stayed low and, although there was some slight warming around midday, it plummeted toward evening and became bitterly cold. One of their worst moments came when they heard gunfire near the village, and feared that the Communists had spotted refugees and were shooting them. But the raw truth was they had scant idea of what had happened to the others: how many had managed to hide or escape, how many had survived, how many had been shot or drowned.

There had been no chance that anyone from their party could find them during the day, and there was next to none now. They could see no point in waiting longer, and needed to get much higher up the mountain before they could feel safe.

An hour or so after dark, with the gunfire finally died down to nothing and no sign of anyone nearby, they decided to move. Their clothes stiff and heavy with ice, they struggled to their feet, turned their backs to the river and began to climb.

13

The Himalayas

In pitch darkness, Tsepa led the little group upwards. Rinpoche had surveyed the slope the previous day and had a fair sense of the route, but no moonlight fell on this side of the mountain and the going was rough and unpredictable, with rocks, boulders, stunted bushes, copses of trees, abrupt rises and steep ravines along the way. And the cold was piercing, far below freezing point.

It was an immense relief to be climbing away from the Communists and their proxies – a relief to be moving at all, getting circulation back into chilled bodies after the day's unending ordeal. But circulation revived feeling and, with it, the ache of overstrained muscles and joints. And although climbing generated enough heat to melt some of the ice in their clothing, there was no evaporation in the frigid conditions. They knew that when they stopped the ice would be back.

The escapee group now consisted only of the lamas and their attendants, Tsepa the guide and his wife, Akong Tulku's younger brother Jampal and the nun he had rescued from the river bank, and the small peasant family who had joined Rinpoche there – thirteen or fourteen people in all, just a few more than the number with which they had set out from Drolma Lhakang eight months before.

They knew nothing of the fate of those from the leaders' group who had been left behind. Their three stalwarts – strong, able, travel-wise men – were missing: they had last seen Urgyan-tendzin paddling back across the Brahmaputra into the firestorm to try to bring over more people; they had left Yonten near the south bank, ferrying refugees from the land strip to shore; and apparently Akong Tulku's older brother Jamyang had, like Tsethar, returned to the river to try to salvage what he could of their family's discarded wealth and possessions. They had no idea what had happened to the fifty or more refugees who had made it across the river, only to panic and run for the mountain, or what fate had befallen the many more left on the Brahmaputra's north bank, trapped in the open by morning.

They climbed for as long as they could, straining to put distance between themselves and their pursuers. Finally, after five punishing hours they could go no further and decided to stop for the night. They had also reached the level of the fir trees, which offered some shelter from the weather while also shielding them from the view of anyone heading their way.

The moon had risen, and although blocked from reaching them on the northern slope, its cold light bathed the Brahmaputra's banks and the mountains that they had come down the previous night. There was no sign at all of the refugees, no campfires to mark their presence, nothing to indicate that anyone had passed that way or that anything of import had happened there; only the occasional shiver of light broke the river's dark surface.

By now the lamas' food provisions were gone, along with their last hopes of replenishing them. They managed to scratch together a few handfuls of *tsampa* from the residue in the food pack, mix it with hoar frost scraped from rocks and leaves, and eat. Finding some hollow logs, they worked their way inside, hoping that the trunks would provide some protection against the cold.

The mere taste of food had lifted their spirits. As they settled down inside their log, Rinpoche's attendant began a conversation with him which he found "magnificent."[174] The monk said that their recent ordeal had been a spiritual lesson for him, that he was feeling quite at ease with their situation and was sure that the worst was behind them. Rinpoche reminded him that they were still in Communist-occupied territory, and that they were being actively hunted and could still be captured the next day. The young man implored him not to talk that way, but Rinpoche said: "this is only talk, we may actually have to go through this experience and if so, will it still be a test of meditation for you?"[175]

Rinpoche raised his voice to ask Yag Tulku's opinion on their situation. The older lama's attention had been elsewhere, and he asked what they had been talking about. After Rinpoche summarized, Yag Tulku, true to form, said that he was sure that the danger was past, and asked what Rinpoche thought lay beyond the mountain. Rinpoche gave what had become his usual reply, that they would find another icy range. He added that it would "provide a still better opportunity for us to practice the *yoga* of inner heat, for this time we will be able to take up the correct posture."[176] Everyone laughed, and the downcast moment was gone.

They tried to sleep, but tension and the stabbing cold kept them awake: in their icy clothes, the log refuges were of little help. Just before dawn, sheer exhaustion tipped them into a doze – almost immediately broken by a loud and urgent whisper from Tsepa: "Wake up, wake up, someone's coming!"

Instantly awake and alert, they could hear the sound of frost crunching underfoot, then a voice. As everyone held their breaths, Rinpoche whispered to Yag Tulku: "You remember our conversation of last night?" In the half-light they could make out a figure coming towards them up the slope. Tsepa stood up and brought his rifle to bear, while Rinpoche and his attendant whispered fiercely to him, begging him not to fire.

As the figure drew near they saw that it was a woman, and then recognized her as one of the peasant couple who had joined them back at Kino monastery. She was followed by her husband and, just behind, by Yonten and Tsethar. After a relieved and jubilant reunion, the new arrivals sat down to tell their story.

※

Soon after dusk the previous evening, around the time that Rinpoche and the others had left the copse of holly trees to begin their climb, the tall river grass on the Brahmaputra's south bank had begun to stir. A number of people who had been trapped there – including Akong Tulku's brother, Jamyang, the youngsters Palya and Drupju, their father and other members of their Washutsong family – were on the move.

They'd had to lie almost totally still throughout the day, hidden deep in the river grass, terrified of being spotted. While almost everyone's clothes had been soaked through during the crossing, the sun gradually dried them out. And one of the family had managed to keep hold of a kettle, which they were able to fill surreptitiously with water and scraps of *tsampa,* and pass quietly from one to another.

Yonten and Tsethar were nearby. Yonten had continued ferrying people across the backwater until the last possible moment, then scrambled into a hiding place; Tsethar, on his salvage mission, had been trapped in the open by daylight before he could even reach the bank, had spotted Yonten and taken cover with him. Their hiding place was close to the track between the backwater and the village that Rinpoche's group had crept through earlier.

Very close to the action, they watched as PLA soldiers and their Tibetan proxies scoured the area. Sometimes their hunters passed close enough to be overheard: it sounded as if they had tracked down and captured several refugees, and the hidden listeners grew increasingly worried lest Rinpoche and the others were among them. They heard too that sizeable quantities of gold coins, silver jewelry and personal possessions had been found strewn along the water's edge, the perceptible wreckage of ruined lives.

Yonten and Tsethar had waited until dusk, then set out up the slope, following the general direction that Rinpoche's group had taken. Yonten, having lost his own boots to the river, was wearing an old pair of Rinpoche's he had extricated from his pack. Within a few minutes they were joined by the peasant family from Kino, and made their way through the nearby village without mishap in the dark, and started up the slope.

They kept going throughout the long night, stopping only for quick rest breaks. With the first light of dawn they began a zig-zag course up the mountain, spreading their search pattern, peering into the gloom for any sign that the leaders' group had passed this way. Edgy and exhausted, they were occasionally startled by the sudden cries of birds shocked awake by the unfamiliar presence of people.

Just before the sun cleared the peaks, Yonten spotted newly made footprints, stamped dark and vivid in the frost. On one of them he recognized the manufacturer's symbol from the rubber heel of Rinpoche's Chinese-made boots. They followed the prints until, not long afterwards, they caught up to the group. For Yonten, meeting everyone again was like a "revival of the dead."[177]

As they concluded their story, Rinpoche grew alarmed. If Yonten could so clearly make out their footprints in the frost, so could pursuers – and no sun would reach their side of the mountain to burn off the frost during the day. Someone might have already picked up their trail, alerted his comrades and be in hot pursuit.

Once again, they had no choice: they must keep climbing hard, and would have to do so in the full light of day. They were all exhausted beyond measure; Rinpoche, who had borne by far the greatest strain, had not slept for three full nights. Yet the going was easier in daytime, and they kept climbing – only stopping, then remaining quite still, whenever someone heard a suspicious sound.

In late afternoon, Tsethar, who had been climbing throughout the night and now the day, felt that they were on the verge of a complete breakdown and urged a halt. The group still had some tea and butter left, and wood was collected and a hole dug for a fire. Rinpoche found the tea wonderfully reviving: "The drink seemed a meal in itself and everyone had a good night."[178]

On December 18, two days from the Brahmaputra, they climbed over bare, open ground.[179] They felt quite relaxed about it. This high above the river there was little chance of being spotted from below, nor was it likely that anyone could track them now. They were confident that they had lost their pursuers. As people began to ease up, Tsethar, the peasant family and Rinpoche's young attendant lagged further and further behind.

At around sixteen thousand feet they came to the crest line. There they stopped, sat down and surveyed the way they had come. Below them lay the shadowed bulk of the slopes they had climbed and, further below, almost insignificant from this height, the Brahmaputra. To the north and east a vast ocean of mountains stretched to the horizon and beyond, to East Tibet and Kham. It was a profoundly moving moment for them all:

> From high up on the mountain we could see the many ranges that all our party had crossed together with such courage and determination, before we became separated at the Brahmaputra. We felt very sad, not knowing what had befallen our many friends and comrades. We could clearly see both the river and its backwater, and through my field glasses I could distinguish a black patch, which I took to be one of our coracles.[180]

Still, standing silhouetted on the skyline, even at this altitude there was some risk of being spotted from below; and after a few minutes, they climbed down from the ridge and headed on, leaving behind their last views of the river, the mountains and the homeland they had known.

Finding a sheltered spot below the crest, they rested there while Tsepa went ahead to reconnoiter. He returned to say that there was a valley ahead that appeared to be quite wild, with no sign of a village or any other human habitation. With the way ahead clear, in bright sunlight the small party headed away from the ridge, beginning their crossing of the great Himalayan divide, the range separating Tibet and the Asian continent from India.

Although they were cheered by the knowledge that from here on they would be traveling in daylight, and might soon be going downhill, they were walking more slowly, drained by their hard-driving climb for the heights. Most of them were painfully thin and worn out, their bodies' reserves seriously depleted; and, while they had no clear notion of what lay ahead, they knew that it was going to be hard, with possibly weeks of journeying to come before they reached the Indian border. In reality, although they had already accomplished a remarkably challenging journey, their most perilous moments were still to come, the full crisis barely a week away.

Descending into the valley, they came across a path which they decided to follow. Before long they spotted footprints, which they stopped to examine; even up here in the Himalayan wildlands they could not take risks. On close perusal the tracks seemed to be Tibetan, old and of no immediate concern. Further along the valley they noticed a herdsman's hut and made their way towards it, hoping to shelter there for the night. As they came up to it, though, they saw that it was broken down, the roof fallen in.

Whatever disappointment they might have felt at finding the hut ruined was made up for by their surroundings. The valley was small and sheltered, almost snug, and they were in a level field that was well protected from wind by the surrounding rocks. Able to fully take their ease here, they slaked their thirst from a nearby stream; then, after laying out their wet and icy clothes to dry, they enjoyed the luxury of a good wash. At dusk they gathered wood and built a fire. For the first time since crossing the river, they were able to warm themselves.

While they relaxed, they considered the course ahead. Tsepa had no knowledge of this part of the country, no idea what route to follow, which direction to take. Rinpoche resorted to mirror divination. The vision's directions were clear: after climbing the snow peak to their immediate west, they would see ahead of them another range with three separate crest lines; they should cross the center one, after which there would be no more high ranges to climb.

As they sat bathed in the glow of the setting sun and warmed by the fire, Yag Tulku – revived by their surroundings and no doubt moved by the thought that they would soon be climbing their last high mountain – gave a short inspirational talk to the others, expressing his confidence that they would reach India. With that, they settled down for the night.

The next day, December 19, would be a long one. They awoke to find that their half-dried clothes had stiffened with ice during the night, and would again weigh them down. With nothing to be done about it, they hefted up their packs and set out for the snow peak to the west. Before long they came to a spur, and shortly afterwards reached the mountain's snow line. The drifts were deep, in places very icy, and the going was taxing and dangerous; it would be very easy to slip, then tumble off the spur.

Everyone was struggling, the previous evening's sunny mood quite dissipated. Rinpoche attempted a joke, suggesting that if they listened closely to the faintly metallic sounds made by the ice on their frozen clothes, they might hear a helpful spiritual message. The others were not amused.[181]

As they ascended, a few villages came into view about four miles away. This was a worry: their dark clothing against the white snow broadcast their presence, and locals might easily see them. Rinpoche felt, though, that with the sun full on the villages while they themselves were in the shadow of the mountain's northern slope, the chances of being seen were small. They climbed on until, around noon, they reached the mountain's crest and then started down its southern side.

The incline was drenched in sunlight and thankfully free of snow. It was instead covered in short, slick grass, almost as slippery as the icy snow, and littered with rocks and boulders. They could find no human paths or animal tracks to aid their way down, and it was treacherous going.

At the bottom of the slope they found themselves in another small valley. Beyond it loomed a heavily glaciered range of mountains which, in the group's weakened state, appeared heart-breakingly high – steep, towering, almost insurmountable. Yet near its summit they could make out three separate and distinct crest lines. They were sure that the central one was the one they should make for, the one indicated in Rinpoche's divination.

When they had first seen the range it had looked fairly close, but it took them far longer to reach than expected. After they began the climb they realised that in their condition it was going to be grim work. Their icy clothes dragged them down, and the higher they climbed, the deeper the snow became – so deep that, if they'd had the manpower, Rinpoche would have again called on men to press the snow down with their bodies. But the only robust men left were Yonten and Tsepa, and the labor would now be too much for them. Instead the pair led the way, forging some semblance of a path through the snow and ice, while the others toiled along behind. Late in the afternoon, a snowstorm hit, cutting visibility and deepening the drifts around them.

They took the storm in their stride. Although their spirits had sunk when they had first seen the mountain and had not risen much during the climb, the snow arrived just as they neared the crest line, when they were realizing that they would make it over. And the storm quickly abated:

> We kept cheerful and eventually reached the top at an altitude of about nineteen thousand feet above sea level. Rising almost perpendicularly to the east of our pass was Mount Namcha Barwa, or the "Blazing Mountain of Celestial Metal"; its crest glittered far above the clouds, for this mountain is over twenty-five thousand feet high.[182]

In around four days, from the banks of the Brahmaputra to where they stood, the spent and starving group had climbed almost ten thousand feet.[183]

Up here the sun was piercingly bright, the sky a fathomless blue. Gazing around them from the crest line, the ice sparkling underfoot, in all directions were high, shining snow peaks. Far to the south the peaks dissolved into range upon range of lower mountains, the furthest tinged a smoky blue. Rinpoche thought that the blue might be jungle, the most distant ranges possibly in India itself. Looking back over the way they had come, they could make out five cairns close to the track they had taken, which they had not seen during the climb, confirming that the route they had taken was the right one.

It was a monumental achievement, the brilliant panorama a splendid, self-existing salute to the moment. After eight months' extraordinarily demanding travel, they had crossed the great Brahmaputra under heavy attack, accomplished an intensely grueling climb of the Himalayas, and scaled their last high mountain range. Now they were on the cusp of the continental divide, about to start down its southern slope.

Pivotal though the moment was, no-one was inspired to give the traditional warriors' cry – the vista had brought home to them just how much further they still had to go. From their current position they would aim to head southeast, following the valleys of the lower Himalayas as they swept down to meet the Brahmaputra which, having looped around Mount Namcha Barwa, was on its long southerly journey to the Indian plains and the sea.

The journey remained arduous in the extreme. Immediately below them the terrain was all desolation – a tumult of deep snow drifts and a glacial debris of rocks and boulders, devoid even of wild animals. The valley seemed almost impossible to reach, the descent from the crest fiendishly steep and slippery, sweeping away below them for hundreds of feet. There was no way to outflank the vertiginous slope: daunting as it was, they had to take it on, and go straight down.

Soon after they began carefully to pick their way down the incline, they almost lost Yag Tulku. His feet slithered out from under him and, before he could react, found himself careening down the slope in a sitting position. Nothing he did slowed him down and, with a sheer drop to the valley floor looming in front of him, it seemed that he was a goner until, just as he was about to careen over the edge, he collided with a small rock just a few feet from the edge. It was enough to stop him and, after taking a while to collect himself, he made his shaky way back to the anxiously waiting group.

At dusk they were still struggling down the slope. But, looking back towards the ridge, in the gloom they saw that, as difficult as their position was, if they had not taken the center crest line indicated by the mirror divination, their situation would have been dire: routes from the other crests led into glaciers that fell away far too steeply for anyone to traverse; if they had chosen either of those routes they would have had to stop and painfully retrace their steps – a potentially calamitous blow in their condition.

Here, though, they were surrounded by cliffs, and could see no way past them. They continued downwards, but the further they went, the steeper was the incline – now made deadly by small rocks dislodged by people behind, each projectile capable of causing injury or worse. They broke up their single file, spreading out across the slope to find their individual routes down.

A shout from Tsepa cut through their tight focus. He had found a way down. He waited while the others made their slow, halting way to him through the gloom, and then led them down between two nearly vertical rocks and into a gentle depression. Here they found a cave surrounded by bushes where they decided to camp.

In the cave they pooled the last of their provisions. Young Jampal still had some of the tea he had salvaged from the Brahmaputra's banks, the nun he had rescued had some scraps of butter and Yonten and the peasant family still had a little *tsampa*. As Rinpoche put it, they had all the basic necessities, and "since we felt that we were safe from any possible unpleasant encounters we made a glorious blaze and spent the evening in devotional chanting."[184]

Rinpoche felt that at last he could relax. They were across the Himalayas, with the Communists almost certainly far behind them, along with everything else: the press of tactical problems, disputes and debates, maybe even undue worries about food, all that was in the past. Things were now raw, elemental: simply keeping going, onwards to India. He wrote: "This was the first night since the beginning of the escape that I slept really peacefully."[185]

The next morning Rinpoche awoke keenly aware that they could not afford a moment's delay. Leaving the cave, they pushed on down the incline. After reaching level ground they came to a snowy expanse with a large lake in its center. After passing the lake and hiking for some while, they abruptly arrived at the edge of an escarpment, its slope falling away steep and sheer. For some time they could see no way to get down. Then they spotted a tiny ravine that they decided to enter and follow: although it was just as precipitous as the surrounding slope, its surface was of rough and uneven stone that gave them some footing. With the younger attendants helping the lamas, some of whom were now in real physical difficulty, they eventually made their way to the bottom of the escarpment.

They had arrived in a small valley that was almost free of snow, and which had a frozen stream coursing down its middle. After the previous days' experiences, the walk along the valley seemed almost too easy. They spotted a few wild animals, including fox and deer, but the area was otherwise quite deserted. In the distance, in the direction they would be heading, they could make out clusters of fir and holly trees. They were clearly reaching lower altitudes. As the sun sank, they chose a campsite sheltered from the weather by rocks and turned in for the night.

On the morning of the winter solstice, five days after crossing the Brahmaputra, they continued their southeasterly journey. Their first objective was a large patch of emerald green vegetation. From far off it looked seductively like grass, but as they neared it they were horrified to see that it was in reality a huge swamp, thick with glutinous mud and quite impossible to cross. The only way around it was through a dense tract of uncommonly prickly thorn bushes: they had to fight for every foot of ground, slicing and hacking their way through with knives and swords. The brutally hard work went on throughout the day, with Yonten and Tsepa taking on the lion's share of the battle. Only in early evening did they finally break through to open ground beyond.

Trudging on, they came to a junction of two rivers. Here they spotted recently-made footprints. Knowing that they were not far from the Doshong La Pass, they wondered if they had found a track leading to it. This was troubling – PLA troops could be in the vicinity – but in the fading light they grew sure that the prints had been made by Tibetan boots. As night fell they set up camp nearby in the best spot they could find, among the reeds near the river.

On December 22 Rinpoche wrote that he "felt more and more puzzled, for everything looked somehow strange ... all utterly unlike anything I'd known hitherto; the air was so much warmer and there were so many unknown trees."[186] On their downhill journey they had reached the area on the range's southern slope where the Assam monsoon, blown north from the Indian sub-continent, collides with the cold Himalayan air and cascades down. Utterly unlike the scrublands and mountains of Tibet, here the sky was heavy with clouds, glaciers spilled into the forests below and the ground was thick with lush vegetation and large, broad-leaf trees.

Around the campfire that evening, they talked things over. Everything now came down to one key question. The region they had entered could obviously support human life, and somewhere in the area there would be people and villages: could they allow themselves to eat up the few scraps of food they had left in the hope that they would soon come across friendly villagers – or, if there were Communists around, should they ration themselves even more severely?

At the mention of Communists, someone wondered aloud whether, in their starving, exhausted, dangerously depleted physical state, it might be best to just give up and hand themselves over, hoping for the best. Few shared this view, feeling that there were unlikely to be Communists this far in the mountains and that, anyway, surrender was out of the question – even if they were to die trying, they must make every effort to escape. After dark the sense of impending crisis was heightened by the rise and fall of a strange cacophony from the forest. As the night drew on, though, they gradually accepted that it was simply the sound of unfamiliar animals, birds and reptiles.

The next day, December 23, things were no easier. In the week since they had crossed the Brahmaputra, the trekking had been unremittingly harsh, the desperate climb up the Himalayas' north face followed by a series of harrowing days over their heights, then down from them. They had hoped that by now the journey would be more straightforward and the landscape's challenges lighter, but the vegetation was dense and obstructive, the going rugged, the daily treks just as daunting.

They were nearing Pema Ko, an expanse of mountains renowned in both India and Tibet as sacred land. It was in reality among the holiest and most venerated of the many sacred Himalayan regions, an area where, in the eighth century, Padmasambhava had meditated and left many hidden teachings. Pema Ko was also notorious for how hard it was to reach, protected as it was by nearly impenetrable terrain that demanded the greatest fortitude and courage to conquer. Over the centuries large numbers of pilgrims had died trying, and their skeletons dotted the ranges around.

The group now came to an area of huge rocks and swollen, fast-flowing streams. There was no way to cross the streams except over rudimentary log bridges which demanded agility and intense focus to avoid falling off. Moreover, the rocks had to be negotiated by means of small, shallow footholds with only rusty chains for handholds – reminding Rinpoche of the bridge to Rigong Kha, although now far more trying in their spent and shaky state. He himself was near the end of his physical resources: "It was so tiring jumping from rock to rock that I was beginning to feel at the end of my tether, hardly knowing how to go on; but I dared not tell this to anyone for fear of discouraging them."[187]

This was Rinpoche's sole remark on his physical condition, or that of the others. The reality was far graver than his words conveyed. For months the leaders had been aware that crossing the Himalayas at the end of a long and difficult journey would be a trial, but its cruel challenges, joined with the effects of starvation and fatigue, were beginning to prove too much, and were crushing them.

For months their bodies had been getting a paltry fraction of the sustenance they needed for what they had been asked to do. Now, in this most arduous stretch of the journey, food intake had dwindled to nearly nothing. They were grievously thin and gaunt, almost emaciated: skin was stretched tight over bones, cheeks hollowed out, jaw lines sharply chiseled, teeth protruding from skulls, eyes sunk deep in their sockets. Critically, their walking had much slowed: depleted energy reserves, strained muscles, joints and ligaments had all taken their toll, and a few of them were nearly crippled, barely hobbling along.[188] Their bodies, burning muscle tissue to keep going, were beginning to shut down. In a final terrible effort, they were wrecking their bodies in order to find food to survive.

Towards dusk they came across a small cave. On its floor were footprints similar to the ones they had spotted before, but they had seen no-one around and decided to camp there anyway. After sharing out the last few scraps of *tsampa* and butter, they settled down for the night. As they did so, Tsethar the bursar expressed what they likely all knew: unless they found a village within a day or so, they would all die. There was a short, reflective pause before a voice called out "Be a strong Khampa and don't lose heart!" and everyone laughed.

On December 24, eight days from the Brahmaputra and a hundred days since they left the Tsophu Valley, they made their way down through a maze of mountains. As they had descended, the ice dripped from their clothes to be replaced by sweat and moisture; here the air swam with mist and humidity, while torrential rain fell without pause – flooding down in waves that hit the drenched earth so hard that water rebounded upwards, rain coming at them from above and below.

Here the countryside was more remote, more alien than anything they had known. They were in sub-tropical jungle, the vegetation a rich, startling tangle of trees, creepers, plants and undergrowth, arrays of orchids, high walls of nettles and almost impenetrable tangles of rhododendrons. They wondered at the first banana trees they had seen; the fruit was somehow inviting, but they had no idea whether or not it was edible, and didn't dare take the chance.

Near evening they found another cave. From its burned-out fires, rearranged stones and pebbles and one or two forgotten personal items, it was obviously a popular one. In spite of the soaked vegetation, they managed to build themselves a fine blaze. Jampal still had a few fragments of his brick of tea left and, after stewing up some squares of leather from their last few bags, they sat down to eat. Rinpoche found the meal thoroughly enjoyable – and then was surprised and touched when Yonten came up with some magic of his own, producing from the recesses of his pack a few final morsels of *tsampa* he had been saving for him. Yonten would eat none himself.

However gloom-laden the bursar's words had been, they had rung all too true. The men who had led outdoor lives, notably Yonten and Tsepa the guide, still had stamina to spare in spite of the heavy loads they had been carrying. But in spite of all their immense effort, the lamas' and monks' sedentary lives had caught up with them. Walking was now almost beyond them, and they were close to the end.

Tsepa volunteered to go off to see if he could find a village and obtain food. They came up with a simple plan: if he could find a village and purchase supplies he would return to the cave, otherwise the group should continue on the next day and he would try to meet them somewhere on the way. Then, picking up his rifle and accompanied by the peasant man, he left the cave and headed out into the mountains.

Yonten might have gone with Tsepa, but decided to stay behind. Neither a monk nor an especially religious man, over the months he had been with Rinpoche his regard for his abbot had immeasurably deepened. He had seen him deal with unfamiliar physical hardship, observed his leadership in the face of almost insuperable demands, been moved by his unflagging friendliness and good humor, and wondered at an equanimity which seemed as still as the sky. Natural respect for his young abbot had deepened into a profound fondness and admiration, and then into devotion. If this was to be the end, Yonten wanted to be with Rinpoche, to take care of him in whatever way he could. He also wanted to be with him for his own sake, to die with his teacher.

The group waited around the fire, finding it hard to settle down to sleep. An hour or so after Tsepa's departure they heard the sound of a gunshot, then nothing. They feared the worst and the night was an anxious one.

In the morning, relishing the fire's warmth and happy for the comfort and ease, they decided to stay in the cave. They spent the day stewing up leather and chanting Buddhist songs and mantras. In the evening, their spirits high, they enjoyed a meal of leather scraps and the last of the tea – Yonten's *tsampa* caches had finally run out – then turned in for the night.

No-one needed to mention that nothing had been heard from Tsepa. Nor did anyone point out that, as uplifting as the rest, chanting and companionship had been, they had lost a day's travel while their failing bodies had weakened, and with the morning light they would be journeying on.

14

Pema Ko to Tuting

Rising soon after dawn on December 26, with a few of the older men being helped to their feet, they hefted up their packs and left the cave. With the sun warm on their faces they made their careful, halting way down the slope to the small valley below. When they reached it, they paused to choose a route up to the next ridge, then set out towards it.

Just as they began their climb they spotted someone coming towards them. As he drew nearer, they saw that it was Tsepa's companion, the peasant man, carrying a large bag of *tsampa*. He also brought a message from Tsepa: the food was for their immediate needs only, and when they had eaten they should go with the peasant to a cave where Tsepa would meet them, bringing provisions he was acquiring in a nearby village.

The group sat down to enjoy goodly portions of *tsampa* and then, somewhat restored, followed the peasant to the cave a few miles away. They were astounded to find waiting for them the donors of the *tsampa* – Akong Tulku's older brother, Jamyang, together with three nuns and a woman refugee. After a jubilant reunion, they spent the rest of the morning exchanging accounts of their adventures.

A few days earlier, Jamyang and his small group had been making their way through the area when they suddenly heard a gunshot –

the same shot heard by the lamas' group after Tsepa left the cave in search of food. The sudden blast among the quiet mountains had scared them out of their wits, and sent them running away from it as fast as their enfeebled legs could take them. A few hours later, still recovering from the shock and exertion, they were overtaken by Tsepa and his companion, walking hard in their quest for food. It turned out that Tsepa, who had been quite unaware of their presence, had fired the shot to warn off a wild animal, a bear or tiger, which he thought was about to attack.

At dawn on December 16, Jamyang and the women, along with Yonten, Tsethar and the Washutsong family, had been trapped near the Brahmaputra. Jamyang, like Tsethar, had returned to the river to try to salvage what he could of their discarded wealth – he had managed to bury five hundred Chinese silver coins in the soft river sand – but then was forced to spend the day hiding immobile in the river grass. After nightfall, he had headed for the mountain, intending to follow Rinpoche's group, but lost his way in the dark and stumbled into a village. Someone heard him, raised the alarm, and he was captured and handed over to the Communists.

The troops took him straight to their headquarters, situated near the river's south bank. There he had been confined with a number of other captured refugees. Their interrogation was systematic and thorough. First, everyone's baggage was searched; the sacred contents of all amulet boxes were thrown away, while all religious books were piled up and destroyed on the spot. Then they were individually questioned to double-check their stories and confirm their identities. Finally, in something of a show, political leaders, lamas and monks were forced to scrub toilets and perform other menial tasks. Later, the entire interrogation was repeated; the Chinese had discovered that Rinpoche, Akong Tulku and other prominent lamas had led the escape and, having failed to find them, thought that they might be concealed among the refugees.

Their captors went on with their rough handling of the leaders, but for the time being treated ordinary refugees well. Within a few days, though, a troubling rumor swept through the refugees: all the able-bodied men were to be sent off to labor camps, while the leaders and older people would go to a concentration camp.

Jamyang quickly came up with an escape plan. During the day, the nuns had been allowed to visit a nearby village to buy food; Jamyang asked one of them to obtain enough *tsampa* for them both, and also to find out how to get to the Doshong La Pass. Then, during the changing of the sentries, he rolled under a pile of straw near the fence, and lay there motionless. After dusk, the nun and a few others joined him carrying an ample supply of *tsampa,* and together they squirmed under the wire and headed for the mountain. Of all the men captured during the crossing, Jamyang was the only one to escape.

He had been concerned that in his Kham clothing he would be identified going up the pass – as the brother of a high lama and an aristocrat, he could expect harsh treatment – but no Chinese soldiers were out braving the winter weather. Along the way the group met a Kongpo family, the only ones from their village who had dared to attempt the climb to the snowbound Doshong La Pass. They told Jamyang that earlier in the year an entire regiment of Communist troops had been obliterated on the pass, buried by a sudden blizzard; it was, the villagers thought, the region's spiritual protectors acting to prevent Communist entry to the sacred land of Pema Ko.[189]

Jamyang's group had found the climb through deep snow terribly hard, but once they were over the pass they had little difficulty and made good time. Meanwhile, several thousand feet above them and a few miles to the east, Rinpoche's group had been struggling through the torturous mountain wasteland; by the time they had reached the subtropical region of the southern Himalayas, Jamyang was a mile or so ahead of them, just near enough for an auspicious link-up.

※

News of Rinpoche's presence swept through the area. Within a few hours Jamyang's Kongpo companions arrived at the cave with a large jug of meat and barley soup, hugely appreciated by the lamas and monks. Shortly afterwards, people from a nearby village came with pork and dumplings. The saviors had arrived none too soon. Another few days and it might have been too late; the refugees' survival had been, as Rinpoche put it, a matter of touch and go.

By now it was obvious to Rinpoche and the others that the mountains around them were well populated – quiet unknown to them on their desolate wilderness route. Late in the day, a monk arrived from a small monastery on the heights above the cave, bringing the group an intivation to move into the monastery. Rinpoche politely declined: apart from anything else, he felt that the area was still too close to Lower Kongpo and the Communists for comfort. Maybe his view was reinforced by the messenger's appearance: "I was surprised to see him wearing a long dagger, which looked somehow wrong for a monk."[190]

They had come to the heart of Pema Ko. With its full expanse spreading from north of the Brahmaputra southwest into India, it is an extraordinary – in some ways unparalleled – place for botanists, explorers and Buddhists alike. Its physical features alone are astonishing. On the northern side of one of the world's highest peaks, Namcha Barwa, where the Brahmaputra makes its stupendous hairpin turn before heading for India, lies one of the globe's deepest, steepest gorges.[191] Here the river flows sixteen thousand feet below the peaks before entering a narrow chasm – then, in just a few miles, plummeting a dizzying six thousand feet down a series of precipitous falls and cataracts in a mighty, crashing tumult of water.

Southwest of Namcha Barwa, Pema Ko is a natural paradise. A profusion of flowers, plants and ferns thrive in old growth forests, including hundreds of species of orchids and what one botanist called a "Rhododendron Fairyland".[192] Many of the plants are reputed to be healing, psychotropic or magical; some talk of a grass so potent that even a dog that chews on it could attain the rainbow body of enlightenment. Although in winter Rinpoche's group did not see the flora's full opulence, they were spared the darker side of the paradise, the malarial mosquitoes, biting fleas, poisonous reptiles and voracious blood-sucking leeches which make their homes here.

For Buddhists, Pema Ko has traditionally been among the most sacred of places. Padmasambhava meditated in its caves, leaving behind many hidden teaching treasures, while many believe that Vajrayogini, queen of Tibetan Buddhist deities, is here – here not in a spiritual form, dwelling resplendent on some snow peak or pervading the valleys with her presence, but here physically, her parts and curves the conformation of the mountains and valleys, her form the form of the land. In this view Pema Ko – "Lotus Displayed" – is Vajrayogini's tangible, earthly body. Her head rests to the north of the Brahmaputra; her breasts, on either side of the river, are Mounts Namcha Barwa and Gyala Peri; her central spiritual channel, aligned with her spine, is the Brahmaputra itself, down which her life energy flows as spiritual nectar, down to the plunging gorge with its roaring, unstoppable flood.

However alluring the land of Pema Ko, many pilgrims have understood that, like Nirvana itself, arriving there was not altogether the point. The place's power, they felt, lay just as much in the deadly dangerous journey needed to reach it – an ordeal that might so ravage and disrupt the everyday sense of personal safety and comfort that it pushed body and mind to the edge and beyond. Then an utter transformation of personal being could occur – a shift so complete that the world's inner sacredness and luminosity could burst through, arising so brightly that there was no going back, ever.

There were no guarantees of success or survival, and obstacles were legion. It was held that Vajrayogini's protectors took many forms, among them snowstorms and wild animals, all of them bent on cutting through ego-clinging. And the chances of dying along the way were high, attested to by the numerous skeletons littering the mountain approaches. Yet many pilgrims have been confident that, in losing one's life on this sacred journey, little would be lost. After all, in his guidebook to Pema Ko Padmasambhava himself had assured them: "*If people die here, they do not take karmic rebirth; they go to the Pure Lands. I do not tell lies. It is like that. Keep it in mind.*"[193]

Rinpoche's links with Padmasambhava and Pema Ko were close ones. The Khampas of East Tibet knew it as a place of special sacredness, but also as a place of refuge. Fifty years before, many Khampas had fled here to escape the ghastly massacres launched by "Butcher Zhao." Safe from his rampaging army in so remote a place, a number of these early refugees settled down to build homes and monasteries. Their offspring must been overjoyed to know that a high lama from Kham was in the area, thrilled to be able to help Rinpoche's group in any way they could.

In Pema Ko Rinpoche may have given us a glimpse of the sort of transformative view inspiring those who came here – and perhaps also the vision underlying his group's journey. In the few days spent in the cave, he composed a song, *Sunshine for a Pauper*, an eighteen-stanza supplication to Yeshe Tsogyal, Padmasambhava's consort;[194] she is understood to be the first Tibetan to attain enlightenment, and is also the human embodiment of Vajrayogini. In the first refrain, Rinpoche sang:

Goddess, your empty form is ineffable, beyond language.
By just seeing your face of innate coemergence, inexpressible in words,
Effortless great bliss blazed, and on the path of liberation
The great joy of the four joys was awakened in the center of my heart.[195]

A few days earlier, while the group sat around their fire in the cave, much of their chanting would have been directed to Vajrayogini, Pema Ko's reigning deity – who was also the chief feminine deity of their own Kagyu lineage. The chants were not offered to some envisioned outer being; quite probably they were not even for their personal survival or the success of their journey. They would have likely been directed to the dispelling of personal obstacles standing in the way of realization of the enlightened qualities of mind, of the wisdom, luminosity and emptiness that Vajrayogini manifested.[196]

There can also be little doubt that, back in the Tsophu Valley, when Rinpoche proclaimed their journey to India a pilgrimage, he had a similar transformative vision in mind. Then he had instructed the refugees that the real journey would be an inward one, that they should strive to see each step along the way as holy and precious; in this way, the journey would be beneficial and personally transformative. From their Buddhist understanding, many would have grasped what he said: that like a lotus arising from mud, the most sacred of visions could arise from the most miserable of circumstances. Then the world is seen in its fullness, as a realm of enlightened energies. Some of those who perished on the way might have done so with that vision bright in mind – might have felt that on such a journey, led by such a teacher, it was a fine, indeed blessed, way to go.[197]

Yet however warm their welcome, and however appealing they had found Pema Ko to be, Rinpoche was determined to continue onwards. Apart from anything else, from any broader visions he may have held, he felt that Pema Ko was no longer secure. The Communists would eventually force their way in, sacrificing any number of soldiers to do so. For Rinpoche, India remained the objective.

As the group prepared to leave Pema Ko, the Washutsong family was just nearing the top of the Doshong La Pass after a long, dreadful climb.

At dusk on December 16, the nine remaining members of the family had emerged from the river grass on the Brahmaputra's banks. From there, Palya's father, Tserge Washutsong, had been able to creep into a nearby village in the darkness where he bought some *tsampa* and acquired information on the Doshong La Pass – the ancient route that would spare them the desperate course that Rinpoche's group had been forced to take, straight up the mountain. Then he gathered his family together and headed for the pass.

Tserge had only managed to buy a single bag of *tsampa* for them all, but that was of no immediate concern: traumatized by the crossing, grieving for the loss of so many of their family, for days no-one could eat a morsel. On the climb, babies and small children were carried inside their mothers' *chubas*; older ones, like twelve-year-old Drupju, had to walk. The snow was deep all the way up, deeper near the top, and every step took acute, focused effort. Gradually their soft Tibetan boots were torn apart by ice and rocks, but they could not stop to repair them, and feet froze and became bruised and cut all over. All the while, the piercing cold intensified. At one point Drupju said that he couldn't go any further, but the family took him by the hand and urged him on.

Palya recalled the climb as the worst part of the entire journey, up "a huge snowy mountain," over up a pass that in summer could take a few days at most to climb, but which in the deep snow drifts took the family nearly two weeks,

After they crossed the pass the walking became much easier, and when they reached Pema Ko they too were greeted with much warmth and kindness – fed well, given someone's home to live in and invited to stay for a month if they liked. Palya talked of how happy all the family were to hear that Rinpoche's group had passed through earlier. She herself was delighted to be able to rest in the fabled land of Pema Ko, and "basically slept for the entire month."[198]

On December 28, Rinpoche's group, now numbering around nineteen people with the addition of Jamyang's group, continued on. Although not all the food they had eaten in Pema Ko had agreed with them – one day they had nibbled on tasty but unfamiliar roast corn, only to have it swell up and cause serious stomach aches – they were well-fed, and had rested enough to continue the journey.

For the first time since leaving the Tsophu Valley, they could travel on well-used paths and rely on their fellow Tibetans for rest, food and shelter. They started out southeast, heading down long, wild valleys between imposing mountains whose slopes were dotted with small villages. This was the landscape that Padmasambhava had described in his guidebook as like many cows' horns, their tips pointing upwards to Pema Ko. Periodically, they came to mountain streams which had to be crossed on bamboo bridges; these were primitively built, often with leaves still attached, and the structures bucked and swayed as they made their way over. Towards evening they found a level spot on the banks of a stream, where they camped for the night.

They had hoped that the going would be easier after Pema Ko, heading downhill on traveled footpaths, but they still had to pass through the sacred land's southern approaches. The next day was harrowing: "Up and down slopes covered with large rocks; in some cases rough steps had been hewn, in others, it was the old story of narrow notches cut in the rock faces."[199] Then they again found themselves in cloud forest, an area so dense in growth that they could see nothing of the countryside around. The rain began to beat down, and they were soon drenched through again, with no way to dry their clothes.

The day's trek had drained the worn-out group, and they decided to rest for a day at a mountain village. Poor as the villagers were, they welcomed Rinpoche and the group with rice cakes and rice beer. The monastics had to decline the alcohol, which upset the villagers' sense of decorum and hospitality, but they were gentle people and the unintended slight was soon forgotten. With no room available in the village itself, crammed as it was into a small, rock-free space on the mountainside, the group camped on a small hill nearby that was well-supplied with water.

On the morning of December 31 they set off for their next objective, the larger village of Pedong, which they could see high on a mountain slope across the valley. Following a narrow path down through the rocks and undergrowth, they reached the valley, and then crossed another flimsy bamboo bridge. As they started up towards the village, it was clear that they faced another severe climb, up a very steep ascent on hard, stony ground – back-breaking in their condition. Occasionally they came across footholds cut into the mountainside, their zig-zag pattern making for easier gradients up the steepest sections. Close to noon they reached a point from where they could see the Brahmaputra, now on its southwesterly course to India. It was a heartening sight – they would soon be joining it – and the scenery on the river's southern side was "very beautiful with patches of cloud and little groups of houses dotted about … everything looked wonderfully green."[20]

The day was warm, and as they climbed they grew hot and increasingly thirsty. There was no water on the mountain, not even puddles, and by early afternoon they were parched and struggling. The previous days' journey had brought home how very weak they still were, in really no condition to travel. Since leaving Tsophu Valley over three months before they'd had only a few days' rest, and if they were to continue they would need more. After talking things over with his fellow lamas, Rinpoche sent a messenger ahead to Pedong village, announcing their imminent arrival and asking the headman if they could rent accommodation for a few weeks.

They reached the village towards dusk, and received the warmest of welcomes, its temperature perhaps raised by the prospect of the rental windfall. The headman took the lead, giving his best room to Rinpoche and the rest of his home to his attendant, and to Yonten, Tsepa and his wife and the peasant family. He cooked all meals for the entire group himself. The others were assigned lodgings throughout the village.

The fortnight in Pedong was both restful and intriguing. The debilitated group found the community's food – mainly meat, vegetable and soup creations – both healthy and nutritious. While he was enjoying one dish, Rinpoche was surprised to hear that the meat was in fact leather, heavily spiced and supplemented with vegetables; leather turned out to be the main source of meat in this remote mountain area. The visitors were also offered a wheat beverage that turned out to be alcoholic. When Rinpoche asked for tea instead, the headman, a gentle, friendly man, told him that there was no water available that night and urged the beer on him, saying that it would be most beneficial to them after their long journey. As politely as he could, Rinpoche declined, saying that the soup had been enough, but the headman was clearly hurt by this refusal of his hospitality.

As the group explored Pedong, they realized why beer was the chief beverage. The village's only source of water lay far down in a valley. Fetching it was women's work: they had to climb down, dig a hole, then wait while water slowly trickled in before beginning the long, loaded journey upwards. With water so laboriously acquired, and with no milk available and winter vegetables in short supply, Rinpoche and the lamas had little choice: they temporarily suspended their monastic vow and began to drink the wheat beer, finding it tasty and nutritious.

Pedong's religious ceremonies were an oddly lax mix of Buddhism and the ancient Bon religion, with copious amounts of liquor served to all. Yet the beer, leather and vegetable diet had no obvious effects on the villagers' health, nor did it disrupt either their cheery, well-structured communal life or the local industry, which Rinpoche described as "very fine and artistic basket work colored with beautiful vegetable dyes."[201]

The villagers told of how, some time before, units of the PLA had set up a regional headquarters nearby, having crossed the Brahmaputra after a long march from the east. After just two years they returned the way they had come – leaving behind them such an unfavorable impression that the villagers were making preparations to fight them using crude bows and arrows should they return; they had also planned to build a series of new bridges rigged to collapse as the Communists crossed.

The two weeks' rest, food and beer did much to revive the group's vigor, and on January 14 they took leave of the sunny community and set out on the next leg of the journey. It was a short one, only four hours to the next village, where they already knew the people, most of whom had trekked to Pedong to meet Rinpoche. In the village they met a lama from Upper Kongpo who had escaped with a number of local people; his stories of brutal persecution tragically matched the many they had heard before.

Trekking on the next day, they reached the Brahmaputra. They followed its course along paths that wound along the mountain slopes among thick vegetation – periodically crossing to the opposite bank over a style of bridge they had not seen before: although still very wobbly, the bridge had been modified with bamboo hoops fixed at intervals along its span, which helped travelers keep their balance. In the afternoon they came to a small village where they decided to stay the night.

They found this community even more interesting than Pedong's. In recent weeks the group had traveled from the familiar mountains and scrub country of their homeland into the cloud forests of Pema Ko. Now they were in the borderlands, a kind of cultural no-man's land, where the outermost reaches of Tibetan culture thinned out and mixed with the first shades of Indian influence. Rinpoche was amused to note that the men wore pajamas, and was intrigued to see Indian coinage and clippings from Indian newspapers tacked to the bamboo walls.

Yag Tulku, though, was outraged by what he saw as the locals' corrupt behavior, saying that he would have been very rude to a local priest, whose sole interest in Buddhism seemed to be the nurturing of magical powers, had Rinpoche not spoken to the man first. Apparently the venerable lama did not get to hear that the community's specialty lay in the concoction of a special paralyzing poison for hunting animals.

The visitors also learned that a sizeable detachment of Indian troops was stationed nearby; they were very friendly to the local people and had invited them to their New Year festivities. Recently, Indian military aircraft had been seen flying overhead. These were dark portents: the villagers were witnessing the build-up to the short, bloody war that would break out between India and China just two years later, beginning with the launching of PLA attacks on Indian outposts in these high mountain regions – one of the most fiercely contested points lay just to the west of the Doshong La Pass.

On January 16 the refugees awoke to their final day in their homeland. It was taken up by a long trek along the mountain path above the river until, in late afternoon, they arrived at the last village in Tibetan territory. Here, close to the Brahmaputra's bank, they set up camp for the night. With ample supplies of water at hand, Rinpoche reimposed the monastic rule against drinking alcoholic beverages – apart from anything else, he felt that "some of the younger people were growing too fond of it."[202]

Just after dawn the next morning they continued along the river bank. At one point the ground turned rockier, when the path curved upwards and headed for a high mountain ridge. As they came to the crest line they saw in front of them a large signboard painted with the white, green and saffron of the Indian flag; above, painted in large Hindi letters was "BHARAT," below, "INDIA."

Rinpoche and the group knew nothing of how they would be received at the border, but the two armed guards approached them with smiles, then shook their hands in a gesture of welcome. The Tibetans' happiness swelled when they spotted a newly built, freshly whitewashed Buddhist *stupa* just within the Indian border.[203] The guards pointed them along the road, indicating that they should continue on to the customs post a mile or so further on. With that, they stepped out of Tibet and into India, into the world beyond.

The customs officers, all soldiers, searched everyone for weapons and other potentially suspicious objects. They first confiscated Rinpoche's binoculars, which had proven such an aid on the journey; then they took Tsepa's rifle, which had been so troublesome. They also tried to divest Yonten of his Khampa knife – it was, after all, more a short sword than a knife – but he would not hand it over. The knife was not only a beautiful object and an heirloom, but very much part of Yonten's identity as a Khampa; like so many of his fellow-Khampas, he had already refused to give it up to the Communists. Finally the officers relented, also leaving him with the sacred Trungpa seals and statues with which Rinpoche had entrusted him at the start of the journey.

With customs cleared, the group entered the NorthEast Frontier Agency, one of the political divisions of India left over from the British Raj. Walking on down the mountain slope, they passed numbers of Indian troops heading the other way, towards the border, and could hear an aircraft passing somewhere high overhead. Yonten also noticed battalions of troops bivouacked in the forests on either side of the road.

Very tired after their long day, the refugees found a campsite as soon as they could, a flat area next to a small stream. Beginning to fully unwind now that they were officially in India, they enjoyed an unusually restful sleep, briefly interrupted by a soldier who came by in the middle of the night to check on them before continuing on his patrol.

Just after the group rose the next morning, another soldier arrived. A friendly sort, he made himself at home by their fire and offered the lamas *cheroots* to smoke – politely accepted by each of them, with no intention of lighting up. As they sat congenially around the fire, the Tibetans discreetly looked the soldier over: with his straight, pointed nose, deep-set eyes and copious moustache he was a novel, even peculiar, sight. Later another soldier joined them whose looks were more familiar; he spoke Tibetan and turned out be Bhutanese. He was even able to confirm the news that they had heard months ago: the Karmapa had made it safely to India, arriving before the Dalai Lama.

Later, a messenger arrived with a courteous message. The group should continue on to a camp about a quarter of a mile further on, where they would be looked after. They found themselves in the camp of an Indian army regiment, as the personal guests of the regiment's second-in-command, the adjutant. Above the camp, waving and furling in the mountain breeze, was the Indian flag, in the center of it the eight-spoked Wheel of Ashoka – the emperor who, over two millennia before, had devoted himself to propagating Buddhism in Asia.

The adjutant spoke fluent Tibetan, enquiring after the lama's names and saying that he understood that they were abbots of important monasteries. He said that he himself was a Buddhist, and that he'd had the privilege of meeting many lamas who had taken the route over the pass. Rinpoche and the lamas were quartered in a comfortable bungalow, whose bamboo walls were covered in elegant basket work, and which came complete with a bathroom and fully equipped kitchen. Settled in their relatively sumptuous quarters, that evening they had their first taste of Indian food, a rice and lentil soup. Again they enjoyed a fine night's sleep.

The next morning the adjutant came to compile a detailed list of the group's possessions, of their home monasteries and the routes they had taken since leaving them. A day later he returned to hand out temporary permits, gave them what he could spare from the regiment's limited food supply and advised them to stay at *dak* bungalows – travelers' inns – along the way. After taking his leave and wishing them well, he requested Rinpoche's blessing.

Early on January 21, the group resumed their journey along the winding path above the Brahmaputra. They came to the first really modern structure they had seen, a strongly built bridge supported by steel cables, which they examined closely. Later they met an Indian official, traveling in fine Imperial style with five porters for his personal possessions. He expressed great sympathy for their having had to flee their homeland, and assured them that, just as the Indian Government had looked after the Dalai Lama and other Tibetan refugees, it would take care of them all too.

Rinpoche's attention was drawn to the official's interpreter, a local headman who carried himself with peacock pride in his official uniform. He was from a local tribe, "a primitive tribe who worship nature spirits … the whole atmosphere here seemed quite different from anything we had known before, with no obvious influences from Tibet or the India side."[204] The area's poverty was extreme, and the *dak* bungalow in which they spent the night was tiny compared to the one they had enjoyed in the regimental camp. Rinpoche, wasting no time, found a few people who had worked in Tibet and asked them to teach him some Hindi.

They were passing through Nagaland, the domain of notoriously bellicose tribes – so adept at war that they had managed to fend off Tibet's great seventh-century military empire; it was not until the British Raj launched a full-fledged expedition against them that they were subdued. The Nagas also once had a fearsome reputation as cannibals and headhunters, with the tribeswomen demanding the dowry of a number of fresh human heads before marriage.

Rinpoche's mild views on the Naga were not shared by everyone. Yonten made no attempt to hide his scorn: with their minimal, vividly colored tribal attire, long spears and ornate shields adorned with bird plumage, their nightly drumming and their glorification of meat-eating, he felt that they lived like wild animals.[205] For his part, young Jampal did not relish the idea of having to travel through a place where, he had heard, "people ate people."[206] Palya, when she came through the area with her family some weeks later, was simply terrified.

Around midday on January 22 they reached the town of Tuting. The place buzzed with activity, swarming with troops and with laborers engaged in building accommodations for Indian officials and a new, large camp for the army. This time the group's welcome was a slender one: they were offered only a bamboo shelter for housing and, with the town's food very limited in the rainy season, were encouraged to make do with their own supplies. But they were able to change their Tibetan coins for Indian currency, and could visit small shops and restaurants where they could buy much of what they needed.

Tuting lay high in the Himalayan foothills, and at first no-one could tell them how to get from the remote town into India proper. They heard that military cargo aircraft flew into the airstrip carrying building materials, provisions and ammunition for the workers and army outposts in the area; there was, though, a long waiting list for places on the return flights.

Being temporarily trapped in Tuting was of little concern to Rinpoche. He was struck by the lightness of the town's mood, how much cheerier its people were than in Tibet's Communist-controlled towns, and wrote that " ... we no longer felt anxious: we were free at last and were able to wander around the town at will."[207]

As local officials came to realize who Rinpoche was, their respect deepened and, within their slim resources, they did their best for him and his party. Their generous impulse could outstrip their reach. The next day, as the group was eating their midday meal, a breathless messenger ran up to say that they should prepare to leave for the airport immediately – there was an excellent chance that there would be seats for them on the evening flight. Shortly afterwards a tractor arrived towing a trailer, into which they all bundled. At the airport, essentially a strip of semi-level ground and a hut, they climbed out with their possessions. They waited for some time without seeing an aircraft or any other activity, and then made enquiries: no-one knew of any flight arriving or departing that day.

Later, a jeep drove up with an invitation for Rinpoche to visit the district administrator. The official received him with great courtesy, then offered him a bag of rice and a handful of vegetables, together with an apology for Tuting's inadequate hospitality. He was confident, though, that there would be a flight arriving the next day that they could board. As Rinpoche left, the man requested that he leave his blessing, so that things would go well for the people of Tuting; he was then driven back to re-join the group and spent the night in the airport hut.

On the morning of January 24 – nine months and a day since Rinpoche, Akong Tulku and their small group had started out from Drolma Lhakang – an official arrived and proceeded to read out a list of names. Rinpoche's group had been given priority: they would be on the next flight out.

When the aircraft arrived later that morning, they looked it over with intense interest. A twin-engine World War II-era Douglas C-47 workhorse left behind by the British, it was the first aircraft they had seen up close. They perused the wings and fuselage, propellers and undercarriage, and watched intently as its cargo of building material was unloaded, and as a few rows of seats were unfolded and fixed to the floor. It turned out that there would only be room for six of them on the flight, and it was decided that it should be Rinpoche, Yag Tulku, Tsethar, Yonten and two attendants. The others would be on a flight leaving later that day.

Around mid-morning the lamas were helped onto the aircraft and shown to the seats just behind the bulkhead, with Rinpoche offered a window seat. Yonten, the attendants and the rest of the passengers were belted to the metal floor where fuel, food and building materials were normally tied down.[208] The engines started, built to a roar the likes of which the Tibetans had never heard, and the aging plane gathered speed, bumped down the strip and took to the air. At first it followed the Brahmaputra's curving valley, straining for height and buffeted by mountain winds and thermals. Many passengers, including Yonten and the attendants, were airsick and retched onto the floor around them, but after a while the aircraft climbed above the highest peaks, then above the clouds, and the air calmed and stomachs stilled.

For Rinpoche the flight was a momentous event, and was where he chose to end *Born in Tibet* and his account of his life in his homeland.[209] It was the final letting go of everything he had known, but also the gateway to an ocean of fresh experiences and luminous possibilities. He described the utter strangeness of it all, flying high above clouds and mountains, gazing far down upon villages and the footpaths leading up to them. All their usual reference points were gone, and they could only gauge their speed by tracking the aircraft's shadow as it dipped and soared over the terrain far below:

> We thought about the teachings of impermanence; this was a complete severance of all that had been Tibet and we were traveling by mechanized transport. As the moments passed, the mountain range was left behind, and the view changed to the misty space of the Indian plains stretching out in front of us.

15

India

Winging over the last of the Himalayan foothills, the aircraft banked to the west and, as it entered Assam province, began its descent before landing at Dimapur airport. There the refugees climbed into trucks and were driven over the Brahmaputra, now flowing broad and sluggish across the great Indian plain. Finally they arrived at their destination, the refugee camp at Missamari.[210]

The camp lay about eighteen miles northwest of Tezpur, an ancient city on the river's banks. It had been hastily set up by the Indian government the previous year as tens of thousands of Tibetans poured over the Himalayas, fleeing the Communists. Previously an army camp, another relic of the Raj, it had not been occupied since the end of World War II and was seriously run down. A few of the buildings could be used by the camp administration, but the rest were dilapidated; bamboo and basketry huts were being built, and in the meantime people found some shelter in old, threadbare tents. Over a thousand Tibetans were already there, with dozens more arriving every day – lamas and monks from all schools of Tibetan Buddhism, aristocrats, political leaders, villagers, peasant farmers, herders and nomads.

The authorities were struggling to cope, and the situation in Missamari's makeshift camp was getting dangerously out of control. The refugees urgently needed medical attention for disease, injuries and frostbite – some had lost fingers, others toes or noses – and for various states of malnutrition and debilitation. There was little to be had. And there was barely enough water to drink, let alone wash in, and it was foul. Food was ample, but it was vegetarian, a far cry from the Tibetan staples of meat, animal fat, tea and *tsampa*. In spite of their desperate need for sustenance, the newcomers found it thoroughly unappealing; no-one knew how to cook it and their bodies struggled to digest what little they were able to eat. Meanwhile, in the nearby town, corrupt officials were pre-sorting the food aid from Western donors, keeping the best wheat for themselves and passing on the spoiled grain to the camp.

As the weeks passed and the flood of refugees continued unabated, conditions went from dire to deadly. Missamari was just six hundred feet above sea level – hot even in the spring and fall, intolerable in summer. Soon malaria, dysentery and tuberculosis were rife, and dozens began to succumb to disease. At times the camp actually shrank in size, with more people dying every day than were arriving. For many Tibetans, sweltering in sun-beaten tents in their dark, thick clothing, it must have seemed as if they had gone from a cold hell to a hot one.

Then, piling suffering upon suffering, far-off bureaucrats issued a decree. Oblivious to conditions at Missamari and struggling to find a way to support the mass of refugees in their poor country, they decided that only those with outside sponsors or sufficient funds could leave the camp. Everyone else must be sent out to build roads, with no distinction made between old and young, lamas and monks. For large numbers of the ailing and wasted refugees, the decree meant death.

By late summer, news of the unfolding tragedy had reached the highest levels. Prime Minister Nehru acted swiftly, asking a personal friend, the director of the central government's Social Welfare Board, to head to the camps and sort out the chaos.[211]

Nehru's choice could hardly have been a better one. Freda Bedi was an extraordinary Englishwoman: brilliant, strong of character and a highly capable organizer, she was also profoundly compassionate. Born Freda Houlston, she had studied at Oxford University in the early nineteen-thirties, where she had been inspired by a talk by Mahatma Gandhi. She had also fallen in love with an

Indian student, Baba Bedi, whose family line could be traced back to the founder of the Sikh religion. Their marriage was a scandal. An upper crust Englishwoman marrying a "person of color" was almost unheard of – the liaison especially threatening at a time when Britain was struggling to hold on to the jewel in its Imperial crown, in the face of growing calls for Indian independence. In 1934 Mrs. Bedi abandoned her homeland and settled in India, where she became active in Gandhi's movement before being jailed by the Raj together with her children. Following Independence she had held a number of high-level government positions and, on an official trip to Burma, had become interested in Buddhism.

In late 1959, Mrs. Bedi arrived at Missamari to begin the gargantuan task of caring for the refugees and cleaning up the mess. She decided to use the camp only as a temporary assembly and holding center, prior to evacuating refugees to healthier camps as soon as possible. While she organized food aid and rooted out corrupt officials in the town, she nursed and cared for the people in the camp, working without electricity late into the night. The refugees quickly recognized her high abilities and compassion, and she became known to one and all as "Mummy-la."

Mrs. Bedi had met no ordinary Tibetans before coming to Missamari, and was struck by their general cheerfulness in the face of their dire situation. People had organized themselves into groups, while throughout the day monastics meditated and chanted with others of their own lineage: Nyingma, Kagyu, Sakya or Gelugpa. She was especially taken by the sweetness, humor and sophistication of the few hundred young *tulkus* in camp, and also by their physical beauty.

As she watched them being sent out to break rocks for roads, she wept.[212] She had come to realize that here, in this appalling place, was a magnificent treasury of Tibetan Buddhism, teachings that would greatly enrich the world's culture, and whose loss would be a calamity. Along with her many other responsibilities, she began to fund-raise for the lamas, at the same time using every stratagem she could come up with to get them taken off roadwork.

When Rinpoche's group arrived at the camp, a few months after Mrs. Bedi began her work, conditions had markedly improved. But they were still shocked by the reeking field of suffering. Diseased people lay everywhere, along with human excreta from people too sick to walk, their families too weak to carry them. To Yonten "it looked like when you go to a nomad place and there is yak dung everywhere, the whole place …"[213] Even now, in late winter, they found the heat overwhelming, and were bewildered by the alien and apparently uncookable food. Yonten recalled: "We all got sick after we ate it. Everyone had a bad stomach problem."[214]

Rinpoche's group caught Freda Bedi's eye the moment they arrived: their haggard appearance, emaciated bodies and the painful, hobbling walk of the older lamas were hard to miss. They were, she thought "in just about the worst state of any of the refugees [she] had encountered."[215] Then, as they told their story – the length and difficulty of their journey, the number of people Rinpoche had tried to bring with him, and the many who had fallen by the wayside – she was profoundly moved. She also felt that there was something unique about Rinpoche, a warmth, intelligence and openness, and what she described as a "radiant purity."[216] She resolved to do whatever she could for the group.

For his part, Rinpoche was happy to meet his first Westerner, delighted that it was a person of Mrs. Bedi's caliber. Soon he too was calling her "Mummy-la." Although they lacked a common language – Mrs. Bedi knew no Tibetan – she noticed his intense curiosity about the West, and started teaching him English. Up to this point, few in the camp had shown much interest in the language, or much facility in learning it. She was stunned by the speed with which Rinpoche picked it up. His aims were clear and focused: he recalled this period as one where "for the first time I had contact with Westerners, and I realized that it was absolutely necessary for me to study their language in order to spread the Dharma."[217]

Within a week of his arrival Rinpoche had become Mrs. Bedi's personal assistant and interpreter. He accompanied her on camp rounds, assessing the refugees' needs and conveying them to her, passing on her instructions to them. From the start, their relationship was deep, warm and mutually beneficial, qualities which would only deepen with time.

Still, in line with Mrs. Bedi's policy of evacuating refugees from Missamari as soon as could be arranged, a few weeks after Rinpoche and his group arrived they were trucked out to another camp.

Buxa Duar lay in the Himalayan foothills of West Bengal, just a few miles from the Bhutanese border. Once the site of a bamboo fort built by the King of Bhutan to protect the Silk Route, the British had rebuilt it in stone to guard against Bhutanese aggression; more recently they had used it to incarcerate members of the Indian independence movement. Although the Raj's white sahibs had loved to hunt here, tigers could still be spotted in the surrounding forests.

Around two thousand feet higher than Missamari, Buxa Duar was far cooler and healthier, and a pure freshwater stream ran through the camp. Even so, the newly-arrived Tibetans found the summer heat enervating and oppressive: Rinpoche and the group resorted to soaking their *chubas* in water, wearing them until the moisture evaporated and then repeating the process, over and over.

As the weeks passed, the refugees' health gradually revived, and they began to gain weight. But it had become tragically clear that the move to Buxa Duar had come too late for Rinpoche's bursar, Tsethar, Yag Tulku and Akong Tulku's brother, Jamyang. Their worn-out bodies had been overwhelmed by Missamari's diseases, and all three had contracted tuberculosis.

Shortly after arriving at the new camp, Rinpoche received an invitation from the Karmapa to visit him in Rumtek, Sikkim, where he was building a new monastery. Rinpoche could not immediately accept: without sufficient funds to support himself, he would not be issued the necessary documents for release. Although Rinpoche's role as Mrs. Bedi's assistant had spared him the lethal labor of road-building, she did not have the authority to release him from the camp. Also, at the time Indian officials were also growing increasingly anxious about China. Its leader, Mao Zedong, had been enraged by India's welcome of the Dalai Lama and the tens of thousands who had followed him; and China-India tensions over border disagreements were ramping up. India wanted to avoid anything that might further irritate Tibet's new rulers, and authorities further tightened restrictions on the free movement of the newly arrived Tibetans.

With no other course open to him, Rinpoche resolved to escape and make for Sikkim. His health was relatively good, as was that of Yonten and the attendant who would accompany him on the journey. Jamyang was already too sick to travel, and Akong Tulku decided to stay behind to care for his brother; he himself was now showing symptoms of tuberculosis – as, shockingly, was his fifteen-year-old brother Jampal, who they realized was also in the early stages of smallpox and dysentery. In spite of their accelerating illness, both Tsethar and Yag Tulku were determined to join Rinpoche, hoping to see the Karmapa one last time before they died.

Escaping was no simple matter. An internment camp not long before, Buxa Duar was surrounded by a high wire fence with a single gate for entry and exit; guards were posted at the gate night and day, and also in watchtowers around the camp. After talking it over with the others, Rinpoche decided to slip out at night via the freshwater stream.

At the upper end of the camp the stream was used for drinking water; at the lower end, where it left the camp under the fence, people did their washing. One morning, Yonten and several monks took their laundry down to the stream to wash as usual. Concealed among the clothes were a few bags of possessions, including their remaining coins and Surmang's sacred relics. While the others busily washed their clothes, blocking the guards' view, Yonten and the attendant quickly buried the bags in the stream's banks. After midnight, Rinpoche and the others crept down to the fence, retrieved the buried bags, and then immersed themselves in the stream and wriggled under the wire.

With only their few coins, a general sense of Sikkim's direction and Rinpoche's smattering of Hindi to help them on their way, the small group set out down the hill towards the town; the night was warm and soon after sunrise their clothes were dry again. Tsethar and Yag Tulku were now very ill, and Yonten had to carry Yag Tulku much of the time; his lungs were far gone, and Yonten could smell his terrible breath over his shoulder. At one point the dying man said to Yonten: "you are so kind to me, and I'm sorry I can't benefit you in this life. I will pray for you and maybe sometime in the future I will be of benefit to you."[218]

In the town and on their own, they entered the modern world. They found their way to the bus depot and, with the help of other travelers, purchased tickets and took a bus to the train station. There they managed to buy tickets on a train west to Siliguri, the journey another entirely new experience for them. After arriving in the town Rinpoche asked a taxi driver to take them to Darjeeling, where he had heard that a lama named Kalu Rinpoche had recently set up a monastery. The driver, misunderstanding Rinpoche's limited Hindi – or maybe suspecting from their appearance that the group could not possibly afford the fare for such a long trip – drove them instead to a Gelugpa monastery in Siliguri. There they were fed, housed and warmly treated.

The next morning, Rinpoche asked the monks the way to Darjeeling. They told him that it was a long journey up into the Himalayan foothills, and that bus tickets would be expensive, certainly more than their coins would cover. But they added that there was a train service to Darjeeling and – no doubt feeling that in desperate times both monastic vows and the law might be bent a bit – instructed them in a well-tested tactic for traveling without paying.

After disembarking in Darjeeling, Rinpoche and the others spotted a Tibetan nun, who helped them find a taxi that then dropped them close to Kalu Rinpoche's monastery. The small building was crammed with lamas and monks, and the only space that could be spared was a single room that they would all share. They stayed on for two weeks, meditating with the other monastics, sharing their experiences of escape and their new lives in India, catching up on the latest information.

Rinpoche learned that the route to Sikkim was straightforward, north along well-traveled roads, then up a track into the high mountain country. But there was a major obstacle, a roadblock at the border, set up to prevent Tibetans refugees traveling into an area that could not feed them. Undeterred, Rinpoche made plans to leave, accompanied by Yonten, Tsethar and the attendant. By now Yag Tulku was failing rapidly and could not be moved; he would stay behind at the monastery, to be cared for by the monks until Rinpoche's return.

When the four reached the roadblock at the Sikkim border there were no police in sight, and they continued on up into the mountains. Tsethar too was now very weak, and Yonten and the attendant took turns carrying him. When they reached Rumtek, the Karmapa greeted them with great warmth, and said how happy he was to hear of their successful escape from the Communists. Rinpoche was given his own room and made to feel thoroughly welcome. After he had rested, the Karmapa told him of his plans for the new Rumtek monastery – and then invited Rinpoche to join him there, to help him to rebuild their Buddhist culture and to train a new generation of lamas.[219] Coming from the head of the Kagyu lineage, the invitation was a high honor.

After two weeks in Sikkim, Rinpoche told the Karmapa he would be going to Kalimpong to give an initiation. It was not clear to anyone else at the time, but in bidding farewell to the Karmapa, Rinpoche was both politely declining his offer of a position at Rumtek and beginning to let go of his life as a high lama in the time-hallowed monastic tradition. He was not turning his back on the Karmapa or the Kagyu school of teachings, but stepping beyond the walls of institutional Buddhism. His vision was forward rather than back, and for that he would have to strike out on his own.

On their way to Kalimpong the group passed through Darjeeling, where they heard that Yag Tulku had died. The news had been expected and they joined in prayers for him, saddened at the loss of their large-hearted fellow lama and comrade on the journey.

Kalimpong, a short trip east of Darjeeling, had been one of the British hill stations to which the Raj retreated during the summer months. The Himalayan snow peaks dominate its northern view, and in the recent two years the town had become a major center for Tibetan expatriates – among them leaders of the Khampa resistance movement, still plotting to oust the Communists from their land. Dozens of lamas who had been able to escape early, with much of their wealth and possessions, had built well-appointed monasteries in and around the town. During their few months' stay in Kalimpong, Rinpoche, Yonten and Tsethar were hosted at several of these new-found monasteries, and also rented a small apartment in the town. Rinpoche spent much of his time with fellow lamas, also lending his support and expertise to the building of a new stupa. Perhaps due to a simple change in plans, Rinpoche never did give the initiation he had told the Karmapa he was leaving for.

Among Kalimpong's recently settled lamas was Khamtrul Tulku, who in late 1958 had tried so hard to persuade Rinpoche to join him on his escape. His journey from East Tibet had been well provisioned and relatively relaxed, and he had arrived in India in good health with much of his monastery's wealth and sacred possessions intact. There he had joined in the work of re-establishing Tibetan Buddhism in its new home, building a monastery and inviting young lamas and monks to join him, sheltering them as they took up their education where it had been cut off. Rinpoche spent a good deal of time with Khamtrul Tulku, exchanging Buddhist news and teachings, and discussing their changed prospects and future path.

Much of Rinpoche's spare time was taken up with mirror divinations. In the aftermath of his escape, his reputation had reached new heights in the Tibetan diaspora. The journey he had led had already attained near-mythic status among people who had made their own arduous treks across the Himalayas. No-one knew of anyone crossing Tibet's seemingly uncrossable wilderness, and with so many people, or had heard of a journey so long, hard and dangerous. Many thought the outcome miraculous – that it had to be due to Rinpoche's divinatory skill – and dozens of Tibetans were showing up to request mirror readings.

Some of their questions concerned legendary historical events or epoch-making future ones; others were urgent and personal. The Washutsong family, which had reached India and was now in Assam, had heard of Rinpoche's presence in Kalimpong – the Tibetan grapevine was up and running in the new surroundings – and Tserge traveled to see his teacher from Surmang days. He asked Rinpoche for a divination on the fate of their extended family, and especially that of his five-year-old daughter left stranded on the north bank of the Brahmaputra. Reading the mirror, Rinpoche said that she was in a green meadow, healthy and in good spirits. Years later, when the daughter finally reached India, she told the family that she had been adopted by loving relatives, who had successfully taken up farming in Central Tibet.[220]

Over the months news trickled in from Surmang and Tibet. Rinpoche's family had followed his instructions and left Surmang for Kyere, and then, under the ongoing Communist onslaught, retreated up into the mountains. For years they would survive there in primitive rock shelters before being able to return.

Yonten's beloved uncle, Karjen, the general secretary of Surmang who had stayed at his post while Rinpoche made his escape, had been thrown into jail where, four years later, he would die from starvation and maltreatment.

Urgyan-tendzin, Rinpoche's advisor – the able monk who had taught the refugees how to build coracles, and who had last been seen heading back across the Brahmaputra to fetch more refugees – had also arrived in India. He had been trapped on the north bank under the storm of gunfire but, alone and able to move fast and inconspicuously, he'd had no trouble evading the Communists and in a month had walked along the Brahmaputra to Tuting.

In later years Yonten would remain in close touch with the Tibetan diaspora, alert for any news of Surmang and its people, and of the fates of the refugees who had joined Rinpoche on his escape. He reported that of the three hundred people who had made the 1959 attempt, forty-eight – including Rinpoche's group and the Washutsong family – eventually crossed the Himalayas to freedom. Some settled in India, Sikkim, Bhutan or Nepal, others made their way to the West.[221]

Among the many new people Rinpoche met in Kalimpong was John Driver, a fellow of St. Anthony's College, Oxford. Driver, who spoke excellent Tibetan, was there to study with one of Tibet's most esteemed lamas, to whom he was deeply devoted. Rinpoche was much taken by his sparkling intelligence and knowledge, and the two soon became firm friends. It was another happy and fruitful exchange. In long sessions together, the Oxford don taught Rinpoche more English and fed him information and insights about the West, while the young lama gave Buddhist teaching in return. For Rinpoche the friendship was pivotal; he wrote that their conversations had "definitely inspired me to go eventually to Europe to teach."[222]

By now Rinpoche was at ease with much of the apparatus of the modern world: aircraft, trains, buses, radios and telephones had been woven into his life's fabric. He had also met his first Christians, missionaries up in the mountains in search of converts among the disoriented Tibetans. Their approach interested him, and he watched curiously as they distributed cartons of powdered milk and canned meat, together with poorly translated copies of the Bible – the handouts frequently accompanied by a commentary which compared their own generous Christian approach to the self-absorbed meditative style of the less-developed Buddhists.[223] As grateful as the malnourished refugees were for the food, few of the untutored people understood the profundities of Christianity, tending to find the doctrines of the Holy Ghost and the Blood of Christ somehow ghoulish and repellent.

After several months in Kalimpong, Rinpoche decided to move on. He would not be returning to the camp at Buxa Duar, nor would he be joining the Karmapa in Rumtek. His vision had expanded beyond the security of life as a high lama in a traditional monastery, broadened even beyond India. The wider world was beckoning, a time he later described as "filled with fascination and inquisitiveness." [224]

But where would he go and what would he do; how would he support himself? It appears that after his arrival in Kalimpong, Rinpoche had written to Freda Bedi in Buxa Duar, explaining his departure and telling her where he was, and that they had kept in touch since. Now he conceived the idea of heading to her home in Delhi. The rest would follow. It seems unlikely that Mrs. Bedi invited him: in her high government position, she could not be seen to collude with someone who had flouted government policy by escaping the camp. But she had written to Rinpoche, with her return address on the envelope. Rinpoche sent a message to Akong Tulku in Buxa Duar, asking him to join him on the journey to Delhi.

Tsethar the bursar was now too ill to travel and would stay in Kalimpong. Within a few weeks he too was dead, an indomitable defender of the Trungpa lineage as he saw it. Rinpoche would also be saying goodbye to the last of his Surmang companions, Yonten, whose life had similarly been devoted to the Trungpa lineage. A strong, highly capable and self-assured man, he became close to Rinpoche during the escape, and had seen to his physical needs and well-being, protecting him wherever he could. At times his presence had been critical to Rinpoche's very survival. As Rinpoche prepared to leave Kalimpong, he wrote to the Karmapa requesting that Yonten and an attendant be given employment in Rumtek.

After saying his farewells, Rinpoche left Kalimpong and joined Akong Tulku somewhere en route, possibly in Siliguri. Akong had recovered from his bout of tuberculosis, but his younger brother Jampal, desperately ill with tuberculosis, smallpox and dysentery, would stay where he was in Buxa Duar, to be cared for by fellow refugees. Jamyang was also far too sick to be moved; the brothers would manage to see each other just once more before he, the group's savior in their crisis in the Himalayas, would also be dead.

From their meeting point, Rinpoche and Akong Tulku made the thousand-mile train journey westwards across the hot, dusty plains of Bihar and Uttar Pradesh. At times, through their carriage window they could see the Himalayas gleaming on the northern horizon. For the first time in their lives the two lamas were completely alone – free of family, lamas, attendants, monks, visitors and officials. After arriving in Delhi, Mrs. Bedi's address in hand, they somehow found their way through the ancient, sprawling city to her home and knocked on the front door.

The appearance of the two young lamas in their saffron and maroon robes, tired and dusty from the long trip, took the Bedis by surprise. Without hesitation Freda Bedi took them into her home, including them as members of the family. There was little room in the dwelling provided by the Central Social Welfare Board, and Rinpoche and Akong Tulku were offered a screened-in veranda, equipped with a single bamboo bench. The veranda would be their quarters for the next several months, where they slept, studied and meditated.

Thanks to Mrs. Bedi's labors, the refugee camps had been thoroughly cleaned up and reorganized, while the initial flood of Tibetans had slowed to a steady stream. While she no longer needed to visit the camps as frequently, she still worked at her social welfare job during the week, but in her spare time she continued tutoring the two lamas in English. All three now understood that learning the language was essential if Buddhism was to be taught in the West.

The Bedis' home was well known in Delhi, its doors unlocked and open to friends, guests or anyone who wanted to drop in – including, apparently, passing burglars and the poor; little of their original furniture remained, the bulk of it having been carried off into the city. Their other visitors included academics and intellectuals, officials and diplomats, artists and bohemians, all of them there to engage in debate and discussion, or in simple celebration of each others' company. Among the many guests that the two lamas met at the Bedis' were Prime Minister Nehru and President Radhakrishnan, both of whom Rinpoche described as philosopher-statesmen, combining as they did spiritual insight with political skill. He also came to know Nehru's daughter, Indira Gandhi, who was good friends with Mrs. Bedi.

Few of the visitors had met a Tibetan lama before, and were fascinated by them, much taken by their friendliness and straightforwardness. They were especially struck by Rinpoche's charm and wit, the twinkle in his eye that went along with a quiet humor and a ready, impish playfulness. Only the Bedi family, though, was privy to the tireless teasing that went on between the two friends, the chaffing sometimes escalating into horseplay and wrestling on the living room floor.

Rinpoche had by now heard several varieties of spoken English: Mrs. Bedi's and John Driver's Oxford diction, the Christian missionaries' American twang, and the Prime Minister's tones, polished at Trinity College, Cambridge. It was clear to him that if he was to master the language he must learn to speak it properly. He began to train himself in Oxford pronunciation, emulating the BBC announcers he heard on radio newscasts, practicing their accent and phrasings afterwards, and surprising Akong Tulku and others by the accuracy of his BBC delivery.

Mrs. Bedi was still haunted by the memory of the young *tulkus* in the camps, the treasury of their training dissipating, their brilliance wasted among the rocks they broke for roads. She pondered ways of sheltering them and preserving their Buddhist teachings. It was clear that some sort of an institution – a real entity with buildings, teachers, staff – was necessary. She also understood that while the government could offer a refuge to homeless refugees, it was not in the business of rescuing and rebuilding religions. She would have to do it herself, using her wide network of contacts in England and India to raise the funds.

Mrs. Bedi found a ready and highly capable partner in Rinpoche, whose English was now good enough to actively join in the planning. Together they conceived of a school which would teach both Tibetan Buddhism and English. It would be called the Young Lamas Home School.

As they discussed their prospective students' needs, Rinpoche described the Tibetan Buddhist teachings to Mrs. Bedi in some depth. As she listened, she came to feel that the basic Buddhism she had known was broader and deeper in its Tibetan form. And so, while they worked on the school project, Rinpoche and Mrs. Bedi occasionally traveled to Rumtek to visit the Karmapa, first for his endorsement of the project, then to consult with him. Mrs. Bedi found herself strongly drawn to the Kagyu leader, more than to anyone she had met. Within a few years she was to give up her government work to become the Karmapa's disciple, later taking orders as a Tibetan Buddhist nun – the first Westerner to do so – with the name Karma Khechog Palmo, the widely-revered Sister Palmo.

By early 1961 the school project had been endorsed by the Dalai Lama and by the heads of the other schools of Tibetan Buddhism, and funds began to flow in. They rented a large house in Delhi and soon about twenty young *tulkus* from all four Tibetan Buddhist schools were in residence. The Dalai Lama appointed Rinpoche as principal and spiritual head, while Akong Tulku took over the school's administration; Mrs. Bedi taught English while continuing to raise funds. Along with the school's two main subjects, the young *tulkus* were taught the basics of how to get by in the modern world, topics which included Western table manners.

It was a fine start, meeting a vital need at a critical time for Tibetan Buddhism. But as summer approached, it became clear that the location would not work. For Tibetans, Delhi would be a furnace – but that was only part of the problem. For young men reared in monasteries in Tibet's remotest regions, modern Delhi would be dazzling, overwhelming. Bicycle rickshaws, taxis and garish billboards were all new and engrossing; the air swam with novel, tantalizing smells, of incense, cumin, coriander, turmeric and cloves, and roared and jangled with the sounds of engines, car horns, bicycle bells, and with shouts and songs from the teeming rivers of humanity; threading through it all was a rainbow of sari-clad women. Only the most disciplined young lama would cope in so seductive a storm. The school would have to move.

After consulting her circle of friends, Mrs. Bedi found a house once owned by British administrators in Dalhousie, north of Delhi. The town was another of the Raj's hill stations, established a century before as a summer retreat for troops and bureaucrats. Spread over five hills that were surrounded by snow-capped peaks, it was high, cool and quiet. In the large Victorian home, more *tulkus* could be accommodated and additional teachers taken on, including Westerners – with, at Rinpoche's insistence, preference given to English nationals with "proper" diction.

During the long winter vacation, Rinpoche and Akong Tulku hired a bus and led the young lamas on a tour of the region, the trip designed to introduce them to their new world. They met the Dalai Lama at his headquarters in Dharamsala, toured a number of Sikh temples and saw the capital at Simla, where they visited several government buildings. The tour ended in Delhi where, thanks to Mrs. Bedi, the entire group was granted an audience with Prime Minister Nehru, an encounter that was much enjoyed on all sides.

By the spring of 1962 the school was well-funded and flourishing, with Rinpoche continuing as principal, Akong Tulku as administrator. Akong's younger brother Jampal was brought to the school from Buxa Duar and joined the young lamas' classes; by now he had fully recovered from his serious diseases, thanks to his youth, the ministrations of his fellow refugees, and the removal of a lung.

Far from Dalhousie, in India's remote northeast, storm clouds were building. Tibet's new overlords were disputing the boundary lines along the India-Tibet border and, still furious at India's welcoming of refugees, were now blaming it for fomenting unrest in Tibet itself. In October, high in the Himalayas, a full-scale war broke out. Indian forces proved no match for the battle-hardened

Communists and were pushed back. PLA troops flooded over the Himalayas, even getting into Assam, just a few miles from the camp at Missamari.[225] Neither country wanted war, though, and the following month a truce was arranged. Soon afterwards, as Rinpoche had foreseen, the triumphant Communists sent troops to occupy the sacred land of Pema Ko.

By now the roles of Rinpoche and Akong Tulku in the creation and smooth functioning of the Young Lamas Home School had been widely recognized, and the Dalai Lama's government in Dharamsala decided to grant them a small salary. The extra funds were gratefully received, enabling them to cover their simple needs and to afford occasional visits to other lamas. It was a mixed blessing: as salaried employees, from this point on they had be working under the authority of the Tibetan government-in-exile.

It was not long before their new status as government employees was put to the test. Dharamsala notified Rinpoche and Akong Tulku that they would be leaving their posts at the school and going to Ceylon (today's Sri Lanka). It was not clear what their mission would be. The move may have been a primarily political one, Dharamsala wanting to get their own Gelugpa lamas in to run the young lamas' school, replacing the two Kagyus. Rinpoche and Akong Tulku were leading figures in a school whose tradition the Gelugpas had never really trusted, never seen as fully legitimate. Rinpoche later humorously described the relationship as comparable to the 1960s police attitude to hippies, although basically without antagonism.

In any event, the two friends may not have given the proposed Ceylon mission much thought. Whatever it might turn out to be, they were not interested. They had heard that the place was very hot, and in any event their sights were now set firmly on the West.

It was a delicate situation, and needed careful maneuvering. As government employees, Dharamsala also controlled Rinpoche's and Akong Tulku's travel documents and passports. Unless a legitimate reason for travel could be found, and unless the government felt comfortable with them as overseas representatives of Tibetan Buddhism, the documents would not be issued.

Rinpoche talked things over with Freda Bedi and John Driver, who contacted friends and colleagues in India and England. Before long, they had secured Rinpoche a Spalding scholarship to study comparative religion at Oxford University. Soon afterwards, whether due to a personal intervention by Nehru himself, at Mrs. Bedi's request, or as an expression of the high regard in which she herself was held by both Indians and Tibetans, Dharamsala released the two lamas from the Ceylonese mission and from government service altogether. They were also promised that their passports would not be a problem.

Rinpoche had done his bit to ensure a smooth outcome. He later talked of the tightly controlled Tibetan political situation in India, and how easily his departure could have been blocked. In his favor he had a reputation in the expatriate community for being bright and learned, while his astonishing escape had brought him renown, impressing the government-in-exile. And since arriving in India he had always worn his monk's robes and maintained his vows, including abstaining from food after noon – although in private he had enjoyed the occasional alcoholic drink with his hosts, the Bedis. Also, in his encounters with the Tibetan government he had been, as he put it, "fantastically yielding and seemingly very nationalistic." So when the time came to apply for travel documents, there was nothing that could be held against him, and he was simple and direct: "I have this grant, and I would like to leave India and go to England." [226]

Although the Spalding scholarship had been awarded to Rinpoche alone, there seems to have been not a moment's doubt that Akong Tulku would accompany him. Both were alight with the idea of going to the West, they were the closest of friends and had shared so much together, even dividing between them the small shreds of wealth that had not sunk into the waters of the Brahmaputra. It was inconceivable that they would part company now. The scholarship was a very modest one, barely enough for one person let alone two, but they would manage somehow. They would be going to Oxford together.

By early 1963, everything was ready for the departure to England. Rinpoche's journey to this point had been a long one. Over five years he had made a series of escapes: from his home monastery of Surmang, from his native land of Tibet, and from the camp at Buxa Duar; then, drawn by the vision of taking the Tibetan Buddhist teachings to the West, escapes shaded into evasions as he abandoned the security of a life in institutional Buddhism, his duty to the government-in-exile and, finally, any allegiance to Tibetan nationalism itself. He was entirely alone, free to follow his course as he saw it.

Both Rinpoche and Akong Tulku were looking forward to the journey, to England and all that lay ahead. After seeing them through the passport process, Mrs. Bedi purchased two steamship tickets to London from the Peninsular and Oriental Steam Navigation Company, fondly known in the old Empire as the P&O. Finally, to ensure their comfortable journey, she asked one of her sons to accompany the two lamas on the long journey south to Bombay.[227]

The farewell to Freda Bedi and her family was a wrenching and emotional one for them all. From their arrival in India, "Mummy-la" had done everything she could for them. It was a very great deal: from her vital help in the camps, through their passage to the modern world and their full entry into it, she had done it all, in every way needed. They would always be grateful to her, Rinpoche later writing: "She extended herself to me as a sort of destined mother and savior."[228]

Some time in late February, the train pulled into Bombay and the two lamas saw the ocean. It meant much to them. Although it was often used in Buddhist texts as a metaphor for the vast and spacious mind – 'Ocean of Dharma' was Rinpoche's Buddhist name – few Tibetans had ever seen the sea. Now there it was, a deep glistening blue stretching beyond the horizon, their way to an alluring vista of unexplored terrain.

The two friends stood on the verge of another journey, one that would pose challenges that would, in their way, be just as fierce and just as monumental as anything they had faced so far – the risks and danger just as great, the potential outcome perhaps greater. Rinpoche mentions no sense of foreboding or anxiety. He was excited by the freshness of it all, by the prospect of being on a ship entirely surrounded by Westerners, of engaging with the strange new world ahead.[229]

They were hosted in Bombay by one of Freda Bedi's friends, who showed them around the city. Then they went down to the docks and embarked on the P&O liner, bright in its white and yellow livery. Within the hour the ship had cast off its moorings, cleared the harbor and set course for Suez, England and the West.

Epilogue

In the first days of the spring of 1987, the Canadian seaport lay quiet under dark and ashen skies. Across the harbor nothing moved, every ship, tugboat and ferry locked in place by a mass of ice which covered the leaden sea from shore to shore. Sometimes heavy fog blew in, muffling sounds and dissolving shapes, blurring all like a fading memory.

In a strange nexus of weather, at the end of March powerful winds had blown ice floes southeast from Labrador and the Gulf of St. Lawrence, then northwest into Halifax's famously ice-free port. Once there the heavy floes, many of them over nine feet thick, were held firmly in place by the wind, thwarting every effort to clear them. Nothing like it had been seen for almost a century; nothing like it has been seen since.[230]

In the city's old Halifax Infirmary, Chögyam Trungpa Rinpoche lay dying. For six months he had been critically ill, and during that time Infirmary staff had graciously accommodated the unfamiliar Tibetan rituals surrounding death, along with the streams of students arriving to see him. At around 8 p.m. on Saturday, April 4, Rinpoche opened his eyes and gazed slowly and serenely around at those gathered at his bedside. Spontaneously, in soft and muted tones, they began to sing an anthem he had composed and, as they reached the last verse, he left this life.

After an ambulance transported the body to Rinpoche's home, his attendants, all of them Westerners, prepared and dressed the body according to Rinpoche's previous instructions, working fast in case *rigor mortis* set in. They need not have worried: the limbs remained loose and flexible well past the usual duration. The body, attired in ceremonial teaching robes, was then placed on a brocade cushion on the teaching throne, sitting upright in meditation posture.

By the next morning the news of his passing had reached Rinpoche's students world-wide, one remarking that "it was as though a huge hole had been torn in the fabric of the universe we had known."[231] The morning edition of Halifax's leading newspaper headlined the news at the top of the front page. Below was a report that the wind had shifted to the northeast, and was joining with the tide to move the ice floes back out to sea. After a weeklong shutdown, the port was returning to everyday business.[232]

Traditionally, when a realized master dies, he is understood to do so in a meditative state, a state not disrupted by death. During this time Buddhists understand that the body does not decay and should be left in place, usually for three days. The period is taken to be highly beneficial for the teacher's students, who can experience a unique stillness and absence of emotions. Rinpoche's students came in their hundreds from across the world to sit with the body. Along with the grief there was a sense of celebration, of who he was and all he had given and, pervading all, "the gaunt, eerie, ancient Trungpa manifestation, eleven lifetimes as one primordial presence."[233]

After a few days an attendant decided to check the placement of a sacred object near Rinpoche's heart. As he adjusted it, his hands suddenly warmed; in the chilly room the rest of the body was icy cold. Astounded, he mentioned it to others, including Rinpoche's widow, Diana, a thorough skeptic about such phenomena. Everyone vividly felt the warmth and, a few days later, physicians confirmed it.

Finally, five days after medical death, the state of meditation was judged to be complete, and the body was lowered from the throne and placed in a brass-colored metal casket. In a formal motorcade,

the casket was driven to the airport, where it was loaded onto a
specially chartered jet and installed in the first class cabin. With fifty
family and students sitting behind, accompanying Rinpoche on this
last journey, the aircraft took off and set course for Vermont.

In mid-March 1963 the P&O liner, inbound from India, had
steamed up the Thames estuary. Rinpoche and Akong Tulku gazed
out at the lines of ships, the endless wharves, cranes and buildings,
the streams of vehicles on rectilinear roads, and at jet aircraft
overhead, their roars filling the sky. They had made a long, almost
cosmic, journey through space and time: from an ancient spiritual
kingdom in the furthest reaches of the Himalayas to their new home,
the modern capital of what had, until recently, been the greatest
empire the world had ever known.

It had been an absorbing voyage for Rinpoche. In the ship's small
world he was, for the first time, entirely surrounded by Westerners,
most of them English. They were of a quite different stripe to those
he had known in India. Most had not quite emerged from the
halcyon days of empire, and many of the old habits remained:
outwardly affable, they were also reserved and distant and, although
they were intrigued to have the exotic Tibetan lamas aboard and
treated them with customary courtesy, the robed Asians were clearly
viewed as "not really one of us." It was a blunt introduction to
England's cool and mannered land.

The two lamas were welcomed at Tilbury Docks by a group of
English Buddhists and then driven to a home in London for a few
days' rest, in an England only just warming up from its coldest
winter in over two hundred years. Rinpoche then spent the summer
meeting people, teaching and leading programs. In the fall, they left
for Oxford and Rinpoche began his courses at the university,
studying comparative religion, philosophy, history and fine arts. In
the evenings he attended English classes, working to develop a
mastery of the language. Akong Tulku, although highly trained in

Tibetan medicine, could only find a menial hospital job, work which in time he grew to like.

Rinpoche's first impression of England had been that it was "very clean and orderly and, on the whole, very strange."[234] But he avidly learned all he could about the land: in Oxford he quickly grew to admire its more ancient, dignified culture; he also appreciated the free expressiveness of modern Western art.

A few months after their arrival he and Akong Tulku were interviewed by *The Oxford Times*, whose reporter marveled equally at their "nightmare journey" out of Tibet and their modesty about it. Asked what their feelings were as they struggled across the Himalayas, Rinpoche said: "We didn't have any. We just wanted to save everybody."[235]

Among the many people Rinpoche met in those early Oxford months was Esmé Cramer Roberts, who proposed that they do a book together. The following week they began work, and in 1966 *Born in Tibet* was published.

The following year an English Buddhist offered to turn over his contemplative center to the two lamas. Rinpoche leapt at the idea: what he really wanted to do was teach Buddhism. The center, lying among the gentle, rolling hills of Dumfriesshire, Scotland, was named Samye Ling, after the first Buddhist monastery in Tibet.

The news spread quickly, and people began to arrive in swelling numbers. Rinpoche was delighted by the enthusiasm, but as the weeks went by he grew dissatisfied. He felt that he was not really getting through to his English students: they seemed to be distracted by the Tibetan-ness of it all – viewing him, as he put it, as a kind of biological oddity, like "an exotic species of bird."[236]

In the late summer of 1968 Rinpoche received an invitation from the Queen of Bhutan to visit her country. During his stay he decided to make a pilgrimage to Tagstang – "Tiger's Nest" – a legendary cave where, more than a millennium before, the great Padmasambhava was understood to have subdued the demonic forces of the degenerate times.

In the cave at Tagstang Rinpoche saw with vivid and overwhelming clarity that he needed to project greater energy, further openness and more affection towards his students. He also realized that the true obstacle to teaching Buddhism in the West was what he called "spiritual materialism." It revealed itself in many forms: the hankering after miracles, the notion that blessings come from somewhere else, somewhere higher, and so on – even the very notion of attaining enlightenment was ultimately a trap. But at its core this materialism was simple: ego's wish to use spiritual teachings to solidify itself, to make the self somehow stronger and more exalted. Rinpoche knew that if Westerners could be trained to unmask this self-deception, they could follow the Buddhist path as thoroughly as anyone else. He left Tagtsang inspired, confident that his students would find the genuine path.

While in Delhi for his return flight, he stayed at the home of James George, the Canadian High Commissioner to India. They were soon good friends. One afternoon Rinpoche was handed a message saying that someone was there to see him. It was Jampal, Akong Tulku's younger brother. He had been in monk's training at the Karmapa's monastery in Sikkim, but detested his Buddhist training and monastic life as much as ever. Hearing that his old chum Trungpa Rinpoche would be at the High Commission, he waited until the Karmapa was away, then fled the monastery and headed for Delhi. He begged Rinpoche to get him out, saying, "Please take me with you." Without ado, and with the High Commissioner's aid, telegrams were dispatched, passports and entry permits swiftly arranged. Jampal said later that "with Trungpa Rinpoche's help I achieved all this in one month – usually people had to wait three or four years."[237]

Before leaving Delhi, Jampal contacted Samye Ling to tell his brother Akong Tulku that he would be arriving there soon. Then Rinpoche and his young friend went to the airport and boarded their flight. However, their destination was not Scotland but Paris. Jampal would not reveal what the two of them got up to in the City of

Light, merely laughing and saying: "Oh, we were just messing around ..."[238]

Rinpoche had begun to relax his monk's vows, exploring the implications of his Tagtsang breakthrough and a full opening to the West. As a boy, he had known that complete openness between teacher and student was crucial, an intuition confirmed when he met his guru, Jamgon Kongtrul, with his naturalness, love, and easy sense of humor. And he knew that it cut both ways: if students fixated on "the glorious image of spirituality" represented by monk's robes, there could be no open, genuine teaching.[239] He was coming to accept that removing his monk's robes would lift an obscuring veil.

A few months later, Rinpoche was driving his car in Northumberland when he blacked out and crashed through the front of a joke shop. At Newcastle General Hospital doctors found his injuries to be so severe that his left side would be permanently, if partially, paralyzed. He was in intense pain, but his mind was crystal clear: he felt relieved, even humorous, and there was a powerful sense of communication:

> When plunging completely and genuinely into the teachings, one is not allowed to bring along one's deceptions. I realized that I could no longer attempt to preserve any privacy for myself, any special identity or legitimacy. I should not hide behind the robes of a monk ... [240]

The accident shattered Rinpoche's last hesitations. He removed his robes and gave himself over to a process he described as like surgery without anaesthetic – peeling away his Tibetan and monastic identities layer by layer, cutting down all the way to the bone ... then, from inside out, allowing Western cultural styles and manners to settle, layer and grow.

Akong Tulku, meanwhile, had become increasingly dismayed by Rinpoche's drinking and his increasingly unpredictable behavior since his return from Bhutan. He was unwilling to join Rinpoche on this ultimate leg of the journey, feeling that it was too dangerous. Rinpoche recorded in his diary his distress at the pain caused to his dear friend by the course he was taking.[241] Later, though, as the two old friends' paths diverged, his attitude hardened and grew fiercer; tension mounted and arguments grew more frequent.

At this point a powerful new element entered the unfolding drama. In the previous years, as he had made his passage to the West, Rinpoche had received vital aid from two Englishwomen: Freda Bedi, who had given him crucial care following the escape, taught him English and enabled his move to Oxford; and Esme Cramer Roberts, who had proposed and co-produced the book that introduced him to the West. Now a third Englishwoman appeared on the scene, one who was to play the most decisive role of all.

In December 1968, just after Rinpoche's return from Bhutan, young Diana Pybus had heard that he would be talking at a Tibetan rally in London. From an upper-crust family, she was boarding at Benenden, one of England's pre-eminent girls' schools (an older schoolmate was Princess Anne, the Queen's daughter). While there she had come across the newly published *Born in Tibet*, found it engrossing and decided to attend the London rally. Looking up at him on the stage in his maroon and saffron robes, Diana felt "an immediate and intense connection ... deep and old ... like coming home." She had never felt anything as powerful, and said to herself: "This is what I've been missing all my life. Here he is again." [242]

From then on, Diana yearned to see Rinpoche. She had an interview with him in London and then attended a meditation program at Samye Ling. After that, though, she ran into an array of formidable obstacles,and it would be another six months before she could see him again. When the time finally came, she did not have the train fare to Scotland; undaunted, she hiked part of the way, then caught a train to Carlisle and, just before it entered the station where she would have to show her ticket, jumped out. She hit the ground hard before rolling down an embankment, and then, after dusting herself off, caught a taxi to Samye Ling. Rinpoche paid the fare.

On January 3, 1970, Rinpoche and Diana were married in Edinburgh. The event crowned an extraordinary year for him. Following his Tagtsang revelations he had completed a journey that was, in its way, as challenging as any he had faced so far – a lone trek across the landscape of the mind to fully embrace the West, to become one with it. Now, with Diana, he had made a splendid union with someone who was spirited and powerful in her own right, someone who would go with him wherever the journey led.

When Diana's mother read of the marriage she fainted. When the Tibetan community in Asia heard of it, and of the fractious events at Samye Ling, there was shock, dismay and much shaking of heads. Freda Bedi and others, though, barely raised their eyebrows. She had received many teachings from Rinpoche during his stay at the Bedi home, and had since taken ordination as a Tibetan Buddhist nun. It was obvious to her that Rinpoche was following the ancient, hallowed path of the *mahasiddhas* – saints who cast off convention and manifested a quality of "crazy wisdom" to bring the raw, rugged and intimately personal quality of the teachings home to students.[243]

Rinpoche himself was fully aware of the risks he was taking, and the likely reaction in both East and West. But his confidence was unshakably high, reflected in a poem, *In the North of the Sky*, which he wrote around this time. Its third stanza begins:

Here comes Chögyam dressed as a hailstorm.
No one can confront him.
It is too proud to say Chögyam is invincible,
But it is true to say he cannot be defeated ...

The stanza concluded: "He escaped from the jaw of the lion."[244]

Newlywed Diana now chose the course for the next leg of the journey, urging Rinpoche to leave Samye Ling and Britain for America. And so in March 1970 they flew to Canada to await their visas, and on May Day crossed into the United States. Then they made for the forested hills of northern Vermont, to an old farmhouse where people were gathered to greet them.

It was auspicious timing. With the Sixties counter-culture peaking, many young people were seeking a deeper, more authentic way of life. Within a few weeks word spread that Trungpa Rinpoche was in Vermont, that he had an easy command of the language, a great sense of humor, and enjoyed hanging out, drinking, smoking and talking.[245]

He was an eye-opener. In contrast to usual notions of a Buddhist holy man as somehow detached from the world, withdrawn into some pure and ineffable inner realm, Rinpoche was startlingly earthy. Far more than they were themselves, he was intensely, vibrantly aware of the details of the world around him, lovingly in touch with it all. And he was passionately curious about everyone he met, about who they were, where they came from. People who spent time with him came to realize that he had no personal agenda at all, that he manifested in whatever way a person's state of mind and situation required: tender and affectionate, stern and dark, drily ironic or impishly playful. He said: "compassion is not so much being kind; it is being creative to wake a person up."[246]

Rinpoche's open, rollicking, unassuming style struck a ringing chord with Americans. People flocked to hear this highly approachable Buddhist master who taught in brilliant English, and in a fresh, direct and humorous way. His love of the arts – he was an accomplished calligrapher, poet, painter, playwright and flower arranger – drew many poets and musicians to him, among them Allen Ginsberg, William Burroughs, Joni Mitchell and David Bowie, to whom he may well have given his stage name.[247]

He also worked closely with businessmen, educators and administrators, psychologists and medical professionals, gardeners, cooks and many others, counseling them to connect more deeply with their own worlds, encouraging them to seek out the inherently valuable qualities of Western culture, those qualities that foster an appreciation of natural human dignity and of traditional culture.

His key teaching, then and later, was of the dangers of spiritual materialism – ego's use of spirituality to puff itself up – and he was scathing about what he called the "love and light" approaches that were on glittering display in the "the spiritual supermarket." He taught that the chief method for cutting through self-deception was sitting meditation … just sitting, relaxing, attending to the breath and making friends with oneself, with both one's neurotic and enlightened nature. It was simple, ordinary and almost unbelievably profound.

Rinpoche's majestic command of the English language enabled him to transmute its ego-based syntax into a vehicle for the teachings of egolessness – a word he coined that is now in the Oxford English Dictionary. Today the words and phrases he used to convey Buddhist terms and concepts in English are employed by most Buddhist teachers in the English-speaking world. Rinpoche was not above deploying slang or idiom if it helped to communicate. When acronyms came into vogue, he coined a few of his own as snappy reminders of equanimity, of not getting carried away by hopes and fears, or the highs and lows of everyday life: "CCL" for Couldn't Care Less and "DRM": Doesn't Really Matter.

Centers devoted to his teachings sprang up around the country, and then in Canada, Europe and beyond. Within the year, he set up home in Boulder, Colorado, and in 1973 he established his international headquarters there. The old Vermont farmhouse was named Tail of the Tiger, and within a few years had become a major meditation center.

Then, in a blur of activity, he created an array of teacher training programs and organizations, all taking their place in a rich, multifaceted society – among them a translation committee, a mediation council, a credit union, an association of health professionals, a theater group, a preschool and an elementary school, and organizations devoted to the study and practice of the Japanese tea ceremony, flower arranging and archery. Still, Rinpoche never seemed hurried, spending his time quietly, humorously, effortlessly.

In 1974 Rinpoche founded Naropa University, later to become a fully accredited college. That year the Karmapa toured Europe and North America and, fully aware of Rinpoche's often controversial style, visited his centers and met his students. The Karmapa then penned a ceremonial proclamation in which he stated that Rinpoche had "magnificently carried out the vajra holders' discipline in the land of America, bringing about the liberation of students and ripening them in the *dharma*. This wonderful truth is clearly manifest."[248] The proclamation, from one of the few authorities qualified to judge, was both a high honor and a consummate recognition of Rinpoche's accomplishments.

The year 1976 was an especially ground-breaking one. Rinpoche introduced the Shambhala vision, teaching on the basic goodness of all beings and on the creation of an enlightened society. Among the texts he composed on these teachings was a summary of the one he had consigned to the Brahmaputra under gunfire. In these teachings he also spoke of monarchs who had ruled in enlightened ways, among them the fifteenth century Emperor Yung Lo of China.[249] Whatever Rinpoche's views of the People's Liberation Army's actions in his homeland may have been, he retained a very high regard for the people and culture of China, and would invariably treat Chinese people he met with the utmost warmth and respect.

Also in 1976, reflecting Rinpoche's consummate embrace of the West, he broke all historical precedent by proclaiming an American, Thomas Rich, as his "dharma heir" – someone fully empowered to carry on his Tibetan Buddhist teachings. Also around this time he created the Dorje Kasung, a military-style service organization tasked with protection and other duties. Its slogan was "Victory Over Aggression," while its training was a close facsimile of the monastic discipline which had served him so well as a boy.

That year Rinpoche was also briefly reunited with Yonten. His old Surmang friend was traveling with Rinpoche's revered teacher from those days, Dilgo Khyentse Rinpoche, whom Yonten had served for many years. One of Yonten's missions had taken him to Tibet, when he was able to visit Surmang. He felt nothing for the place: its buildings were tumbled ruins, its community an empty husk, its art and sacred texts scattered to the winds; and everyone he had known there had either fled or died.

Rinpoche and Diana were by now the parents of three sons, but Diana also found the time to take the Shambhala teachings in a fresh and deeply authentic direction. From the age of four, she had loved horses and riding, and now saw that they offered excellent vehicles for mind-body discipline. She took it to the highest level, becoming one of the few women ever accepted for training in Vienna's famed Spanish Riding School. Diana later described how, in dressage training, the rider relies on her own inborn capacity for wakefulness to fully communicate with the horse, gently encouraging his willingness to work while enhancing his natural movements, so that "he feels good in his mind about it."[250] At this point, the horse's movements are beautiful and he and the rider become one, merged in a lovely, regal unity.

In 1979 Rinpoche assured the future of the Shambhala teachings by ceremonially confirming his eldest son Ösel as his Shambhala heir, the teacher empowered to carry on his vision of basic goodness and enlightened society. Sixteen years later, Ösel would fully take on that mantle and, with the name Sakyong Mipham Rinpoche, has steered the teachings forward into the new century. Today he is a well-known meditation teacher with many devoted students around the world, also guiding a number of projects on social transformation and other humanitarian issues. Like his father he is an accomplished poet, author and artist. He is also an athlete, and among his books on the practical application of Shambhalian teachings is *Running with the Mind of Meditation.*[251]

During the winter of that year Rinpoche was teaching in Nelson, British Columbia, when he was given a Lhasa Apso. From the start, the small, shaggy dog refused to have anything to do with anyone else. Yumtso, as Rinpoche named her, grudgingly went for walks with people or disdainfully sniffed the food they offered her, and then bounded back to Rinpoche to sit at his feet. He gave her the tenderest morsels from his plate and took her everywhere he went. When he taught she sat under his chair, sitting up, awake and still, gazing out at the audience. Some time later, Rinpoche offhandedly mentioned to an attendant that Yumtso was his bursar, and said nothing more on the matter. The attendant took him to mean that Tsethar the bursar, who had died in Kalimpong nearly two decades before, had been reborn and found his way back to his abbot.[252]

The following year, 1980, the Karmapa again toured the West and ordained several monks at his center in Woodstock, New York.

Among them was Jampal. Throughout the seventies he had been hell-bent on hedonism, drinking and carousing his way through Scotland, Europe and North America. But he'd had his fill, finally surrendering to, and requesting ordination from, the Karmapa. He then entered a series of intensive retreats, emerging almost skeletal, but with his mind luminously clear. Today, as Lama Yeshe Rinpoche, abbot of Samye Ling, he is a highly respected teacher, well known throughout Europe and Asia. Like a spirited wild horse that needed much kindness and space before he could be tamed, he had received both from Trungpa Rinpoche, whom he credited with having had the greatest effect on him of any teacher he had known.[253]

By the early 1980s, Rinpoche had been widely recognized as a major figure in the introduction of Buddhism to the West. He had transmuted the English language into a vehicle for the teaching of egolessness. He had presented the teachings of Tibetan Buddhism in all their richness and depth, doing so in a fresh and contemporary way. He had fully laid out the Shambhala vision for the creation of an enlightened society. And he had founded a host of organizations, including a university, an abbey for monastics and major meditation centers in North America and Europe; hundreds of centers studying his teachings had sprung up around the world. He had given over five thousand talks, the vast majority of them archived as video and audio recordings; books transcribed from them would later sell over a million copies, with many more editions yet to come. Most of this had been accomplished in around ten years.

During the early 1980s Rinpoche was spending much of his time in Nova Scotia, Canada, which he called "the province of no big deal."[254] It was a place he had grown to love for its beauty and ruggedness, and for the gentle culture of its people. It was, finally, where he would settle.

His health, though, was in obvious decline. Like many Tibetans in the West, he suffered from high blood pressure and diabetes brought on by the low altitudes and unfamiliar food, conditions which were exacerbated by drinking, by the daily strain of the paralysis and by a lifetime of unstinting exertion. His failing body seemed only to boost his action: he conducted two major teaching programs, then moved his home from Boulder into a courtly residence in Halifax's South End, and brought his organization's international headquarters to a building nearby.

In late September 1986 Rinpoche suffered respiratory failure and cardiac arrest, and was taken to the city's old Infirmary. For six months his condition swung up and down, but then sharply worsened, and he was moved into the Intensive Care Unit.

❋

In Burlington, Vermont, the metal casket holding Rinpoche's body was transferred from the aircraft to a motorcade, then driven across the state and up into the wooded hills, to the meditation center with its old farmhouse where Rinpoche had first taught in North America.

In the shrine room the body, still in meditation posture, was transferred from the casket to a wooden reliquary box, which was then filled with a compound of salt, camphor and a variety of herbs mixed to an ancient formula; every few days the mixture was replaced. The body remained there for a period that included the traditional forty-nine days from death, and was then cleaned with saffron water and moved into a reliquary box of bare cherrywood.[255]

On the early morning of May 26, thousands of people filled a small meadow above the center. There, surrounded by forested hills that formed a natural amphitheater, a twenty-foot-high Buddhist cremation stupa had been built, painted brilliant white and surmounted by a gold spire, then ornamented by a famous Tibetan painter.[256] Around it, positioned as an open square, were large white tents adorned with colorful Tibetan symbols.

The major media had sent crews to record an event never before seen in the West, the full formal cremation of a high Tibetan lama, and reporters and cameramen were scattered across the meadow and in the surrounding woods. Then the dignitaries arrived, preceded by leaders of Tibet's Buddhist lineages. Dilgo Khyentse Rinpoche, who had taught Trungpa Rinpoche as a boy at Surmang, would be presiding over his cremation. Among the honored guests were James George, the former Canadian High Commissioner to India, and four nurses who had recently attended Rinpoche in the Halifax Infirmary.

As the ceremony began, thick mist cloaked the surrounding hills. From deep in the woods, an approaching bagpiper could be heard playing a lament; from somewhere behind him, like a somber heartbeat, came the slow cadence of a bass drum and, from further back, the low, haunting wail of Tibetan horns. Slow marching directly behind the piper was an honor guard, followed by a party of Tibetan monks, and then the canopied, silk-curtained reliquary box carried on the shoulders of eight uniformed students; just behind it were Diana and her young family, and a group of Rinpoche's close students. As the piper stepped out onto the open meadow, the mist slowly drew back from the hills, revealing a brilliant sky flecked with white clouds.

In complete silence, the crowd watched as the procession made its slow, ceremonious way under a Japanese Torii gate to the cremation stupa, and then as the reliquary box was carefully placed inside. At that point, Shibata Sensei, the heir to twenty generations of Imperial Bow Makers to the Emperor of Japan and now Rinpoche's student, performed a stark and moving ceremony in front of the stupa, one only conducted when an emperor dies: plucking an empty bow in the four cardinal directions and then offering straw sandals for the pyre.

At around 11 a.m. the fire was lit. As the flames took hold flags were raised, and the roar of a highly charged cannon rocked the hills around. For a while the fire burned with great intensity, orange flames shooting into a bright sky now completely free of clouds. Then, as it died down, a few people glanced upwards. Soon everyone was looking up, pointing to the sky. A perfect circle of rainbow light surrounded the sun, while an array of rainbow shapes spread out across the vivid blue – signs traditionally associated with key events in the life of a great master.

Skeptics in the crowd might have pointed out that the "rainbows" were probably high altitude cirrus ice crystals, tiny prisms refracting the sun's rays, while their on-cue appearance at the ceremony's climax could, at a stretch, be written off as mere statistical coincidence. Newspapers reporting the event did not cavil: one front page headline read "Rainbow Seen at Ceremony," another "Rainbow Cheers Followers of Buddhist Leader," while a third simply reported what all had seen: "as the fire died down a dramatic series of rainbows filled the sky."[257]

Curiously, two lamas present also downplayed the rainbows, perhaps to cut through the flutter of excitement, maybe because such things were normal on these occasions. Their eyes had anyway been more on the unfolding of events: the timely lifting of the covering mist, followed by the unfurling of clouds shaped like white silk Tibetan offering scarves, then the rainbow displays and, finally, three hawks circling directly overhead, which the lamas said were goddesses who had taken birdlike form to welcome Rinpoche home.

No-one, not even those closest to him, would ever claim to know what Rinpoche might say or do. But those who had met him or heard or studied his teachings – especially those on the pitfalls of spiritual materialism – might not find it too hard to imagine him looking over his glasses at the day's supernormal events, or those of the weeks and years before, and saying to whoever was with him, simply and kindly and without the faintest touch of irony: "DRM" – doesn't really matter.

However that might be, by mid-afternoon the ceremonies were over, and dignitaries and monastics, family and friends, students and admirers, television crews and reporters had made their way down the hill, then to their work and homes across the globe. By nightfall the place was empty of crowds, its events a memory.

Within a few days the woodland meadow was as still as it had ever been. At its high point now stood the white stupa, in plain and open union with all around it, solid and indomitable on Vermont's good earth.

Acknowledgements

This book has been years in gestation, and many people have helped to bring it to fruition.

I would like to express my heartfelt thanks to Diana Mukpo, for her permission to re-tell the story and to include Trungpa Rinpoche's maps and drawings, and for her encouragement, which turned a plodding walk into a trot. Thank you, too, to Gesar Mukpo for his inspiration and leadership on our Kathmandu expedition.

Survivors of the escape generously shared their recollections with us. The late Akong Tulku Rinpoche, Lama Yeshe Losal Rinpoche, Yonten Gyamtso, Palya Washutsong (Pasang Dolma) and Drupju Washutsong all added a fresh, personal and often revelatory dimension to what we knew. It was a privilege to meet them, and I am profoundly grateful to them all.

Without the unstinting support of Walter and Joanne Fordham, whose wisdom and friendship have guided the project from the outset, this story might not have seen the light of day. I would also like to thank Carolyn Gimian for her guidance, and her archival, literary and publishing help; also James Gimian for his ready support and publishing advice. Thanks also go to Johanna Demetrakas for generously sharing her interview material.

The book owes much to Ruth Nicola, for whose companionship and fine literary eye I am deeply grateful; and to Kent Martin, whose friendship, support and insights have been invaluable. Thank you too to Barry Boyce, Jeanne Riordan, Kathy WagnerLiza Matthews, Diane Metzger, Bob Ziegler, Don Winchell, Jim Lowery, Deborah Kaetz, Jutta Stawitz and Steve Ritchie, all of whose skills and generosity have added greatly to the book, and to its printing and publication.

Others have contributed much to this project, and I would like to thank the Shambhala Archives, James Hoagland and the Shambhala

Trust, the Hemera Trust, the Nova Scotia Archives, Larry Mermelstein, Ani Jinba, Petra Mudie, Lyndon Comstock, Jim Lowrey, Andrew Rock and Nancy Natilson, John Perks, Mark Nowakowski and Clark Warren.

A number of friends offered generous support. I am most grateful to John Leon and Rowena MacLeod, Michael Chender, Barbara and Denault Blouin, Chris Magnus, Hedy Bookin-Weiner, Michael Naugler, Steve Brooks, Kay Crinean, Anna Taylor, Hermine Geertrui Rodenburg, Marion Stork, John Neill, Martin Janowitz, Sally Walker and Jan Wilcox.

I would also like to thank Ronald Barnstone, Christine Bauman, Edmund Butler, Kathleen Calkins, Lucille Celestino, Steven Daniels, Ruth Dillon, Robert Bruce Dodds, Richard Freeman, Nancy Green, Newcomb Greenleaf, Norbert Hasenoehrl, Stephen Holder, Christopher St. John, David Joiner, Robert Kennedy, Rinus Laban, B. van Lieshout, Deborah Luscomb, George Marshall, Marvin Moore, Stefan Mulder, Natural Health Inc., Loring Palmer, Richard Peisinger, Rebecca Peloso, Trime Persinger, Leda Powers, Kathleen Pew, Otto Pichlhoefer, J.T.M. Pollmann, Andrea Pucci, Leah Regulinski, Hal Richman, Esther Rochon, Ruby Shoes Productions, Jean Spencer, Tjandra Soegiarto, Vera Schoelmerich, Rose Sposito, Susan Szpakowski, Agnes Tam, David Veleta, Irene Vliegenthart, Kunga Washutong, John Weber, Samten de Wet, George Woodard and Sarah Woodard, and Nick Wright.

Many other friends have supported the project and, although limited space prevents the inclusion of all their names, their help has been invaluable in furthering it. Thank you.

This book is the fruit of people's help and generosity, and its merit is shared with all. Where it fails, the responsibility is mine; friends may, though, feel reassured to know that survivors' accounts, images and videos will be archived, awaiting the time when this shining story finds the author, scholar or filmmaker it deserves.

APPENDIX

In the North of the Sky

In the north of the sky there is a great and dark cloud
Just about to release a hailstorm.
Mind, children,
Mind, young puppies and kittens,
That your heads are not injured.
But these hailstorms are merely pellets of ice.

There are hundreds of magicians
Who try to prevent storm and hail
In the course of time
All the ritual hats, altars and ritual garments
Have been blown away by the force of these hailstorms.

Here comes Chögyam dressed as a hailstorm.
No one can confront him.
It is too proud to say Chögyam is invincible,
But it is true to say he cannot be defeated.
Chögyam is a tiger with whiskers and a confident smile.
This is not a poem of pride
Nor of self-glorification:
But he is what he is.
He escaped from the jaw of the lion.

"Clear away," says the commander,
"You are standing on no-man's land,
We do not want to shoot innocent people."
We cannot alter the path of the shell.
The bomb once it is released knows its duty;
It has to descend. Chögyam knows his course....

Chögyam Trungpa. *The Collected Works of Chögyam Trungpa*, Vol. 7. Ed.
Carolyn Rose Gimian. Shambhala Publications. Boston. 2004. 303.

Resources

A variety of resources can be found here:

www.fromlionsjaws.ca

- Maps, including large-size, downloadable version of Chögyam Trungpa's hand-drawn maps.

- Galleries of images – Chögyam Trungpa and other survivors of the escape, and key figures appearing in the story; also images of scenery on the route.

- Google Earth files of paths and placemarks, downloadable, enabling the reader to track the route, see the terrain they faced.

- Discovering the Route – an illustrated account of what it took to locate places and find the refugees' route.

- A one-page overview of the escape's place in history.

- Links to a one-hour video of the escape – which comes with a strong spoiler alert, and a list of errata.

Selected Reading

Trungpa, Chögyam. *Born in Tibet.* Shambhala Publications. Boston, 1985.

Trungpa, Chögyam. *Crazy Wisdom.* Shambhala Publications. Boston, 1991.

Trungpa, Chögyam. *Journey Without Goal, The Tantric Wisdom of the Buddha.* Shambhala Publications. Boston, 2000.

Trungpa, Chögyam. *The Mishap Lineage: Transforming Confusion into Wisdom.* Shambhala Publications. Boston, 2009.

Mukpo, Diana J. *Dragon Thunder: My Life with Chögyam Trungpa.* Shambhala Publications. Boston, 2006.

Baker, Ian. *The Heart of the World, A Journey to Tibet's Lost Paradise.* Penguin Books. New York, 2004.

Brauen, Yangzom. *Across Many Mountains, The Extraordinary Story of Three Generations of Women in Tibet.* Vintage Books. London, 2001.

Chan, Victor. *Tibet Handbook: A Pilgrimage Guide.* Moon Publications. California, 1994.

Diemberger, Maria. *Tibet, The Roof of the World Between Past and Present.* White Star. Vercelli, Italy, 2002.

Feigon, Lee. *Demystifying Tibet: Unlocking the Secrets of the Land of the Snows.* Elephant Publishers. Chicago, 1996.

Fields, Rick and Cutillo, Brian (transl.). *The Turquoise Bee, The Lovesongs of the Sixth Dalai Lama.* HarperCollins. New York, 1998.

Fugard, Sheila Meiring. *Lady of Realisation.* Biography of Sister Palmo. 1st ed. Cape Town. Maitri Publications, 1984. Library of Congress, No. Txu 140-945, Cape Town: Electronic Ed., 19 April 1999.

Goldstein, Melvyn C. *The Snow Lion and the Dragon: China, Tibet, and the Dalai Lama.* University of California Press. 1999.

Hilton, Isabel. *The Search for the Panchen Lama.* Penguin Books. London, 1999.

Jarvis, Tim. *Chasing Shackleton: Re-Creating The World's Greatest Journey Of Survival.* HarperCollins, NY. 2014.

Knaus, John Kenneth. *Orphans of the Cold War: America and the Tibetan Struggle for Survival.* PublicAffairs, New York, 1999.

Laird, Thomas. *The Story of Tibet, Conversations with the Dalai Lama.* Grove Press. New York, 2006.

Nalanda Translation Committee (transl.). *The Rain of Wisdom, the Vajra Songs of the Kagyu Gurus.* Shambhala Publishers. Boulder and London, 1980.

Patterson, George N. *Tragic Destiny, The Khamba Rebellion in Tibet.* Long Riders' Guild Press, 1959.

Rinchen Khandro, Ani. *Kagyu Samye Ling: The Story.* Dzalendara Publishing. Eskadlemuir, Scotland. 2007.

Schell, Orville. *Virtual Tibet, Searching for Shangri-La from the Himalayas to Hollywood.* Metropolitan Books. New York, 2000.

Shakya, Tsering. *The Dragon in the Land of Snows: A History of Modern Tibet Since 1947.* Columbia University Press. New York, 1999.

Talty, Stephan. *Escape from the Land of the Snows, The Young Dalai Lama's Harrowing Flight to Freedom and the Making of a Spiritual Hero.* Crown. New York, 2011.

NOTES

ABBREVIATIONS:
CT: Chögyam Trungpa
BIT: Born in Tibet
YG: Yonten Gyamtso
LYR: Lama Yeshe Rinpoche

Prologue

[1] Stephan Talty, *Escape from the Land of the Snows, The Young Dalai Lama's Harrowing Flight to Freedom and the Making of a Spiritual Hero:* Crown, New York, 2011.

[2] Talty, 198. [3] CT, *Born in Tibet,* George Allen & Unwin, London, 1966, currently published by Shambhala Publications, Boston. While the current work draws heavily on Trungpa's account, *Born in Tibet* will be cited only for specific quotations or excerpts from the book, taken from the 1985 edition.

[4] Unknown to the author a French colleague, Eric Rugani, had come to similar realizations about the escape and had embarked on the identical journey, using Rinpoche's account and maps along with satellite imagery to find the escape route. Although there are differences between our versions of the escape route, these are relatively minor, and our independent work has effectively confirmed the route. The two routes, along with the author's and Eric's narratives of the project are available for downloading and viewing and on the book's website. (See Appendix: *Resources*).

[5] BIT, 230-1. If there are any doubts about the difficulties such under-editing can present to the reader, they might be laid to rest by the following. In the video version of the river-crossing episode, the narrator states "Only fourteen made it across that night." It's a dramatic and shocking statement, but it turns out to be untrue. In the middle of the long descriptive paragraph mentioned, Trungpa Rinpoche clearly states that fifty refugees made it to the strip of land near the south bank. Yet of the sizeable number of people who saw the movie – a good proportion of whom had previously read *Born in Tibet* – no-one seems

320

to have noticed the video's error. The highly significant fact had apparently been missed by all, buried in the midst of a dense and over-long paragraph.

⁶ CT, *The Mishap Lineage: Transforming Confusion into Wisdom:* Shambhala Publications, Boston, 2009. 101.

Judith Smith was present when Rinpoche recounted the story in Boulder in 1978, just before he left to lead the yearly Seminary, which that year was held at Lake Louise, Alberta (personal communication, May 3, 2013).

⁸ Drupju Washutsong interview, Walter and Joanne Fordham. Portland, Oregon. June, 2013.

⁹ Tim Jarvis, *Chasing Shackleton: Re-Creating The World's Greatest Journey Of Survival.* HarperCollins, NY. 2014.

¹⁰ Additional works consulted for this account: Shackleton, Ernest, *South: The Story of Shackleton's 1914–17 Expedition,* London: Century Publishing, 1982 [1919]; Huntford, Roland, *Shackleton,* Athenaeum, 1986; and Smith, Michael, *Shackleton,* Oneworld, 2014.

¹¹ In the precarious circumstances and under the prevailing naval discipline, the latter version is highly credible. Later in the journey, an experienced officer, Frank Wild, appointed by Shackleton to command the marooned crew in his absence, having noticed that food was being pilfered, calmly announced that he would shoot anyone caught in the act; no further food was stolen (Smith, 341).

Chapter 1

¹² Sir Thomas Holdich, cit. in Schell, Orville, *Virtual Tibet, Searching for Shangri-La from the Himalayas to Hollywood,* Metropolitan Books, New York, 2000, 7-8.

¹³ cit. in Diemberger, Maria, *Tibet, The Roof of the World Between Past and Present:* White Star, Vercelli, Italy, 2002. 6-7.

¹⁴ cit. in Schell, 17.

¹⁵ cit. in Schell, 15.

¹⁶ cit. in Schell, 16.

[17] BIT has the birthdate as 1939. This is based on the traditional Tibetan approach, which calculates birthdate from date of conception. Trungpa Rinpoche later corrected the date to 1940, the "Year of the Dragon." Western dates are used throughout here.

[18] CT, *The Mishap Lineage, Transforming Confusion into Wisdom:* Shambhala, Boston, 2009, 63.

[19] BIT, 27.

[20] BIT, 28.

[21] Chökyi Gyatso was later contracted to "Chögyam" and it was as Chögyam Trungpa that he became known in the West.

[22] For the sake of brevity, Chögyam Trungpa Rinpoche, as both the chronicler of the story and its protagonist, will be referred to in the text as "Trungpa Rinpoche" or by the shorthand "Rinpoche," an honorific term, like "Dalai Lama." Referring to him simply as "Chögyam" or "Trungpa" alone would be seen as a sign of disrespect. For clarity, other incarnate lamas who appear in the narrative are referred to in the longer and more formal style, e.g. "Akong Tulku," "Yag Tulku."

[23] CT, *The Mishap Lineage,* 53.

[24] Rick Fields and Brian Cutillo (transl.), *The Turquoise Bee, The Lovesongs of the Sixth Dalai Lama:* HarperCollins, New York, 1998, 20.

[25] BIT, 31.

[26] BIT, 44.

[27] CT, *The Mishap Lineage,* 49.

[28] BIT, 47.

[29] BIT, 47.

[30] CT, *The Mishap Lineage.* 69.

[31] CT. Foreword to Nalanda Translation Committee (transl.), *The Rain of Wisdom, the Vajra Songs of the Kagyu Gurus,* Shambhala Publications, Boulder and London, 1980, xi.

[32] CT, *Crazy Wisdom:* Shambhala, Boston, 1991, 48.

[33] CT, *Journey Without Goal,* 97-99.

[34] Sakyong Mipham Rinpoche, Trungpa Rinpoche's son and the heir to his Shambhala tradition, succinctly made this aspect of Rinpoche's training clear in his 1994 Foreword to *Born in Tibet,* p.7; there he talked of Westerners' view of the training of a high lama as harsh and medieval, when in truth it is the training's blunt simplicity and "realness" that so fully prepared the young lama for the many challenges he would face later.

[35] BIT, 51.

[36] BIT, 52.

[37] BIT, 51.

Chapter 2

[38] Edward Balfour, *The Cyclopædia of India and of Eastern and Southern Asia,* Vol. II, Bernard Quaritch, London,1885, 299. Google E-book. Retrieved July 23, 2014.

[39] Lee Feigon, 43.

[40] Feigon, 51.

[41] CT, *Mishap Lineage,* 50.

[42] The modern transliteration. In BIT Trungpa Rinpoche renders the name as "Ma Bu Feng."

[43] Cited in *Ma Bufang.* Validated Wikipedia entry: Retrieved November 11, 2014.

[44] Melvyn C. Goldstein (1991), *A History of Modern Tibet, 1913-1951: the Demise of the Lamaist State.* University of California Press. 321. ISBN 0-520-07590-0. Retrieved August 5, 2013.

[45] "Foreign News: The Northwest Falls." *TIME*. Monday, Oct. 03, 1949. Retrieved August 5, 2013.

[46] Chen Jian. *The Tibetan Rebellion of 1959 and China's Changing Relations with India and the Soviet Union.* Cold War Studies at Harvard University. Retrieved July 25, 2013.

[47] BIT, 91.

[48] BIT, 63.

[49] BIT, 116.

[50] BIT, 117.

[51] BIT, 119.

[52] The U.S. had extensively supplied Chiang Kai-Shek's republican forces with arms both during World War II and later.

[53] George N. Patterson, *Tragic Destiny: The Khamba Rebellion in Tibet*, The Long Riders Guild Press, 1959. 174.

[54] BIT, 120.

[55] BIT, 127.

Chapter 3

[56] Garab, *Glimpses of Trungpa Rinpoche*. Video documentary, Lyndon Comstock.

[57] BIT, 137.

[58] Akong Rinpoche interview by Johanna Demetrakas, Samye Ling, 2008, for *Crazy Wisdom* feature documentary. Crazy Wisdom Productions, 2011.

[59] YG, interview, Boudha, April 30, 2012

[60] Garab, *Glimpses of Trungpa Rinpoche*.

[61] Op. cit.

[62] Akong Rinpoche, personal communication, September 6, 2013.

324

[63] This view was partially confirmed, a few months after the chapter draft was completed, when the author read an interview conducted by Walter Fordham with Karma Senge Rinpoche, Trungpa Rinpoche's nephew, conducted in July, 2005. Karma Senge talks of Trungpa Rinpoche's having had a vision of Mahakala, a protector deity, warning him against returning to Surmang. Subsequently, Trungpa Rinpoche delayed returning, saying that they "should just take it a bit slow, and it may just turn out that [they] wouldn't need to go to Dütsi Tel [Surmang]." Karma Senge, *Don't go to Dütsi Tel.* Chronicles of Trungpa Rinpoche. Retrieved November 6, 13.

[64] Denma Translation Group, *Sun Tzu, The Art of War: A New Translation.* Shambhala Publications. Boston, 2001.

[65] BIT, 137.

[66] YG, April 18, 2012.

[67] YG, April 18, 2012

[68] BIT, 138.

[69] YG, April 18, 2012.

[70] BIT, 143.

[71] YG, April 20, 2012.

[72] BIT, 146.

[73] BIT, 147.

[74] YG interview with Surmang Khenpo, Boudha, November, 2010.

[75] YG, April 18, 2012.

Chapter 4

[76] YG interview with Surmang Khenpo, Boudha, November, 2010.

[77] It is conceivable that when Rinpoche worked on the book, he adjusted these durations and directions away from the actual ones, to prevent any chance of the landowner and other friends in the area from being tracked down and persecuted.

[78] BIT, 159.

[79] YG interview with Surmang Khenpo, Boudha, November, 2010.

[80] BIT, 161.

[81] BIT, 83.

[82] BIT, 163.

[83] BIT, 163.

[84] BIT, 166.

Chapter 5

[85] BIT, 168.

[86] BIT, 169.

[87] BIT, 169.

[88] BIT, 169.

[89] YG, Surmang Khenpo interview, Boudnath, Nepal, Nov. 2010.

[90] YG interview, Boudnath, Nepal., Apr. 30, 2012.

[91] YG, Apr. 19, 2012.

[92] YG, Apr. 18, 2012.

[93] YG, Surmang Khenpo interview, Boudnath, Nepal, Nov. 2010.

[94] BIT, 171.

[95] BIT, 172.

[96] BIT, 174.

[97] There are a number of extenuating factors that may have played a role, but in the end we don't know why Yag Tulku chose so flagrantly to ignore Rinpoche's pleas for secrecy and to keep his traveling party small. Yet he'd ignored him earlier, when Rinpoche interrupted the Treasury Teachings to meet Khamtrul

Tulku concerning the escape, and it's hard to avoid the feeling that, like Tsethar the bursar, Yag Tulku didn't always consider Rinpoche's views worthy of full adult consideration. If this was indeed the case, in the course of the journey Yag Tulku's attitude would change profoundly.

[98] BIT, 179.

[99] Although the text was to be lost during the escape, the vision came to light again later, in Rinpoche's Shambhala teachings presented in North America in the 1970s and '80s.

[100] BIT, 180.

[101] YG interview, Boudnath, Nepal, Apr. 18, 2012.

[102] YG interview, Boudnath, Nepal, Apr. 25, 2012.

[103] According to the Office of the Dalai Lama, His Holiness did visit Bodhgaya in 1959, but it was not on a date that appears to coincide with the mirror divination. (Office of His Holiness the 14th Dalai Lama official website: Retrieved 14/01/14.) A Tibetan might respond to this apparent lack of empirical confirmation by pointing out, with unarguable logic, that the mirror deity, Dorje Yudronma, did not inhabit an earthly realm, and that the Dalai Lama she wanted to join at Bodhgaya was not necessarily the current, earthly one.

[104] Palya Washutsong interview, Boudnath, Nepal, Apr. 28, 2012.

[105] BIT, 181.

Chapter 6

[106] YG interview, April 18, 2012.

[107] BIT, 185.

[108] BIT, 185.

[109] YG, interview, April 20, 2012.

[110] We have not yet been able to establish this lama's identity, and the name may be a pseudonym. As Rinpoche had heard nothing from "Lama Urgyan" at the time of writing *Born in Tibet*, it's possible that he had been captured by the

Chinese, the pseudonym chosen to conceal his identity; perhaps it was also employed to shield him from revelation of the miscalculations Rinpoche described in his account. The famous Tulku Urgyen Rinpoche was already in Sikkim well before June 1959.

[111] BIT, 188.

[112] BIT, 187.

[113] BIT, 190.

[114] YG, April 20, 2012 interview. Yonten said that he'd seen the tracks, and that they were much like those of the fabled yeti. When questioned further on the subject, he seems to have sensed some skepticism and laughed, saying that he didn't care whether or not we included his account.

[115] Drupju, Palya Washutsong's 12-year-old brother was one of them, and was highly disappointed that the tracks were gone by the time he got there. Drupju interview, Walter and Joanne Fordham. Portland, Oregon. June, 2013.

[116] BIT, 191.

[117] BIT, 191.

[118] Crazy Wisdom, 51-2. With thanks to Walter Fordham for bringing this reference to my notice.

[119] YG interview, April 20, 2012.

[120] YG interview, April 20, 2012.

[121] YG interview, April 20, 2012.

[122] Palya Washutsong interview, May 4, 2012.

Chapter 7

[123] YG, interview April 20, 2012: this is another case of Rinpoche's blurring of the facts to protect those still in Tibet in the early-1960s.

[124] BIT, 195.

[125] BIT, 197.

[126] BIT, 198.

[127] BIT, 199.

[128] BIT, 199.

[129] BIT, 199.

Chapter 8

[130] BIT, 203.

[131] BIT, 204.

[132] BIT, 205.

[133] BIT, 206.

[134] LYR interview, Samye Ling, Eskdalemuir, October 18, 2012.

[135] A widely-held Tibetan view, somewhat informed by Buddhist cosmology, held that the world consisted of twelve flat realms, one upon the other, the whole perched on top of a cylinder.

[136] BIT, 208.

[137] BIT, 208.

Chapter 9

[138] BIT, 209.

[139] YG interview, April 22, 2012.

[140] YG interview, April 21, 2012.

[141] BIT, 213.

Chapter 10

[142] Both Yonten Gyamtso and Palya Washutsong, who heard it from her father, recalled that Rinpoche was now resorting to mirror divination almost daily, usually in the morning before setting out on the day's trek. It's probable that

the omission from his account of his regular mirror divinations at this time was due to his collaborator, Esme Roberts, who was dubious about the more esoteric and magical aspects of his recollections.

[143] BIT, 216-7.

[144] BIT, 216-7.

[145] BIT, 218.

[146] Akong Tulku, Yonten Gyamtso and Akong Tulku's younger brother Jampal were also aware of the losses.

Chapter 11

[147] BIT, 222.

[148] YG interview, April 22, 2012.

[149] None of the interviewees referred to their suffering on the journey, except briefly in passing as a summary remark. It took a few pointed questions for Palya Washutsong to say anything at all about it (Palya Washutsong interview, May 4, 2012.)

[150] Palya Washutsong interview, May 4, 2012.

[151] BIT, 222.

[152] BIT, 223.

[153] BIT, 223.

[154] BIT, 223.

[155] The narrative is slightly unclear here. Rinpoche refers to "The nun … now completely broke down," seemingly referring back to the "one woman" he'd had to discipline at the Serkyem Pass. BIT, 223/4.

[156] BIT, 224.

[157] BIT, 224.

[158] BIT, 224.

Chapter 12

[159] YG interview, April 24, 2012.

[160] BIT, 228.

[161] Rinpoche makes no mention of numbers at this point, as any figure he revealed might expose those left behind in the mountains, perhaps still intending to escape. Nor could any of the interviewees offer much more than a rough estimate, pointing out that the circumstances made it impossible to gauge with any clarity how many refugees remained with the lead group. Offered just as hesitantly as the interviewees' rough estimates, my best sense from the combined accounts is that around 200 refugees may have reached the Brahmaputra.

[162] BIT, 229.

[163] BIT, 229.

[164] BIT, 230.

[165] BIT, 230.

[166] YG interview, April 24, 2012.

[167] LYR interview, October 18, 2012.

[168] Chögyam Trungpa Rinpoche, *Shambhala Day Address 1979. Chronicles of Chögyam Trungpa Rinpoche*, audio recording: (Retrieved 23/02/15).

[169] Palya Washutsong interview, April 28, 2012.

[170] This number suggests that at least six of the eight coracles had made it across by this point. We know that at least one further group arrived (Tserge Washutsong's second load of family), so that as many as sixty or seventy people may have made it as least as far as the strip, and eventually onto the south bank.

[171] LYR interview, October 18, 2012.

[172] While Rinpoche himself said nothing more on the matter, every one our interviewees spontaneously expressed this view when giving their accounts: that the refugees' presence had been revealed to the Communists by the bull-

stealing episode. Although only the historical PLA military log could fully confirm this view, both the survivors' informed sense of the situation, and their consensus, must be given due credit.

It appears to be fully supported by events: the refugees had been quickly discovered by well-posted pickets, while only a previously alerted and armed force could have so quickly brought down such a concentrated, heavy and sustained weight of fire – the massive attack well under way as the very first coracle neared the Brahmaputra's south bank. It seems almost certain that the bullock incident had indeed given them all away at their most vital and vulnerable moment, sabotaging everyone's chances of escape, and leading to the injury or death of an untold number of people.

[173] BIT, 232.

Chapter 13

[174] BIT, 233.

[175] BIT, 233.

[176] BIT, 233.

[177] YG interview, April 24, 2012.

[178] BIT, 234.

[179] From the day they crossed the river, Rinpoche's account in *Born in Tibet*, drawn from his diary, provides specific dates.

[180] BIT, 234.

[181] In mentioning this incident as an example in a later teaching session, Rinpoche remarked that it was a pity that his fellow travelers had not allowed good humor to lift their spirits in the hard conditions they were facing.

[182] BIT, 236.

[183] By way of comparison, they had apparently reached an altitude a few thousand feet above Mount Everest's climbers' base camps (respectively 16,900 ft., 17,598 ft.; *Wikipedia*. Retrieved November 11, 2014) This takes *BIT's* figure, made without the aid of modern technology, at face value. Without knowing

the exact route they took or the specific range they climbed, it is hard to confirm the accuracy of Rinpoche's 19,000 ft. figure, which he apparently gauged by comparison with the official 25,531 ft. altitude of Mt. Namcha Barwa.

[184] BIT, 236/7.

[185] BIT, 237.

[186] BIT, 237.

[187] BIT, 238.

[188] While Trungpa Rinpoche makes no mention of it, the group's physical condition at this stage of the journey is clear from various sources. In his interviews Yonten affirmed both their physical state and their appearance, Akong Rinpoche described the group as "crippled," while Freda Bedi/Sister Palmo described their exhausted, emaciate state later in India as among worst she'd seen of all the Tibetan refugees. Human and scientific experience, based on their exertions and the scant nutrition they'd had, reinforce these reports.

Chapter 14

[189] Ian Baker, Introduction by His Holiness The Dalai Lama. *The Heart of the World: A Journey to Tibet's Lost Paradise.* Penguin Books, London, 2004. 107.

[190] BIT, 241.

[191] Ian Baker, in Ben Preston. *Author and Adventurer Ian Baker to Speak About His Travels in Tibet.* Santa Barbara Independent, October 4, 2008. Retrieved September 29, 2014.

[192] Victor Chan, *Tibet Handbook: A Pilgrimage Guide,* Moon Publications, California, 1994. 713.

[193] Naomi Levine, *Journey to the Hidden Land of Pema Ko.* Elephant Journal, Aug 21, 2011. Retrieved September 25, 2014.

[194] Although Rinpoche didn't date the supplication, this time and location seem likely: the coda states that he'd nearly lost his life, implying that it was now saved, and also specifies the cave's precise location – in "the hidden land of Pema Kö. In a natural rock cave near the sacred place of Pema Shelri" –

whereas prior to December 26 they appear to have still been unclear about where they were.

[195] CT, *Sunshine for a Pauper: A Spontaneous Song of Supplication to the Mother-Lineage Guru of the Great Secret.* Nālandā Translation Committee. 2015.

[196] Buddhism's nontheistic approach does not account for deities external to mind.

[197] In spite of all Pema Ko's personal links and qualities, though, Rinpoche's narrative barely mentions it just touching on it in a short sentence before moving on. This omission was likely at the urging of his collaborator on the book, uncomfortable with the details he described. It could not have stemmed from a need for secrecy, as Padmasambhava's own guidebook to Pema Ko described routes, locations and qualities in detail, as did those of many teachers who'd written their own versions.

[198] Palya Washutsong interviews, April 28, 2012; May 4, 2012.

[199] BIT, 242.

[200] BIT, 242.

[201] BIT, 243.

[202] BIT, 246.

[203] Stupas are traditional Buddhist structures, usually a hemispherical mound surmounted by a tower representing enlightened mind, and frequently containing the funerary relics of saints and teachers,

[204] BIT, 247

[205] YG interview, April 25, 2012.

[206] LYR interview, October 18, 2012

[207] BIT, 248.

[208] In his account Rinpoche talks of seats being screwed in after the cargo was unloaded, while Yonten Gyamtso and Lama Yeshe both described being belted to the bare floor. These C-47s were military cargo aircraft, their role being chiefly to supply the official camps and army outposts in the area; with cargo

334

being the overwhelming priority, only a few collapsible seats for officials would have been flown back and forth.

[209] BIT, 248.

Chapter 15

[210] Material for this chapter was compiled from several sources: Yonten Gyamtso's recollections (Interviews, Kathmandu, April-May 2012; *Account of Trungpa Rinpoche's escape from Tibet and arrival in India*. Recorded by Surmang Khenpo, November, posted on *Chronicles of Trungpa Rinpoche* website, 9 March 2011); Rinchen Khandro, Ani. *Kagyu Samye Ling: The Story*. Dzalendara Publishing. Eskdalemuir, Scotland; Tenzin Palmo. *Mummy-la: The Life and Accomplishments of Freda Bedi*, in Karma Lekshe Tsomo, editor. *Eminent Buddhist Women*. SUNY. 2014; and Fugard, Sheila Meiring. *Lady of Realisation*. Biography of Sister Palmo.1st ed. Cape Town: Maitri Publications, 1984, Copyright © Library of Congress, No. Txu 140-945, Cape Town: Electronic Ed., 19 April 1999, (Accessed 11 November 2014.) For general historical information: Maxwell, Neville *India's China War*, New York, Pantheon 1970.

[211] Tenzin Palmo. *Mummy-la: The Life and Accomplishments of Freda Bedi*. In Karma Lekshe Tsomo, editor. *Eminent Buddhist Women*. SUNY. 2014.

[212] Sheila Meiring Fugard. *Lady of Realisation*. Biography of Sister Palmo. 1st ed. Cape Town: Maitri Publications, 1984. Copyright © Library of Congress, No. Txu 140-945. Cape Town: Electronic Ed., April 19, 1999. Accessed November 11, 2014. 16.

[213] YG, *Account of Trungpa Rinpoche's escape from Tibet and arrival in India*. Recorded by Surmang Khenpo, November, posted on *Chronicles of Trungpa Rinpoche* website, March 9, 2011

[214] YG, March 9, 2011.

[215] Akong Rinpoche. *Kagyu Samye Ling: The Story*. Dzalendara Publishing. Eskdalemuir, Scotland. 2007. 14.

[216] Sheila Meiring Fugard, *Lady of Realisation*.

[217] BIT, 251.

[218] YG interview, March 9, 2011.

[219] YG interview, March 9, 2011.

[220] Palya Washutsong interview, April 28, 2012.

[221] YG interview, April 22, 2012.

[222] BIT, 251.

[223] CT. *1979 Mahayana Seminary Transcripts*. Vajradhatu Publications, Boulder, CO. 20.

[224] BIT, 251.

[225] Maxwell, Neville *India's China War*. New York. Pantheon. 1970.

[226] CT, *The Mishap Lineage, Transforming Confusion into Wisdom*: Shambhala, Boston, 2009, 62.

[227] modern Mumbai.

[228] BIT, 251.

[229] This extrapolates from his general teachings on Buddhist practice, specifically from his comment that the voyage was "an exciting journey made even more so by being completely surrounded by Westerners." BIT, 252.

Epilogue

[230] On Apr 22 1894 heavy gulf ice completely blocked Halifax harbor. It was subsequently closed by ice in the winters of 1925 and 1934, but these conditions were due to local freezing rather than Arctic pack ice, occurred in mid-winter rather than early spring, and the ice was light and soon cleared. Ref. Mudie, Petra. *Historical Record Of Incidence Of Sea Ice For The Scotian Shelf And Gulf Of St. Lawrence c.1769-1962*. National Research Council – Institute for Marine Dynamics, Canada. April 30, 2002

[231] Vajradhatu Sun, June/July 1987, Boulder Colo., Vol. 8, No. 5. 1

[232] *Chronicle Herald*. April 6 1987. Vol. 39, 81. 1

[233] Martin Janowitz, *Reflections on the Samadhi of the Vidyadhara*. Vajradhatu Sun, June/July 1987, Boulder Colo., Vol. 8, No. 5. 5

[234] BIT, 252.

[235] *Flight from Tibet into India. The Oxford Times,* April 3, 1964. Clipping courtesy of Roger Davison, received April 3, 2016.

[236] Diana J Mukpo, *Dragon Thunder: My Life with Chögyam Trungpa.* Shambhala Publications. Boston. 2006. 73

[237] LYR interview, October 18, 2012.

[238] LYR interview, October 18, 2012.

[239] CT. *The Collected Works of Chögyam Trungpa.* Vol. 1. Shambhala Publications. Boston. 2004. 265.

[240] BIT, 254.

[241] CT, *Diary of Trungpa Rinpoche, 1967-68.* Shambhala Archives. Halifax, Nova Scotia.

[242] Diana J Mukpo, *Dragon Thunder,* 3.

[243] Sheila Meiring Fugard, *Lady of Realisation,* 36.

[244] Trungpa, Chögyam. *In the North of the Sky. "The Collected Works of Chögyam Trungpa"* Vol. 7. Ed. Carolyn Rose Gimian. Shambhala Publications. Boston. 2004. 303. The poem is included in the Appendix.

[245] Much of the information for this phase of the story was drawn from Walter Fordham's biography on the *Chronicles of Chögyam Trungpa Rinpoche.* Retrieved November, 8, 2014.

[246] CT, *The Collected Works of Chögyam Trungpa.* Vol. 6. 541.

[247] An American student, Jack Niland, recalls a 1965 conversation between Rinpoche and David Jones, as he was then, in which the young Englishman said that he was aiming to become a famous musician, but needed a new name, something that would stick. Rinpoche looked at him and said, "Like a knife. What do they call those big knives?" Jones answered: "A bowie knife?" Rinpoche nodded. In another version of the name's origin, John Lyons, in his book *America in the British Imagination: 1945 to the Present,* speculated that David Jones adopted the name in homage to Jim Bowie, the Texan rebel in the movie *The Alamo.*

[248] HH Gyalwang Karmapa. *Proclamation to all Those Who Dwell Under the Sun Upholding the Tradition of the Spiritual and Temporal Orders. Garuda IV.* 1976. 86–87.

[249] The modern romanization of the name is Yongle. Retrieved Septemeber 11, 2015.

[250] Diana J Mukpo, *Dragon Thunder*, 271.

[251] Sakyong Mipham. *Running with the Mind of Meditation: Lessons for Training Body and Mind.* Harmony. 2013.

[252] Account drawn from personal communications from John Perks (Maj., retd.), October 21, 2013, and Jeanne O'Riordan, October 11, 2013. While writing her account Jeanne discovered a Tibetan belief that the bodies of the Lhasa Apsos could be entered by spirits of deceased lamas while they awaited rebirth into a new body, which was completely new information to us. In Tibet Lhasa Apsos were never sold, and the only way to acquire one was as a gift. *Tushita Lhasa Apso.* Retrieved January 26, 2015

[253] LYR interview. October 18, 2012.

[254] CT, *Whycocomagh?* New Glasgow, Nova Scotia June 1977. *The Collected Works of Chögyam Trungpa.* Vol. 7. Shambhala Publications. 447.

[255] The period described in the *Bardo Thodol*, or *The Tibetan Book of the Dead*, between death and rebirth or reincarnation.

[256] A *purkhang*, constructed with many of the design features of a traditional stupa, but with openings on one side for the reliquary box, and at the top for the fire and the smoke.

[257] Respectively, *Caledonian Record, Daily Camera, Burlington Free Press*, May 27, 1987 editions. Shambhala Archives. Halifax, Nova Scotia.

CPSIA information can be obtained
at www.ICGtesting.com
Printed in the USA
LVOW12s2251010616

490865LV00003B/159/P